C0-AVL-915

After Pinochet

UNIVERSITY PRESS OF FLORIDA

Florida A&M University, Tallahassee
Florida Atlantic University, Boca Raton
Florida Gulf Coast University, Ft. Myers
Florida International University, Miami
Florida State University, Tallahassee
University of Central Florida, Orlando
University of Florida, Gainesville
University of North Florida, Jacksonville
University of South Florida, Tampa
University of West Florida, Pensacola

After Pinochet

The Chilean Road to Democracy and the Market

EDITED BY SILVIA BORZUTZKY
AND LOIS HECHT OPPENHEIM

University Press of Florida
Gainesville/Tallahassee/Tampa/Boca Raton
Pensacola/Orlando/Miami/Jacksonville/Ft. Myers

Printed in the United States of America on recycled, acid-free paper

11 10 09 08 07 06 6 5 4 3 2 1

Library of Congress Cataloging-in-Publication Data
After Pinochet: the Chilean road to democracy and the market / edited by Silvia Borzutzky and Lois Hecht Oppenheim.
p. cm.
Includes bibliographical references and index.
ISBN 0-8130-2959-7 (alk. paper)
1. Chile—Politics and government—1988- 2. Concertación de Partidos por la Democracia (Chile) 3. Democratization—Chile. 4. Chile—Economic conditions—1988- I. Borzutzky, Silvia. II. Oppenheim, Lois Hecht.

JL2631.A57 2006
320.983—dc22 2005058236

The University Press of Florida is the scholarly publishing agency for the State University System of Florida, comprising Florida A&M University, Florida Atlantic University, Florida Gulf Coast University, Florida International University, Florida State University, University of Central Florida, University of Florida, University of North Florida, University of South Florida, and University of West Florida.

University Press of Florida
15 Northwest 15th Street
Gainesville, FL 32611-2079
http://www.upf.com

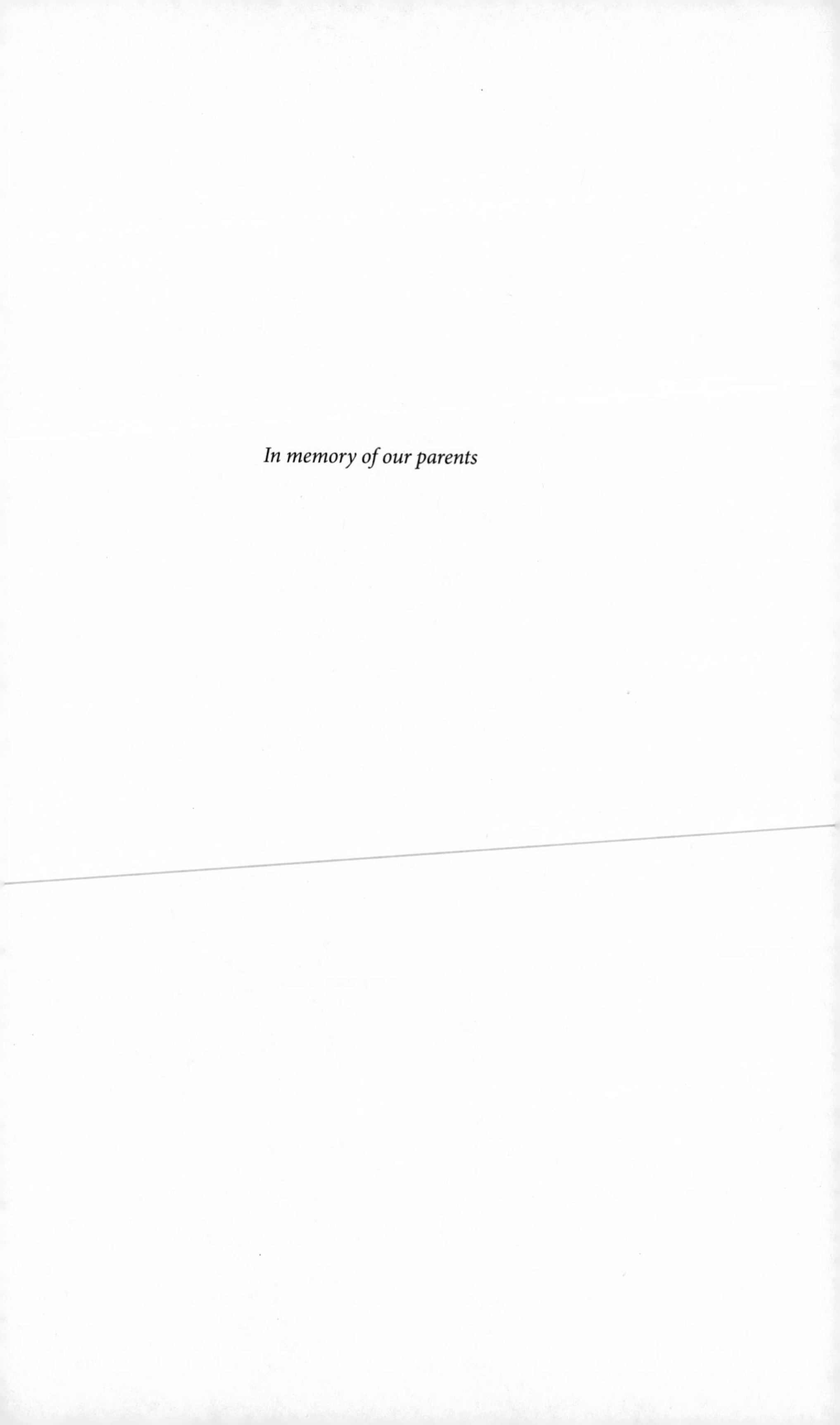

In memory of our parents

Contents

Tables

Abbreviations

AFP — Administradora de Fondos de Pensiones (Pension Fund Managing Corporation)
ALCA — Area de Libre Comercio de las Américas (Free Trade Area of the Americas)
APEC — Asian Pacific Economic Cooperation
CEDAW — Convention on the Elimination of All Forms of Discrimination Against Women
CEP — Centro de Estudios Públicos
CEPAL — Comisión Económica para América Latína y el Caribe
CERC — Centro de Estudios de la Realidad Contemporánea
CNI — Centro Nacional de Informaciones (National Information Center)
CODEPU — Corporación de Promoción y Defensa de los Derechos del Pueblo (Corporation for the Promotion and Defense of the Rights of the People)
COSENA — Consejo de Seguridad Nacional (National Security Council)
DICOEX — Dirección para la Comunidad de Chilenos en el Exterior (Office for the Community of Chileans Abroad)
DINA — Dirección Nacional de Inteligencia (National Intelligence Directorate)
DIRECON — Dirección General de Relaciones Económicas Internacionales (General Office for International Economic Relations)
EU — European Union
FASIC — Fundación de Ayuda Social de las Iglesias Cristianas (Social Aid Foundation of the Christian Churches)
FLACSO — Facultad Latinoamericana de Ciencias Sociales (Latin American School of the Social Sciences)
FONASA — Fondo Nacional de Salud (National Health Fund)
FTAA — Free Trade Area of the Americas
GATT — General Agreement on Trade and Tariffs
GDP — gross domestic product
INDAP — Instituto Nacional de Desarrollo Agropecuario (Institute for Agrarian and Livestock Development)

ISAPRE	Institución de Salud Previsional (Health Maintenance Organization)
JOCAS	Jornadas de Conversación en Afectividad y Sexualidad (Conversation Sessions on Affection and Sexuality)
MERCOSUR	Mercado Común del Sur (Common Market of the South)
NAFTA	North American Free Trade Agreement
PC	Partido Comunista de Chile (Communist Party)
PDC	Partido Demócrata Cristiano (Christian Democratic Party)
PH	Partido Humanista (Humanist Party)
Plan AUGE	Plan de Acceso Universal con Garantías Explícitas (Guaranteed Universal Health Access Plan)
PPD	Partido por la Democracia (Party for Democracy)
PR	Partido Radical de Chile (Radical Party)
PRAIS	Programa de Reparación y Atención Integral de Salud (Program of Reparations and Comprehensive Health Care)
PRSD	Partido Radical Socialdemócrata (Social Democratic Radical Party)
PS	Partido Socialista de Chile (Socialist Party)
PSD	Partido Socialdemocracia Chilena (Social Democratic Party)
RN	Renovación Nacional (National Renovation party)
SERMENA	Servicio Médico National de Empleados (Employees Health Services)
SFF	Sociedad de Fomento Fabril (Federation of Industry)
SNS	Servicio Nacional de Salud (National Health Service)
TPA	Trade Promotion Authority
UDI	Unión Demócrata Independiente (Independent Democratic Union)
WTO	World Trade Organization

Introduction

LOIS HECHT OPPENHEIM AND SILVIA BORZUTZKY

The protracted period of military rule in Chile under General Augusto Pinochet Ugarte (1973–1990) has now been superseded by a long period of democratic governance under the Concertación de Partidos por la Democracia (Coalition of Parties for Democracy, or Concertación; 1990–present). The Concertación coalition drew together under its wide umbrella two major historical antagonists, the Socialist forces and Christian Democratic parties, along with a few smaller parties.[1] In the years since 1990 there have been attempts to critically evaluate the success of this coalition in terms of its major goals of achieving greater democratization and economic equity, especially after the euphoria in the immediate aftermath of the end of military rule died down. To date, however, there has not been any overall assessment of Concertación rule.

The focus of this volume is to provide such an assessment; individual chapters analyzing specific issue areas that the Concertación has had to tackle are united by a shared perspective on Chile under the Concertación. Our general conclusion is that the Concertación coalition, through shifting political and economic contexts since 1990, has done its best to reform the neoliberal political, economic, and social model that was implemented by the military government. Over the years, Concertación leaders have acted pragmatically, keeping in mind the critical issue of governability, which included the problems of civil-military relations and deeply felt divisions arising out of decades of human rights abuses, as well as questions about not only the fairness of the neoliberal model, but also the paucity of economic alternatives. In the end, Concertación leaders chose not to alter the basic free market organization of Chile's economy and society, even though this meant that the underlying unequal social relations the neoliberal model generated would remain in place and continue to be supported by Chilean institutions. Today, after three presidents and fifteen years of Concertación governance, the long-discussed transition is over, and a new political, social, and economic order is in place.

The essays in this book, which examine diverse aspects of this new order, each focus on one of two themes that arise from our general perspective. The first is that of the consequences of the penetration of the market model in society; the chapters that deal with public policy issues—including health care, pensions, trade and macroeconomic policy, and foreign policy—elucidate consequences in these arenas. The second is that of the slow pace and piecemeal process of political reform, despite the Concertación's goal of achieving greater democratization. This theme is reflected in the chapters that deal with justice and human rights violations, reform of the political and party system, and church-state and civil-military relations. Taken together, these chapters provide an overall vision of what the Concertación both has attempted to do and has been able to achieve during three presidential terms.

We also give special attention to the third Concertación president, Ricardo Lagos (2000–2006), not only because his is the most recent administration, but also because as the first Socialist president of Chile since the 1970 election of Salvador Allende Gossens, Lagos raised expectations for reform. We believe that many of these expectations were unrealistic because in the intervening thirty-plus years since the Allende administration, Chile has become a different country; in addition, Lagos ran as the head of a broad political coalition of centrist and left parties that had a very different agenda from Allende's Chilean Road to Socialism. It is, however, fair to say that the Lagos administration policies, like those of the Concertación in general, represent a significant step in the very long process of democratic consolidation in Chile, if not of economic change. To the extent that Lagos himself played a significant role in the struggle against the Pinochet dictatorship, his election closes a thirty-year circle, from the election of Salvador Allende in 1970 through military rule, back to democracy, and to the election of a second socialist as president.

Our analysis of the Lagos administration, as well as of the administrations of his predecessors, takes into account the two themes that are threaded throughout the book: the slow political reform process and the maintenance of the free market model. The two previous Concertación presidents, Patricio Aylwin (1990–1994) and Eduardo Frei Ruiz-Tagle (1994–2000), both Christian Democrats, confronted a series of thorny issues as they attempted to reassert Chile's democratic tradition and create a somewhat more just and equitable society after seventeen years of military rule. Most important, they had to confront a legacy of authoritarianism and inequality resulting from the policies of the Pinochet regime, which increased the gap between rich and poor and between a small political elite and a large excluded majority. In essence, the Concertación coalition's core mission was to restore the rule of law, to strengthen democracy, and to bring a degree of equity to Chilean society. The process of democratic transition turned out to be much more protracted than the Concertación had imagined in 1990, however, leading the coalition to focus its efforts on political reform and ameliorating poverty without changing the fundamentals of the free market model.

In order to understand the challenges that the Lagos and future Concertación governments face, it is necessary to look briefly at the past. In 1970, Chile's long history of democracy appeared to be capped by the free election of a Marxist socialist as president, namely Salvador Allende Gossens. Allende had a long political history, having served as minister of health in the 1930s Popular Front government and for many years in the Chilean Congress, including a stint as president of the Senate. Allende was elected in 1970 as the head of the Unidad Popular, or Popular Unity, a coalition of Marxist and non-Marxist parties. The coalition's stated purpose was to begin a peaceful transition to socialism through the democratic system. Because Allende was elected during the Cold War, however, he faced not only domestic hostility, but also resistance from the United States, spearheaded by President Richard Nixon and National Security Advisor Henry Kissinger.

After three years the Chilean Road to Socialism, which was plagued by economic and political crises, ended in a bloody military coup, on September 11, 1973. What followed were seventeen long years of military dictatorship under General Augusto Pinochet Ugarte. Pinochet was determined to change the face of Chile. He persecuted so-called leftists, attempted to depoliticize the country, and instituted an economic strategy designed not only to undo the Popular Unity's attempted transition to socialism, but to implant the market in Chile. As a result, the regulatory and social welfare functions of the state that had been created over the course of the twentieth century were dismantled. In order to depoliticize the country, General Pinochet outlawed political parties and labor unions and destroyed many of the existing political institutions. Under his watchful eye a new authoritarian constitution was written and approved in 1980. The 1980 constitution created a "protected democracy" that concentrated power in the hands of the executive, included the military as a political player, and limited democratic practices. It also established an eight-year presidential term of office[2] and called for a plebiscite to be held by 1988, designed to renew Pinochet's presidential mandate.

Pinochet was disappointed and surprised when the Chilean people voted against his remaining in power in the now-famous October 1988 plebiscite. Following the rules he himself had set down, Pinochet was forced to allow open presidential and congressional elections in December of the following year. Thus, the political opponents of Pinochet were able to take office in March 1990 and to begin another chapter in Chilean history.

Winning the election was one thing, being able to rule effectively in the aftermath of a long military dictatorship was quite another. General Pinochet maintained that he had, in fact, fulfilled the goals that he had set for himself in the 1970s. In his own words, *misión cumplida*, or mission accomplished. Thus it was that President Patricio Aylwin, who won the first presidential election held since 1970, faced, at least initially, an uncertain future. General Pinochet did not go quietly into the night. He kept his position as commandant of the armed forces and head of the army and, after retiring from the armed forces in 1998, served in the Senate, as stipulated in the 1980 constitution. Moreover, Pinochet and his followers maintained an unrepentant and unapologetic position about human rights abuses, and instead touted the military regime's success in transforming Chile's economy into a model of the free market. He declared the new economic system an unqualified success, even though levels of poverty and income inequalities had worsened markedly during his tenure. Pinochet had also created a new political system that contained a number of undemocratic features, which he attempted to cement in place by approving a series of last-minute laws designed to make them virtually impossible to change. These laws were later dubbed *leyes de amarre,* laws designed to tie one's hands. The hands to be tied were those of Pinochet's opposition, the Concertación coalition.

As a result, President Aylwin, the first civilian elected president in thirty years, faced a number of challenges. First, he had to deal with a truculent military, and he endured several instances of saber-rattling in his attempts to make the military subordinate once again to civilian rule. Second, his administration confronted the legacy of human rights abuses left by the Pinochet regime. Third, it sought to undo the many undemocratic features of the constitution. Finally, Aylwin worked diligently to restore Chile's international image after seventeen years of exclusion and international criticism.

The issue of human rights was controversial from the start, and one that made the military uneasy. Even so, Aylwin moved quickly on this front. He named a human rights commission, the Rettig Commission, to investigate cases of human rights violations that had ended in death. Aylwin accepted the conclusion of the Rettig Commission that almost three thousand people had been killed by the Pinochet regime. Although the commission did not have any authority to deal with torture, the most prevalent form of abuse, it estimated that thousands of others had been tortured by the regime. President Aylwin also challenged the military by rejecting their contention that there could not be any judicial investigation of these cases because the military had passed an amnesty law protecting it against prosecution for abuses committed during the 1973–1978 period. Aylwin proposed the interpretation, later accepted by many, that the amnesty law could only apply once there was a finding that a violation had taken place. Thus, an investigation was necessary in order to grant amnesty.

Aylwin also attempted, without much success, to democratize nondemocratic facets of the Pinochet political system, such as the binomial electoral system that gave undue weight to minority political coalitions or parties[3] and the presence of nonelected senators, which tilted the Senate toward the right. On the other hand, he was able to make headway in the area of local democracy by reinstituting elections for local officials.

Aylwin also sought to restore Chile's image in the world community; under the Pinochet regime, Chile had become synonymous with human rights violations to many. In that area, Aylwin made much headway. His overall goal was to return Chile to its status as a democratic nation; that is, to make democracy and the rule of law a fact once again.

In terms of economic policy, neither Aylwin nor the presidents that followed him did much to change the basic economic strategy, which was based on the primacy of the free market and an economy open to foreign trade and investment. Aylwin and his successors tried to soften the worst consequences of the market model by creating a series of programs to protect the poorest sectors of the society, with the goal of diminishing the numbers of those living in poverty. These policies did have a significant effect on poverty rates, although they did not modify income distribution overall.

The second Concertación president, President Eduardo Frei Ruiz-Tagle, continued the general policy framework of his predecessor. During the Frei administration there were continuing attempts to bring to justice those responsible for gross violations of human rights. In this context, Aylwin's interpretation of the amnesty law was adopted by courageous judges, such as Judge Juan Guzmán Tapia, who began to prosecute dozens of military officers implicated in human rights abuses. Judge Guzmán also succeeded in imprisoning the former head of DINA (Pinochet's National Intelligence Directorate), General Manuel Contreras, after he had been convicted of involvement in the assassination of former Allende Minister Orlando Letelier in Washington, DC. Contreras' imprisonment was no easy feat given his close association with General Pinochet.[4]

President Frei continued to adhere to the free market approach, which, until 1998, generated high rates of economic growth. A major component of the economic strategy was to strengthen Chile's international economic relations through negotiating trade agreements, and under Frei efforts to sign bilateral, plurilateral, and multilateral trade agreements flourished.[5] Frei also focused on what he called "modernization of the state," which involved attempts to reform aspects of the state, most notably the judicial system. Like his predecessor, Frei also attempted unsuccessfully to push the Concertación Party's political reform agenda, such as the elimination of appointed senators.

It is important to note that for the first decade of Concertación rule, the center-left coalition won elections with a strong majority, with percentages in the mid to high fifties. This solid majority began to erode by the latter half of the 1990s, however. The first indication of erosion occurred with the congressional elections of December 1997, when the coalition's total dipped to just over 50 percent. The trend became evident in the 1999–2000 presidential contest, when Ricardo Lagos faced Joaquín Lavín. Lavín, who was mayor of Las Condes, the richest municipality at the time, belongs to UDI (Unión Demócrata Independiente, or Independent Democratic Union) the most right-wing and pro-Pinochet political party in Chile. Although Lagos won a runoff election against Lavín in January 2000, an easy Concertación victory could no longer be taken for granted.

The near defeat of the Concertación coalition in the 2000 election fueled a growing debate about its purpose, agenda, viability, and future. As a result, Ricardo Lagos, who wanted to project himself as the first president of the new millennium, faced old as well as new problems when he took office. Particularly during the first few years of his administration, Lagos had to deal with the consequences of erosion of support for the Concertación. Today, however, Lagos finds his own popularity at a record high, and support for the coalition hovers around 50 percent. The Concertación has struggled during the Lagos years to define its purpose, which is far less clear today than it was at the coalition's inception. In the early 1990s, when the internal military threat was palpable, many Chileans saw the Concertación, which had formed as a large coalition encompassing virtually all political parties opposed to military rule,[6] as representing their desire for a change from the dark past. Today, the purpose of the coalition is less obvious, given that there is a new political order with a set of functioning political institutions, the rule of law has been reestablished, and the human rights abuses of the past have ended.

In terms of civil-military relations, Lagos has been the fortunate beneficiary both of the work of previous Concertación presidents and of changes within the military itself. The current commandant of the armed forces and head of the army, General Cheyre, has stated publicly that the armed forces should never again engage in politics, while Lagos' selection of Michelle Bachelet as minister of defense, an audacious choice given her background as a Socialist whose father had been assassinated for his opposition to the military government, improved relations between the executive and the military. In addition, Lagos confronted another major area of controversy related to the armed forces when he convened a human rights commission to investigate cases of torture during the Pinochet dictatorship. The commission's report, which confirmed 30,000 cases and included graphic details of torture techniques, sent shock waves through Chilean society. As a result, many on the political right could no longer refuse to believe that there had been an institutional policy of torture. Armed forces head General Cheyre issued a second significant statement, this time acknowledging the armed forces' role in systematic human rights abuses.

Like his predecessors, Lagos also continued to push for political reform of the 1980 constitution. He scored a major victory in late 2004 when he reached agreement with the political right on a series of constitutional reforms designed to enhance civilian authority by eliminating a number of authoritarian enclaves in the constitution. These include restoring to the president the right to fire the military heads of the branches of Chile's armed forces and the elimination of all nonelected senators. The latter constitutional provision had for years thwarted the popular will by giving undue weight to the political right. A third change to the 1980 constitution limits the powers of the National Security Council, which in essence had provided the military with an avenue to intervene in political affairs. Another major undemocratic feature, the binomial electoral system, was not eliminated but was transformed from a constitutional provision to a law, which will make it easier to amend or eliminate in the future. Taken together, this set of political reforms is the most sweeping to be achieved by the Concertación to date and resolves most of the outstanding political reform issues.

In the area of economic policy, Lagos faced another challenge during his initial years in office. When he assumed office Chile was in the midst of an economic downturn that continued well into his term of office. From 1990 to 1998, the economy had grown dramatically, at a rate of about 7 percent a year. That rapid rate of growth had silenced the question of whether a center-left coalition could manage the economy well, a concern arising from the Allende government's disastrous economic policies. This period of rapid growth ended in 1998 as Chile experienced the repercussions of the Asian crisis. By 2002 there was increasing debate, both within the Concertación and outside of it, over how to reactivate the economy. Some argued that the free market model needed to be expanded, while others argued that the government needed to initiate some new spending policies. With the reactivation of the economy at the end of 2003, this debate died down. The underlying issues remain, however: Should the free market be extended? If so, how much, and are there modifications that need to be made? For instance, Lagos' call in early 2004 for a royalty fee on the mining industry raised questions among foreign investors about his adherence to the market model, while his government's expansion of free trade negotiations indicates maintenance of the basic free market and open economy approach.

Another set of relevant economic issues has to do with questions of equity. The economic model has succeeded in inserting Chile into the international economy, reducing the level of poverty, and improving living standards, but these economic advances have not improved the distribution of income. In reviewing economic data, we see that the absolute poverty rate has decreased from more than 40 percent of the population in 1990 to 18 percent by 2004, which is a substantial decline. However, economic growth has not decreased the gap between the rich and the poor, which is still very large. Today, the poorest 10 percent of the population receives 1.3 percent of the wealth, in contrast to the richest 10 percent, which captures 41 percent.[7] It appears that this unequal income distribution is an unavoidable consequence of the economic model, and there seems to be little the Concertación can do to improve income distribution without drastically transforming the economic model.

It is also interesting to note that Chile, which has been a major proponent of the free market and open economy model within the region under both Pinochet and the Concertación, finds itself more and more out of step with its neighbors in the region. Most have not reaped the same benefits as Chile from this approach. The elections of Luis Ignacio "Lula" da Silva in Brazil and Nestor Kirchner in Argentina, along with President Hugo Chávez' continued rule in Venezuela, together signal change in the air. A more critical stance toward neoliberalism seems to be returning to the region. It is not clear what this will mean for Chile, which has held firm to its free market and pro-U.S. orientation despite signs of increasing Chilean isolation.

The question of the purpose of the Concertación remains perhaps the most crucial issue for the future. Over fifteen years of Concertación rule, there has been growing wear and tear on the coalition and, with it, an erosion of support. In addition, political maneuvering for party ballot slots in both the October 2004 municipal elections and December 2005 congressional elections, as well as competition for the presidential nomination, have created serious strains on intra-Concertación party relations.

It is not the Concertación alone that faces serious political issues. Within the opposition Alianza por Chile (Alliance for Chile) there are significant problems as well, given intra-coalition tensions between its constituent parties, the UDI and National Renovation (RN). These intra-coalition tensions raise concerns about the viability of both the large political coalitions extant in Chile today. On the other hand, the current binomial electoral system, which favors large electoral coalitions, creates incentives for the maintenance of the political status quo, for both the Concertación and the Alianza.

In a larger sense, the Concertación's major challenge is to reinvent its agenda and purpose after a decade and a half in power. The Concertación faces a crisis of definition: No longer is its purpose to reawaken Chile as a democratic nation; no longer is it defined as the opposition to the Pinochet regime; what, then, is its raison d'être? Why should its representatives be elected to office? How will the Concertación define its course for the next decade? If its economic policy is not very different from that of the opposition—and there are Concertación economists who could easily be mistaken for economists of the political opposition—what is its purpose and agenda? As the younger generation outnumbers the generation that is defined by the Allende and Pinochet experiences, how will the Concertación reach out to them? These are major challenges for the Concertación in the future.

We hope that this book will provide a clear image of Chile between 1990 and 2004. In our analysis of Chile under the Concertación, we focused on two central, interlocking themes: the nature and consequences of the Chilean free market model and the different dimensions of a slow and protracted process of political reform. Our analysis sketches a political coalition that has maintained the fundamentals of a free market model, one that would not likely change dramatically under an opposition, right-wing government. Concertación governments have adopted policies that base continued economic prosperity on the growth of the export sector of the economy, fueled by private capital and the continuous process of privatization of public goods. Because this model generated enormous social inequalities during the Pinochet regime, the Concertación designed programs to soften its impact, resulting in a dramatic decline in rates of poverty. At the same time, Pinochet's changes to health-care and pension plans, which resulted in wholesale privatization of the former and partial privatization of the latter, have not been altered. What has been done is to continue the process of privatization while increasing the regulatory capacity of the state in some areas.

On the political front, instead of attempting to overturn the political institutions created by Pinochet in the 1980 constitution, the Concertación worked to slowly reform the most antidemocratic aspects of the political system. It began by democratizing municipal government through the election of city councils and direct election of mayors. Judicial reforms wrought other changes, including modifying the composition of the Supreme Court, and the recent reform package will undo some of the more obnoxious features of Pinochet's constitution by eliminating appointed senators and restoring the president's authority to remove heads of the armed forces branches. Civil-military relations have also evolved over the course of the three Concertación presidencies, from tension and saber-rattling during the Aylwin years to an explicit recognition of the subordination of military to civilian authority during Lagos' administration. After years of struggle for some measure of justice, hundreds of cases against military officials are underway, and two human rights reports, one dealing with those who died at the hands of the military and the other documenting the tens of thousands who were brutally tortured by the military, have been made public. Thus, there is a new institutional order that retains features of the military period but has been modified and recast under the Concertación. In sum, the two interlocking themes of piecemeal political change and deepening of the market model are central to both the political and economic transformation of Chile between 1990 and 2005 and the organization of the different chapters in this volume.

The Structure of This Volume

The book had its genesis as a panel at the March 2003 Latin American Studies Association conference. The panel looked at diverse aspects of the Concertación government of Ricardo Lagos. As the panel project evolved into a book, however, the focus became broader.

The book is organized around the two themes we have identified as central for understanding Chile today: the continuation and consolidation of market economic policies on the one hand, and the incompleteness of the process of democratic consolidation on the other. The initial chapters analyze those areas where as of 2004 there has been a piecemeal transformation and where Chilean democracy still needs to make progress; following chapters analyze the ongoing consolidation of market policies and their effects on the society and its future. The first part includes chapters on human rights, civil-military relations, the role of the Catholic Church, and the political party system. The chapters in the second part deal with economic and foreign policy, and social security and health-care policies.

Human rights issues have occupied a preeminent place in Chilean politics since the end of the Pinochet regime. A central concern of this book is the extent to which Chile's transition to democracy has been consolidated. It is our belief that Chile will not become a full democracy unless there is a full reckoning with the legacy of death and torture left by the military. Elizabeth Lira's chapter, "Human Rights in Chile: The Long Road to Truth, Justice, and Reparations," covers the evolution of the human rights problem since 1990 and the policies pursued by the Aylwin, Frei, and Lagos administrations to deal with the legacy of human rights abuses. The chapter provides an in-depth analysis of the impact of these policies, as well as the attitudes and responses of the military to accusations, trials, and incarceration of military leaders. According to Lira, although Chile has come a long way since 1990, the country is far from having resolved the issue of human rights. The chapter demonstrates that thirty years after the coup, there is still no common narrative and perhaps there never will be a national interpretation of the abuses of the past. However, recent policies and the changed attitude of a new generation of military leaders have at least allowed Chileans to deal with some of the more damaging consequences of the abuses committed in the past. The chapter discusses the tensions and contradictions that have existed during this protracted transition period between the search for truth, the need to repair the damage caused by the Pinochet regime, and the legal and judicial constraints that were set in place by the Pinochet regime. As Lira argues in her chapter, "The contradictions have been not only political, but also moral and philosophical."

Gregory Weeks' chapter, "Inching toward Democracy: President Lagos and the Chilean Armed Forces," deals with the issue of civilian supremacy over the armed forces. Weeks argues that although there have been only partial institutional changes geared at restructuring relations between civilian leaders and the armed forces, Lagos has made significant strides in the normalization of civil-military relations. His success is due in large part to the actions of Michelle Bachelet, Lagos' defense minister until late 2004. A critical element in the transformation of civil-military relations has been the erosion of General Pinochet's power over the military and society, as well as the appointment of a new commander in chief of the armed forces, General Juan Emilio Cheyre. The chapter provides a comprehensive analysis of the evolution of civil-military relations since 1990 and argues that democratizing Chile is a massive undertaking requiring changes not only in the constitutional and legal structures, but also in the attitudes of Chilean society. Weeks concludes that despite the lack of major constitutional reforms, Lagos has been successful in fostering greater trust between civilians and the military, has made the Ministry of Defense more relevant, and has been able to negotiate some reforms. In brief, despite the fact that substantial reforms are still needed, the Lagos administration has been able to move the military toward acceptance of democracy and democratic institutions.

Patricio Navia's chapter, "Three's Company: Old and New Alignments in Chile's Party System," examines the evolution of Chile's political cleavages since 1989. Navia argues that the pre-1970 system characterized by a three-way political and ideological division (leftist, centrist, conservative) was replaced after the transition to democracy by two coalitions. The first is a conservative coalition consisting of the parties associated with the Pinochet regime. The other is the Concertación, a coalition of centrist and leftist parties that emerged out of the opposition to the Pinochet regime and is led by the Christian Democratic and Socialist parties. Navia examines to what extent this political alignment is likely to survive the oscillations of Chilean politics, and what the chances are of a reemergence of the three-way division of the past. He also questions how firm the structure of the existing alignment is. Using electoral and polling data, Navia highlights the push and pull of these two tendencies in the current political environment. The larger issues here are the binomial electoral system and its effect on the transition to democracy, as well as the role that the leadership of the Christian Democratic Party may have in the preservation of the current political party system. With the third Concertación government entering the end of its term, with political maneuvering gearing up for the 2005 presidential and congressional elections, and with strains and tensions visible in both coalitions, Navia's questions are not only pertinent, but also critical to the evolution of Chile's democracy.

William M. Lies' chapter, "A Clash of Values: Church-State Relations in Democratic Chile," represents a unique contribution to analyses of the complex and critical relationship between the very powerful Catholic Church and Chilean politics. Lies outlines the transformations the church in Chile has experienced since the beginning of the transition to democracy and pays special attention to the interfaces between church doctrine and the public policy process. The very active role that the Chilean bishops played during the Pinochet regime has continued, but their agenda has changed dramatically. Whereas during the Pinochet years the church adopted a very critical stance against the regime and openly supported the opposition movement and the formation of the Concertación, the conservative leadership of the church in the 1990s developed a very different political agenda. This comprehensive political agenda ranges from divorce to environmental issues and from the right to life to workers' rights. Lies argues that Chilean Catholics are increasingly dissenting from their own bishops, raising questions about the effectiveness of the church and pushing the bishops toward very open intervention in the policy process. In his comprehensive analysis of the church's process of adapting to democracy, Lies concludes that while the church was successful in organizing the opposition to the Pinochet regime, it has been much less successful in the legislative realm.

Lois Hecht Oppenheim's chapter entitled "Chilean Economic Policy under the Concertación: The Triumph of the Market?" discusses the manner and extent to which the Concertación governments have continued applying the market model and the modifications made to the model since 1989. Oppenheim begins by discussing the economic legacy of the Pinochet regime and the constraints faced by Concertación policy makers as they assumed responsibility for overseeing the economy. The focus of the chapter is on the salience of trade policy and the efforts to ensure the growth of the export economy, which, she argues, is the most important engine of economic growth for Concertación policy makers. The success of the strategy is clearly seen in the diversification of Chile's economic partners and the signing of trade agreements with the European Union, the United States, South Korea, and other nations. Oppenheim also raises questions about the viability of the model, given that it is based on the exportation of nonrenewable resources and that it generates economic inequalities. She concludes by examining the extent to which the free market approach under the Concertación matches the military's neoliberal model as well as by evaluating the sustainability of the model and its effect on Chile's economic future. Oppenheim's analysis of trade policy reveals the extent to which market economic principles have penetrated the entire society.

"Peace at Home, Turbulence Abroad: The Foreign Policy of the Lagos Administration," by Joaquín Fermandois, provides an insightful analysis of the unique international situation of Chile since 1990, with a special focus on the policies of the Lagos administration. Many of the administration's efforts in the foreign policy area have centered around economic issues, specifically the signing of free trade agreements with the United States and the European Union. This chapter complements Oppenheim's analysis of free trade policy. However, while the former chapter focuses on the economic importance of these agreements, the latter focuses on the centrality of these agreements for Chile's foreign policy. Fermandois also elaborates on the contradictions posed by the success of Chile's foreign economic policy. Namely, while Chile stands as a success story in the international economic system, the country's relations with its Latin American neighbors have experienced numerous crises.

Silvia Borzutzky's chapter, "Cooperation or Confrontation between the State and the Market? Social Security and Health Policies" summarizes the major reforms enacted by General Pinochet and examines the policies that the Lagos administration has pursued in both the social security and the health-care sectors. The central issue under examination here is the tension between market policies and the need to deal with persistent socioeconomic problems. Are the policies of the Lagos administration strengthening the market? What is the role of the state in the provision of social benefits? Ultimately these policies appear to have deepened the process of privatization and reflect the Lagos administration's commitment to market-oriented policies. Borzutzky also examines societal reactions to these policies, arguing that while the process of marketization of social security is widely accepted, the same processes in the health-care area have encountered major opposition. She concludes that whereas in the social security area the market has been strengthened, the situation in the health sector is quite complex and unclear. No doubt the success of the health-care policies will depend on the impact of the Plan AUGE, an initiative designed to reduce inequities in health care, and the willingness of the public sector to finance the plan. The chapter, as well as this volume, concludes that the Lagos administration seems to be driven more often than not by a market logic, and within this logic the central issues tend to be competitiveness and efficiency rather than distribution issues.

Together, these chapters provide a coherent and comprehensive view of how

Chile has traversed the road toward democracy and the market. The road has undoubtedly been long, and the interlocking processes that Chileans have had to deal with have been complex and challenging.

Notes

We wish to thank the two anonymous reviewers for their very insightful and helpful comments on the chapters in this volume.

1. Since December 1989, the Concertación coalition has won both presidential and congressional elections, including the elections of presidents Patricio Aylwin (1990–1994), Eduardo Frei Ruiz-Tagle (1994–2000), and Ricardo Lagos (2000–2006).

2. This term was shortened to six years at the beginning of civilian rule and further reduced to four years in 2004.

3. The binomial system is based on two-member districts where, in order to win both seats, a two-candidate slate must gain two-thirds of the popular vote. Thus, a minority coalition could win the second seat with only slightly more than one-third of the vote. Assuming that this outcome occurs in multiple districts, it results in an overrepresentation of the minority.

4. Contreras hid out in the south of Chile, aided by military colleagues, and later claimed he was too ill to serve time, a claim supported by military doctors.

5. *Bilateral* refers to agreements between two countries, *plurilateral* to regional agreements, and *multilateral* to global agreements, such as those coming out of the General Agreement on Trade and Tariffs (GATT) that created the World Trade Organization (WTO).

6. The coalition does not include the Communist Party, whose exclusion the Christian Democrats had required.

7. Gonzalo de la Maza, "Modernization a la Chilena: Integration and Exclusion," *ReVista: Harvard Review of Latin America* 3, no. 3 (2004): 25–30.

PART I

The Arduous Road to Democracy

1

Human Rights in Chile

The Long Road to Truth, Justice, and Reparations

ELIZABETH LIRA

This chapter examines the tensions between the conflicting historical impulses to forgive and forget past human rights abuses on the one hand, and to seek justice, truth, and reparations on the other.[1] The long historical pattern of tension between these competing goals reached new proportions in the aftermath of the military coup against the government of Salvador Allende and the unprecedented acts of violence, torture, and death perpetrated against its supporters. These tensions, which have played themselves out under the Concertación governments since 1990, highlight both the degree of democratic advances and limitations on democracy extant in Chile today.

Since the beginning of the Republic of Chile (1814), contenders for control of the state have justified their actions during all major political conflicts in the name of *la patria* (the homeland). The contending factions and parties had different visions of and dreams for *la patria*. Soldiers, militia, and civilians died on all sides for *la patria*. No one fought against *la patria*. These political conflicts divided families and polarized society. They were the cause of suffering and very extensive damage in general. In the name of *la patria*, a number of forms of political repression were carried out: preventive detention of political opponents, extra-judicial executions, abuse and torture of prisoners, exile, confiscation of property, and other forms of political persecution. Nevertheless, the crimes and abuses against political adversaries of the moment were perceived as a minimal cost in comparison to the importance of saving *la patria*.

Once the most intense moments of conflict were over, there were calls for reconciliation. Political reconciliation was achieved by a succession of consensual amnesties and reparation laws. Amnesties were negotiated to put an end to conflicts and to ensure a peaceful society.[2] Reparation, as part of political reconciliation, usually reintegrated those who had been defeated, that is, the losers. Reparation meant that dismissed employees (*exonerados*) were given positions within the military, in universities, in public schools, or as government bureaucrats. They were also given posts in presidential cabinets, in the legislature, and in the judiciary. Some of them received pensions.

From the 1820s until the early twentieth century, political reconciliation in Chile was marked by efforts both to suppress and to reconstruct social memory. From the perspective of the victims this was done to facilitate impunity, and from the perspective of the perpetrators it was done to give political absolution for crimes committed during the political cataclysm. These "social memory" and "official history" aspects of political reconciliation were long term. They occurred through the rewriting of government-approved history texts, during public ceremonies and celebrations, and in numerous subtle symbolic "reconciliations."

Chile's political class did not believe that forgetting (*olvido*) was literally possible, but its members insisted on the necessity for legal, political, and symbolic starting over. This was not reconciliation between people at an emotional or psychological level. Neither was it reconciliation between parties and factions at an ideological or programmatic level. Such reconciliation was neither possible nor expected. Political reconciliation meant that certain issues were not addressed in the political arena or, if they were, that policies on sensitive matters did not exceed certain limits that might endanger the newly reconstructed *concordia*. Such reconciliation required moderation, prudence, and common sense (*cordura*). It required pretense and public masks. It meant *fictive harmony* and pragmatic toleration of differences, an end to violent conflict, accommodation to the "rule of law" (whatever that law was at the moment), and governability. Above all else, political reconciliation was political pragmatism at its best—and worst.[3]

During the Pinochet military regime (1973–1990) different voices, especially the Catholic Church, demanded reconciliation. But it was only at the end of the dictatorship that political reconciliation seemed to be an objective shared by the majority of political leaders. However, it was not clear whether they shared a common meaning and understanding of the implications of such reconciliation. Chilean history had never witnessed such a violent and prolonged political repression. No nineteenth-century conflict could compare to the events in Chile after September 11, 1973. Human rights lawyers, who had fought an unprecedented legal battle in the courts after 1973, had made the major difference, even though the judiciary rejected more than eight thousand writs of habeas corpus up until 1989. One thing was clear: The capacity of the historical pattern had been exceeded by the numerous claims made by many groups after 1989, who demanded "truth," prosecution of "victimizers" (who were heroes for Pinochet supporters), and "social justice." In contrast, the reintegration of the losers into the political system, renewed efforts at political reform, and other forms of reparation for victims (branded as subversives by supporters of the military regime) all go hand in hand with the historical emphasis on legitimizing political order and ensuring governability.

The government program of the Concertación de Partidos por la Democracia (Coalition of Parties for Democracy, or Concertación), written in 1989, addresses the issue of human rights in its opening chapter. It asserts that human rights violations have serious consequences not only for the victims, but also for the political future of the country as a whole. It also states that a full democracy is not viable unless Chile confronts these consequences.

The policies aimed at achieving truth, justice, and reparation, initiated in spite of military and political constraints, have been struggling against societal expectations of impunity and oblivion. The contradictions have been not only political, but also moral and philosophical. The historical precedent for political reconciliation loomed over human rights issues during the transition. Political reconciliation is still an unfinished process.

This chapter illustrates some of the tensions produced as a result of the political initiatives, the search for truth, reparation laws, and judicial constraints during the three governments of the Concertación. My purpose is to show that in the case of Chile, reconciliation and truth are contradictory and often incompatible processes. In other words, those who seek reconciliation do not want to search for the truth. Consequently, the human rights policies of Ricardo Lagos' government can be understood only within the larger context of the three governments of the Concertación.

Human Rights Policy during the Aylwin and Frei Governments

When Patricio Aylwin became president of Chile in 1990, he stated that the government's goals concerning human rights were to establish an official truth regarding past human rights violations; to provide reparations for the victims; and to guarantee legal, social, and political conditions that would prevent the recurrence of human rights violations. During his first statement to the Plenary Session of the National Congress on May 21, 1990, he said, "I am undertaking the complex task of healing the wounds that remain from the past. This requires us to address three issues, which we are now tackling with a sense of fairness by ways of reason and law: the so-called 'political prisoners,' the exiled, and political murders."[4]

To address the issue of truth, President Aylwin created the Truth and Reconciliation Commission (Rettig Commission) in April 1990 to investigate and uncover the truth about what had happened to persons who had disappeared after being arrested by the government (called *detenidos desaparecidos,* or detained-disappeared), who had been executed, or who had been killed as a result of political violence. The commission's report documented these cases and made concrete recommendations for reparations.

These recommendations gave rise to Law 19.123 of 1992, which created the Corporación de Reparación (Corporation of Reparations). As a means of acknowledging and compensating for damages caused by the state, the corporation established a reparation allowance to be given to family members of the detained-disappeared and of those who had been executed for political reasons. When the Corporación de Reparación was disbanded in 1996, this task was taken up by the Programa de Continuidad de la Ley No. 19.123 (Program for the Continuation of Law 19.123), now the Human Rights Program of the Ministry of Interior.

The Truth and Reconciliation Commission also recommended the creation of a health and mental health program for the victims. This recommendation led to the creation of the Programa de Reparación y Atención Integral de Salud (Program of Reparations and Comprehensive Health Care), or PRAIS. The program began under the auspices of the Ministry of Health in 1991 and as of 2005 continues to provide free general and mental health care for all victims.

In August 1990 the Oficina Nacional de Retorno (National Office of Return) was created by Law 18.994 to facilitate the repatriation of people who had been exiled. Subsequently, two additional laws were passed that complemented the first: Law 19.074 of 1991 established conditions for the recognition of degrees and qualifications earned abroad. Law 19.128 of 1992 granted tax exemptions to allow returning Chileans to bring with them luggage, merchandise, and works of art. The Oficina Nacional de Retorno functioned until 1994.

The Aylwin government also promised to free political prisoners imprisoned under the dictatorship, and undertook various initiatives to do this. New laws abolished the military's jurisdiction to try civilians in military court for certain crimes under the Military Justice Code. Changes were also introduced to the Arms Control Act and to the Terrorist Conduct Act. These laws were commonly known as *leyes Cumplido* (Cumplido laws), named after Justice Minister Francisco Cumplido. In 1991, the government also ratified amendments to Article 9 of the constitution, which authorized the president of the republic to grant pardons to those who had been convicted of certain crimes under the Terrorist Conduct Act. A total of 169 pardons were granted. The last prisoners were released in March 1994 by the commutation of their prison sentences into banishment.

In 1993, the executive branch created the Programa de Reconocimiento al Exonerado Político (Program for the Recognition of Politically Dismissed Persons) through Law 19.234, overseen by the Ministry of the Interior. Law 19.234 established pensions and social security benefits for those who had been dismissed from their jobs for political reasons. In 1998, Law 19.582 broadened the categories of possible beneficiaries, and in June 2003 the period for filing claims was extended for a year, under Law 19.881.

In 1995, during the administration of President Eduardo Frei (1994–2000), the government established a program to compensate peasants who had gained lands through agrarian reform, then lost their land rights under the 1973 Decree Law 208. The Instituto Nacional de Desarrollo Agropecuario (Institute for Agrarian and Livestock Development, or INDAP) administered this program and handled the claims of peasant organizations seeking compensation for having been expelled from land. The president also awarded discretionary pensions to these peasants.

The Aylwin and Frei governments had been pressured to put an end to the issue of human rights through political means. Right-wing sectors sought political agreements that would put an end to discussions of human rights issues and insisted upon application of the amnesty decree *sin más*; that is, without the circumstances surrounding the forced disappearance of persons being investigated. Some people thought it would be possible to close the human rights issue, arguing that this was the way that social peace had been achieved in the past. Those who were responsible for human rights violations argued that social peace was contingent on strict application of the amnesty decree and on an end to discussions of human rights.

The general secretary of the government at the time, José Joaquín Brunner, referred to the challenges facing the nation as follows: "We need to construct—President Frei's phrase is most fitting—a healthy historic memory. This does not mean that we forget the past, but neither does it mean that it is a memory full of wounds."[5] The right-wing opposition, however, continued to push for a *ley de punto final* (full stop law) or for a guarantee of a strict application of the amnesty decree (Law 2.191 of 1978), arguing that this was the only way to achieve political reconciliation. Minister Brunner responded that it was not in his power to intervene in these cases, that interpretation of amnesty was the responsibility of judges, and that it was not "a blindness of the government." He believed that a *ley de punto final* made even less sense: "The so-called *ley de punto final*, which would put an artificial end to cases that are still open or that have their own dynamics, produces no results and we would hit our heads hundreds of times against the same wall. Surveys show that only 14 percent of the people agreed with this solution."[6] According to Brunner, the solution depended on coming to "rational agreements through the convergence of different positions in order to achieve legal and constitutional stability for the few but very complex and delicate tasks that lie ahead."[7]

In spite of these arguments, the lack of information about the fate and whereabouts of the detained-disappeared had become a problem with no apparent solution.[8] Various efforts to obtain information about their whereabouts had failed. While many insisted on repeating the historical pattern of impunity, doubts continued to grow about the conviction that social peace depended on impunity and that political reconciliation depended on making a fresh start.

It seemed that the subject of human rights had disappeared from the political agenda. Nevertheless, in 1996 a trial was initiated in Spain against Pinochet and the Chilean military junta for violating human rights. In March 1998 Pinochet stepped down as commander in chief of the armed forces and was sworn in as senator for life. He fought off a constitutional accusation in the Chamber of Deputies, which failed to pass. In addition, Pinochet overcame around three hundred complaints filed against him in court for disappearances, executions, torture, and other crimes. The general secretary of the Communist Party, Gladys Marín, presented the first lawsuit in January 1998, accusing Pinochet of genocide, kidnapping, illicit association, and illegal burials. On October 16, 1998, Pinochet was arrested in London by order of Spanish Judge Baltasar Garzón and was detained for 503 days. Suddenly, human rights were at the top of the political agenda, and the controversy over whether justice or impunity was the key to social peace surfaced during the trials, in Congress, and in daily politics.

In August 1999, at the end of Frei's presidency, Defense Minister Edmundo Pérez Yoma organized the Mesa de Diálogo (Round Table Dialogue) on human rights. The Mesa de Diálogo included representatives of the commanders in chief of the armed forces, civilians, human rights lawyers, and representatives of churches and the Freemasons, presided over by Defense Minister Mario Fernández. The Association of Relatives of the Disappeared, the Communist Party, and some left-wing organizations rejected the Mesa de Diálogo, organizing street protests to denounce what they saw as a new initiative to negotiate impunity.

Meanwhile, Pinochet returned to Chile in March 2000, days before Ricardo Lagos took office as president of Chile, and the Mesa de Diálogo ended in June 2000. In the final accord, the armed forces recognized that "state agents" had violated human rights during the military regime. The armed forces committed themselves to look for information about the detained-disappeared over the following six months. They repeatedly affirmed that they had no documents whatsoever on these cases, and therefore would question retired military personnel and all those who might be able to provide at least some information.

The application of the amnesty decree continued to be a critical issue. On behalf of victims of Operation Condor (Operación Cóndor)[9] and the Caravan of Death (Caravana de la Muerte),[10] human rights lawyers Héctor Salazar, of

FASIC,[11] and Hugo Gutiérrez, of CODEPU,[12] presented a report emphasizing the obligation of the Chilean authorities to investigate the cases of the detained-disappeared. This report, prepared by Amnesty International and the International Commission of Jurists, exposed the incompatibility of the amnesty decree, Law 2.191 of 1978, with international law.[13]

Human Rights Issues under the Government of Ricardo Lagos

President Ricardo Lagos was elected president in a runoff election in January 2000, gaining 51.31 percent of the vote. His government took office in March in the midst of the tensions caused by Pinochet's return from the United Kingdom and pressure from various sectors to bring him to trial. When Lagos addressed his supporters in the Plaza de la Constitución on the day he took power, the only slogan the crowd shouted in response to his speech was "¡Juicio a Pinochet!" (Bring Pinochet to trial!).[14] After five months, the Supreme Court confirmed that Pinochet would be stripped of his immunity for the Caravan of Death case.

On January 5, 2001, President Ricardo Lagos received the armed forces' "Report on the Disappeared," produced as an outcome of the Mesa de Diálogo. In response to this report, the president of the Association of the Relatives of the Detained-disappeared declared,

> This report will show whether or not the armed forces decided to accept their responsibility and whether they are providing the information we know they have, and which did not take them six months to find. This information has always existed. . . . The armed forces have the obligation to the country to assume institutional responsibility for the crimes committed in the past. . . . The truth we want and which we hope will be provided, especially by the armed forces, is to know what happened to each and every one of our relatives who were detained and disappeared. We do not want them to tell us again that our family members are dead, because it has taken us many years to come to terms with the pain of knowing that perhaps we will never see them alive again. But we need to know where, how, when, why, and who. We do not want generic truth but case-by-case answers. We know who violated human rights, and they have to take responsibility for their actions. We hope this will happen with this report, presented to the president of the republic.[15]

The report identified 180 disappeared persons and claimed that their bodies had been thrown into the sea. The report also gave information on another twenty unidentified individuals, allegedly buried in certain specific sites.[16] Aside from the great uproar the report provoked, the most important political outcome was the armed forces' acknowledgment of responsibility for disappearances and the fact that they described them as acts meriting condemnation (*actos repudiables*).[17] The newspaper *La Tercera* published part of the armed forces' report.[18] Although some political sectors valued this admission, the information was considered not only insufficient but also erroneous, given the inaccuracies and mistakes found in more than fifty cases, which were publicized by the Socialist Party and CODEPU.[19]

The Pinochet Foundation and some retired military officers expressed dismay, reiterating that they had had no idea that such actions had taken place. Senator Julio Canessa, former vice commander in chief of the army, responded to the armed forces report as follows:

> We do not accept that the state's fundamental institutions be divided. There are no armed forces of yesterday and others of today. There is no Carabinero Police of yesterday and another of today. There is no Supreme Court of yesterday and another of today. In the struggle to prevent Chile from being reduced to an ideological colony, each performed in good faith what they believed to be their duty. . . . And they continue to do so. Therefore, we uphold the honor of men of arms and of all uniformed men whose honor has been questioned. We also recognize the value of the politicians who in their time confronted the totalitarian aggression and then patriotically contributed to the task we all shared of rebuilding the country.[20]

The Search for Truth

Neither the Truth and Reconciliation Commission report nor the armed forces' report alone was able to provide the entire truth. The complete documentation on individual cases that the relatives of the detained-disappeared were demanding could only be obtained through the judicial process. The president of Chile sent the armed forces report to the Supreme Court, which assigned judges and magistrates who would take sole responsibility for investigating the denunciations in it. For example, Judge Héctor Carreño was appointed to investigate the information that the navy had provided about the remains of six Communist Party leaders who had been arrested and disappeared in 1976. The report stated that the six had been buried in the hills of Cuesta Barriga. Carreño's search yielded bone fragments, revealing that the bodies had been removed. The same scenario occurred in almost all of the cases investigated by the appointed judges.

The credibility of the armed forces report, already eroded by the identification of inaccuracies after only a few days in the public eye, would be further weakened in May of that year. One of the high-profile cases was that of Juan Luis Rivera Matus, a Communist union leader who was arrested and disappeared in 1976. The armed forces report stated that his body had been thrown into the sea; however, his remains were unearthed at Fuerte Arteaga. After the Medical Legal Service confirmed his identity, his bones were given to his family for burial. This case gave rise to many questions about the accuracy of the report.

In the first week of November 2000, Judge Juan Guzmán, in his capacity as chief investigator for the complaints filed against Augusto Pinochet, started the search for several Communist Party leaders and members who had been detained in 1976 and apparently had been buried in Patio 28 of the General Cemetery of Santiago. The autopsy reports logged in cemetery records enabled the judge to confirm that these bodies had been mutilated and bore clear signs of torture, bullet wounds, and cuts.[21] Given the seriousness of these revelations, Socialist Senator José Antonio Viera Gallo argued that if any of these corpses had been removed after 1978, then these cases could be treated as crimes that were not protected by the amnesty decree.[22] Nevertheless, it was no longer possible to bring charges because the statute of limitations had run out.

The appointed judges had managed to uncover evidence establishing that the disappearances had been part of a cover-up for the deaths of people who had died from torture after being detained. They also established that they were part of a systematic policy directed against members of certain political groups, who were generally arrested in the street, without eyewitnesses. The perpetrators believed that if the detained person disappeared without a trace and no body was found, it would not be possible to investigate the crime. These would therefore constitute "perfect crimes." Paradoxically, these perfect crimes turned out to be the most substantial evidence of the criminal policies implemented by, and the involvement of, the armed forces and the military government. The judges ruled that the generic statement in the January 2001 report that bodies had been thrown into the sea was not sufficient evidence that the detained-disappeared were actually dead. Instead, if the remains of the detained-disappeared were not found, the crime would be classified as "permanent kidnapping," making the amnesty decree inapplicable.

Family members and the government continued to insist that the search for the truth about individual victims had to continue, to find out the final destiny of each and every one of the detained-disappeared and under what circumstances he or she had died. The armed forces' admission that they had thrown unidentified bodies of detained people into the sea did not constitute sufficient proof, for either the family members or the judges. Therefore, the legal term *kid-*

napping continued to be a nightmare for the perpetrators. Nobody tried to affirm that the detained-disappeared were alive, but neither could anybody prove in front of a judge that they were, in fact, dead.

The appointment of special judges and the unwillingness of the Supreme Court to apply amnesty and statutes of limitations opened a new route to truth. Unlike in other nations that had offered amnesty in exchange for evidence, as South Africa had done, or that had simply closed the issue, as Spain had done, in Chile the judicial road, initiated by the Comité de la Paz (Peace Committee) in 1973 and later continued by the Vicaría de la Solidaridad (Vicariate of Solidarity), continued to play an important role. The value of the judicial inquiries and the existing evidence became manifest with the course of years, not only in the courts but also in public opinion. After the Mesa de Diálogo, the special judges were able to carry out their investigations in military regiments and on military premises, reconstructing the story of what had happened.

Several new denunciations caused an uproar in 2003, but these resulted from investigations that had been underway since 2001. The special judges had managed to obtain fragmented and sparse information, but they had undoubtedly made significant progress in unraveling what had happened and in the quest for truth.

Justice

The truth that was gradually emerging would open the road to justice, thus reducing social impunity. Judge Juan Guzmán continued to investigate the Caravan of Death case, which led to various complaints being filed against Pinochet. In the caravan case, fifty-six executions and nineteen disappearances had occurred in various cities in Chile when General Sergio Arellano Stark's delegation passed through them. In July 1999 the Supreme Court reinterpreted the amnesty decree, ruling that it could not be applied in these nineteen disappearances. According to the ruling, the deaths of these victims could not be officially certified, given that their bodies had never been found. According to Chilean law, kidnapping constitutes a permanent crime until the person reappears or the remains are found. The five army officials responsible for this operation were arrested and accused of kidnapping.

The plaintiffs' lawyers asked, in March 2000, for the revocation of the immunity privileges Pinochet held as a lifetime senator. In May, the Santiago Court of Appeals ruled, by a vote of thirteen to nine, that Pinochet should be stripped of his immunity as lifetime senator. The Supreme Court upheld this ruling on August 6, on grounds of "reasonable suspicions" that Pinochet had been the intellectual author of the Caravan of Death and that he had then participated in covering up the crimes. His defense lawyers argued that Pinochet should undergo medical examinations to show whether he was fit to stand trial. Despite a medical diagnosis that Pinochet presented "a light to moderate dementia of vascular origin," Judge Juan Guzmán put the former dictator on trial on February 29, 2001. Judge Guzmán wrote in the accusation,

> To call to trial, to indict or prosecute our fellow human beings is far from blaming or dishonoring. It implies that we put to use the jurisdictional path prescribed by the law, enabling us to make use of all the appropriate channels, appropriate measures, and periods of time that exist to help the accused prove his innocence. It helps us to conclude with a definite finding of guilt or innocence unless the contrary can be confirmed.
>
> Now, should innocence not be established, at least the defendant will have had a trial with the right to due process where he can try to prove he is not guilty. In both cases, most definitely, we will comply with the imperative of justice our law guarantees to achieve a common good and social peace.

In view of the evidence, the judge concluded that "sufficient suppositions against him lead the court to believe that he participated as intellectual author in the crimes of kidnapping and first-degree murder," which is why "[we] put Augusto José Ramón Pinochet Ugarte on trial as intellectual author of the crimes of kidnapping and murder."

On July 9, 2001, the Sixth Chamber of the Court of Appeals ordered the temporary and partial dismissal of charges against lifetime senator Pinochet, applying the regulations from the Code of Criminal Procedure, which had not yet taken effect. These regulations exempt an individual from trial on the basis of madness or dementia. In 2002, Pinochet was acquitted once and for all for the Caravan of Death case. On two other occasions, efforts were made to strip him of his immunity but, once again, the petitions were denied on grounds that Pinochet had been diagnosed with subcortical dementia.[23]

Apart from the Caravan of Death case, there were other cases in which the investigations were advancing faster than ever before. The investigation of the murder of Tucapel Jiménez, a union leader who had been found beheaded in his own car in February 1982, suddenly progressed when the judge who had been in charge of the case for seventeen years was replaced. Ten army officers were charged, among them four retired generals. Major General Carlos Herrera Jiménez declared in front of the judge, "I felt honored to have been chosen to carry out this important mission, considering that the man was a traitor who had sold out to foreign interests. He belonged to international Marxism."[24] Herrera confessed to the crime in great detail and was sentenced to life in prison. With the passing of time, his attitude about the crime changed, and he asked the family for forgiveness on the national television program "Medianoche" in April 2001, "It is good that Mr. Jiménez understands that for a long time I was proud of having served my country this way. With the passing of time and with thirteen years of prison in my body, I have come to understand that it was a disgraceful, absurd, and irrational murder that has no justification. From that moment on, I started carrying a heavy cross."[25]

Retired General Ramsés Alvarez Scoglia was also convicted of the Tucapel Jiménez murder; at the time of the murder he had been chief of DINA (Dirección de Inteligencia Nacional, or National Intelligence Agency), the organization that had planned, ordered, and covered up the crime. This trial demonstrated once again that the repression carried out in this and other cases had been part of a regime policy, refuting the persistent assertions of civilian and military authorities of Pinochet's regime that the crimes had been the result of "individual excess." If the actions of Herrera Jiménez had been a case of individual excess, they would have led to some kind of disciplinary measure. On the contrary, according to his testimony, he had been congratulated.

Other cases like that involving DINA's chemist, Eugenio Berríos, also led to the DINA. This case, Operación Albania, involved a group of agents from the Central Nacional de Informaciones (National Intelligence Center, or CNI). The murders of four leftist leaders—journalist José Carrasco, Abraham Muskablit, Eugenio Rivera, and Gastón Vidaurrázaga—on September 8, 1986, involved CNI agents.[26] Retired Major General Carlos Herrera was also convicted of killing truck driver Mario Fernández in 1984 during a torture session. The accused perpetrators were convicted in the majority of cases and belonged to the DINA or the CNI.[27] Around three hundred cases were in progress or under investigation by judges in 2002.

The other perspective on justice was represented by Miguel Retamal Fabry, defense lawyer for the military officials accused of human rights abuses. He addressed several of the critical issues in these cases. In a recent editorial, for example, Retamal analyzed the fifteen-year prison sentence given to General Manuel Contreras, as well as the ten-year sentences for Brigadier Generals Marcelo Moren Brito and Miguel Krassnoff Marchenko. The latter were convicted of the crime of kidnapping a person who had last been seen at Villa Grimaldi. In Retamal's opinion, bringing a charge of kidnapping "a person who no one in his right mind believes to be alive, if nearly thirty years have passed since he was last heard of," was a "legal fiction, which infringes on the most basic principles of criminal responsibility under our laws; and worse, the ruling contradicts the explicit text of the amnesty decree that applies to the period of time in which the events happened."[28] Retamal pointed out that the visiting investigative judges and the specially appointed judges had not allowed the collection of evidence about the crime, thereby preventing the closure of the indictments against seventy-eight members of the Chilean army. He described the relationship between the accused and their institution of origin as highly complicated and contradictory, and he denounced the "political world" for having an ambivalent position about prosecuting human rights abuses.[29] He ended by stating that public opinion seemed to be mainly in favor of investigating, bringing to trial, and perhaps sentencing those accused of human rights crimes, even though, he said, "no serious study has been conducted in respect to what the general public thinks about this situation." On the other hand, the indictments and arrests had converted the Telecommunications Command Center of Peñalolén into a "detention center" for the ex-military personnel accused of human rights violations.[30]

In summary, thirty years after the military coup, victims of the regime finally received justice through the recognition and acceptance that the violent acts against them had really occurred and that they had had horrible consequences for hundreds of thousands of people. Specifically, the facts had been reconstructed through hundreds of trials; these trials had identified the individuals responsible for the crimes and the circumstances under which the crimes had been committed. The political justifications that human rights violations were the price "of saving the country from the clutches of international communism" no longer rang true. Now these abuses were labeled by the court system as crimes. The pressures to limit the judicial investigations were diminishing in face of the facts that were coming to light. Judges now could determine when to close the cases. At the end of 2004, more than four hundred cases were still open in the tribunals, and the application of the amnesty decree was discussed in every trial. However, it is uncertain when these cases will come to a close and whether they will ever be fully resolved.

Reparation

Those who had suffered under the military regime demanded recognition of their status as victims and recognition that their rights had been violated. Some victims still have the strong feeling that no policy, no matter how well conceived, could ever compensate for the death of their loved and lost ones and the suffering in their own lives.

By the end of Patricio Aylwin's presidential term, the government regarded the chapter on political prisoners of the dictatorship as closed.[31] Former political prisoners had to deal with the issue on their own as if it were a private matter, supported by a few human rights lawyers and nongovernmental organizations, especially CODEPU. Former political prisoners were in a critical situation. The majority of them had suffered humiliation, torture, prolonged imprisonment, and job loss, and many had been forced to leave the country in order to save their lives. However, in their opinion, as well as in public opinion, the country had been very miserly in recognizing these damages during thirteen years of democratic transition.

At the end of the 1990s, some groups of former political prisoners organized themselves to obtain moral, social, and monetary reparations. These groups sought

1. to reactivate investigations and seek justice by filing criminal complaints against those responsible;
2. to file civil complaints to obtain financial compensation for having been subjected to torture;
3. to create services to facilitate mental health and social rehabilitation of the victims; and
4. to reconstruct and chronicle the prisoners' experiences in various detention centers in the form of novels, testimonies, documentaries, historical writings, and videos and films.[32]

As part of these attempts to gain reparations for the suffering caused, the organizations filed complaints against Augusto Pinochet and others for the harm caused to victims of prolonged imprisonment and torture. The criminal complaints demanded justice, but the victims also expected recognition from the state and compensation for the moral, psychological, physical, and social damages and suffering caused by the torture and abuse. They presented civil suits, hoping to obtain compensation for the damages and injuries caused.

In 2003, different groups of former political prisoners increased the visibility of the problem by claiming discrimination vis-à-vis other human rights violations, an effort in which the Comisión Ética contra la Tortura (Ethics Commission against Torture) played a significant role. The commission set the goal of achieving the enactment of a comprehensive reparations law for those who had suffered torture and asked the government to set up an investigative commission of truth, justice, and reparation for the survivors of torture in Chile. In 2003, the president of the republic agreed to form this commission.

Former political prisoners joined together to form the Coordinadora de Organizaciones de Ex Presos Políticos de Chile (Coordinating Organization of Ex-political Prisoners of Chile). After the government's announcement that it would draft a reparations measure for victims who had not been included in other programs, they presented their own proposal for comprehensive reparations to the president. This document, written by the coordinadora, emphasized that without truth, justice, and comprehensive integration, there would be no solution to this human rights problem. Other groups of former political prisoners also sent proposals to the government. Among them were people who had been imprisoned on Dawson Island, who organized as the Proyecto de Información de Derechos Humanos Dawson 2000 (Dawson Human Rights Information Project 2000), and people from the region of Magallanes, organized as the Agrupación Cultural y de Derechos Humanos Orlando Letelier (Orlando Letelier Cultural and Human Rights Association) in Punta Arenas.[33]

At the same time, Socialist Senators Carlos Ominami and Jaime Naranjo and Deputy Fulvio Rossi proposed a reparations law to compensate those who had been political prisoners between September 11, 1973, and March 11, 1990. They advised the government to form a commission made up of government representatives, former political prisoners, and members of the judiciary. This commission would define who would qualify as beneficiaries. Ominami, Naranjo, and Rossi also proposed holding a public ceremony in which the category of former political prisoner would be officially recognized, as well as to declare all former detention and torture centers in Chile national sites and to build monuments and memorials.

A draft agreement to provide reparations for former political prisoners of the military regime was presented in June 2003 in both the Senate and the Chamber of Deputies. The Chamber of Deputies bill stated that torture was one of the most serious violations of human rights and an "expression of utmost regression in the way that human beings relate to each other" and that the imprisonment and torture of thousands of Chileans "were the result of a state policy implemented by the de facto government headed by General Augusto Pinochet Ugarte." The draft agreement stated that these people needed "health care designed for rehabilitation," and that compensation for the torture victims was "a debt Chilean society owes these fellow citizens."[34] The government's response was a proposal of August 12, 2003, entitled "No Hay Mañana Sin Ayer" (There Is No Tomorrow without Yesterday).

The Quest for Reparations through Civil Lawsuits

During the 1990s, several civil lawsuits had been brought against the Chilean government seeking compensation for the disappearance of persons, political executions, and torture and serious physical harm. These lawsuits had diverse outcomes. The majority were turned down and appealed. Toward the end of 2002, there were only about 180 active lawsuits, although many of them covered several cases.

Nevertheless, a close examination of the fundamental arguments offered by the plaintiffs and the counterarguments presented by the State Defense Council in challenging the suits illustrates once again the persistence of antagonistic versions of what had happened in the country during Pinochet's regime. The civil lawsuits covered a wide range of situations that had caused the claimants serious harm, including a collective suit concerning exile, which was filed in late 2000.

One of the lawsuits, presented on behalf of Leopoldo Letelier Linque and twelve other Chileans, sought damages resulting from their being "forced by actions of violence to seek diplomatic protection in various embassies in Chile, between 1973 and 1974." On May 29, 2001, the State Defense Council challenged the lawsuit, arguing, "the prohibition to return to the country was legislated by the competent authority, in accordance with the norms of the time and supported by decrees passed in the years in which the events occurred. That is, the administrative authority adjusted to the legal framework of the times of the proceedings in question." The plaintiffs' lawyer, Adil Brkovic, commented on this response: "It makes absolutely no sense that the State Defense Council, directed by someone who had been exiled, says that exile was legal because it had been backed by a decree. It was a decree of the dictatorship! With this kind of reasoning, executions were legal and everything else the dictatorship did was legal, because it was all put on paper. Does putting it on paper make it legal? If so, what is the difference between a democratic state and a dictatorial state?"[35] The debate on the legality of laws passed by the dictatorship was not only relevant to human rights violations mentioned in the civil lawsuits.[36] On the one hand, the increasing number of civil lawsuits showed the victims' perception that the reparation policies implemented up to 2003 were inadequate. On the other hand, lawsuits became a political strategy for lawyers to force the government to increase financial reparations and to include former political prisoners in the reparations process.[37]

Gestures of Reparation

A group of seventeen high-ranking officers and forty lower-ranking officers had been tried and convicted of treason against *la patria* in 1973 for their opposition to the military coup. In June 2003, Air Force Commander in Chief General Osvaldo Sarabia reinstated these officers. This initiative improved his reputation with members of the air force, including with officers in exile, such as Sergio Poblete, who at the time lived in Belgium.[38] Sarabia's action allowed the officers to recover their institutional identity cards. Sarabia recalled that the process leading to reinstatement began shortly after he became commander in chief, in conversations with the former officers who lived in Chile and abroad. As Air Force Captain Raúl Vergara recalled, initial efforts at rapprochements had begun under former commander in chief General Matthei and had continued under his successor, General Ramón Vega. Vergara described the emotional difficulties of this process:

> From our perspective, the perception of this process has special characteristics. In terms of belonging, we have mixed feelings of love and resentment. On the one hand, we yearn for the air force to become a homogeneous institution, free from the prejudices of the past, and we hope for an almost maternal acceptance. We think of reunification as the return of the prodigal son, of the son who was spurned and stigmatized but is forgiven and is accepted back into the maternal bosom that had refused him over such a long time. On the other hand, in our reinstatement we would like to be recognized as winners, as heroes. We need recognition for the constitutional principles we upheld when dismissed from the ranks during the coup. We would like the institution to acknowledge the correctness of our cause and the error of the military winners of 1973. We want the air force to apologize to you for the blows, injuries, and abuses inflicted in their name, and we hope that the gates of the institution be wide open.[39]

He claimed that these feelings were common in the air force. It is highly likely that many air force members who had suffered severe consequences for not supporting the 1973 military coup could identify with these words. On the one hand, they saw themselves as victims of the "suffering, pain, and physical and mental privation stemming from the rigor and the cruelty we were subjected to." On the other hand, they saw themselves as winners because of the "clarity of their decisions, their adherence to principles, and their ability to resist with head held high and unbending spirits."[40] Vergara emphasized

> In both attitudes the common spirit, however, is that the feelings of both belonging and recognition are two sides of the same coin. The exclusion has kept us in a state of pain and absence. For military men, formed and molded in both values, with a total and absolute bond to the institution, this exclusion has a special and unique connotation. This explains our ceaseless, insistent, and persistent quest all these years for retribution, without ethical ties and with military honor.[41]

Defense Minister Michelle Bachelet[42] announced in 2003 that since 2002 the Ministry of Defense had been reviewing all of the cases of officials who had been forced to leave the armed forces for political reasons after September 11, 1973: "Two subsecretaries are in charge of a committee that works on two levels with dismissed military personnel. In the first instance, they aim to restore economic benefits and retirement pensions as provided in the law for public employees dismissed for political reasons. Second, they try to restore their honor and their relationship with the institutions."[43] This process, which had been quietly underway, was one more example of the ongoing efforts on behalf of other groups of Chileans affected by the aftermath of the military coup.

Former Exiles and Chileans Living Abroad

Acting as if the flow of returning Chileans who had been exiled after 1973 had ended, the National Office of Return closed its doors in September 1994. At the end of 1996, the laws that recognized university degrees and professional qualifications earned abroad and that exempted returnees from paying taxes expired. The final evaluation carried out by the National Office of Return confirmed the need to develop a policy for all Chileans residing outside of Chile. While campaigning for the presidency, current president Ricardo Lagos picked up this initiative, stating in his speeches that "the Chilean community outside our borders comprises virtually a fourteenth region that demands the legitimate right to participate in rebuilding the country. We are convinced that an initial and symbolic step in that direction must be the recognition of their inalienable rights as citizens, first of all by granting them the right to vote in presidential elections."[44]

The result was the creation of the Dirección para la Comunidad de Chilenos en el Exterior, or DICOEX (Office for the Community of Chileans Abroad), in the Ministry of Foreign Affairs. It acknowledged that the community of Chileans abroad might well constitute a fourteenth national region and explicitly recognized the Chilean diaspora.[45] Among other initiatives, DICOEX started a census in 2002 to ascertain how many Chileans are living abroad. DICOEX opened the possibility of building a bridge between the exiles, whose numbers in 1982 were conservatively estimated at around 200,000, and their homeland. By 1994, no more than 50,000 former exiles had returned to Chile.[46]

"There Is no Tomorrow without Yesterday": The Reparations Proposal of President Ricardo Lagos

On August 12, 2003, President Lagos presented a proposal to the nation to give reparations to victims of several types of human rights violations. The new feature of his proposal was that it recognized that the consequences of human rights violations could not be repaired with one solution or with a complete closing of the issue, as had been previously advocated:

> It is the duty of all Chileans, and especially my duty as head of state, to create convincing measures that help to create a nation whose soul is united in peace for the new generation of Chileans, a nation whose conscience has taken the right steps necessary for truth, justice, and reparation. Chile

will only be able to aspire to a dignified, solid, and democratic future if it is capable of doing so upon a foundation of social peace, solidarity, and the unity of all Chileans.[47]

Lagos pointedly stated that his government would not accept a proposal that established an end to the reparation process and that he would leave it up to the courts to interpret the amnesty decree. Lagos' proposal outlined the following objectives:

- To uncover that part of the truth that is still unknown and that it is an ethical imperative to reveal—the location of the detained-disappeared persons and of executed persons—and to clarify the circumstances of their disappearances and deaths.
- To persist in ensuring the independence, expediency, and efficiency of the tribunal's actions in the search for justice and in the application and interpretation of the law. This requires pushing for legislative initiatives that facilitate and speed up judicial investigations.
- To broaden and improve reparation measures applied up to now and to expand these in cases where there are any gaps or to include situations that deserve to be included.
- To improve, through legislative initiatives, institutional designs, and actions, the protection, promotion and guarantee of full respect of fundamental human rights.[48]

To achieve these objectives, Lagos proposed that some judges would remain assigned exclusively to human rights cases and to those cases that were connected and that could be collectively placed in the hands of one judge. This was complemented with legislative initiatives to speed up judicial investigations and the handling of information.[49]

During the month of September 2003, different sectors of society remembered and commemorated the fact that thirty years had passed since the military coup. As part of the initiatives toward reconciliation, the president opened to the public the doors of Morandé 80, the presidential palace, which had been closed by the military regime. The government also restored the image of Salvador Allende. The memories relived after thirty years show that a common history does not exist and that it might never emerge, not even in descriptive terms. Contradictions and discrepancies in interpretation cut across deep loyalties that have given meaning to the lives of different groups over the past thirty years. These contradictions have coexisted in a shared place. The capacity to separate the legacy of death and the pain of that past from a future offering hope and life, however, is still very far away.

Concluding Thoughts

The Comisión Nacional sobre Prisión Política y Tortura (National Commission on Political Imprisonment and Torture), also known as the Comisión Valech, named after its president emeritus, Bishop Sergio Valech Aldunate, was created in November 2003. An important step in the process of uncovering the truth, this commission was set up to compile a meticulous list of persons who had been deprived of freedom or tortured for political reasons and to ascertain what they had experienced. This recognition, President Lagos said, "will permit persons who have not received any other form of reparation to receive an austere and symbolic compensation."[50] In the meantime, Pinochet was deprived of his immunity in the Operación Cóndor case, and his accounts in the Riggs Bank were frozen.

President Ricardo Lagos received the Valech Commission's report on November 10, 2004, and officially announced its findings to the Chilean people on November 28, 2004. The report declares that torture was a government policy during the military regime. It describes the methods of torture and the places it was conducted. Lagos told Chileans that they now understood the "magnitude of the suffering, the insanity of the intense cruelty, the immensity of the pain" that have affected the lives of thousands of persons and their families.

In December 2004, Congress approved a law that would provide an "austere and symbolic" monthly payment as compensation to the thousands of people imprisoned and tortured during the military regime. The far more important moral reparation emerged from the recognition of the military government's moral, political, and penal responsibilities in this massive violation of human rights. For the victims, it is a vindication of their efforts to keep the cause of truth and justice alive in a society that has largely preferred to dismiss and forget this dark and violent past.

Notes

1. This paper was translated from Spanish by Jennifer Herbst.

2. Brian Loveman and Elizabeth Lira, *Las suaves cenizas del olvido: la vía chilena de reconciliación política 1814–1932,* 2nd ed. (Santiago: Ediciones LOM DIBAM, 2000), chap. 1, pp. 11–54.

3. Ibid.

4. Speech given by President of the Republic Patricio Aylwin Azócar to the National Congress in Valparaíso on May 21, 1990. See Patricio Aylwin, *La transición chilena. Discursos escogidos.* (Santiago: Editorial Andrés Bello, 1990), 31.

5. María Eugenia Oyarzún, "Gobierno fijará muy pronto su posición frente a la reconciliación," *La Tercera* online edition, August 14, 1995, www.latercera.cl.

6. Ibid.

7. Ibid.

8. According to figures from the Corporación Nacional de Reparación y Reconciliación, 1,145 people had been detained and afterwards disappeared during the military regime. See Corporación Nacional de Reparación y Reconciliación, "Informe a su excelencia el presidente de la república sobre las actividades desarrolladas al 15 de mayo 1996," 36.

9. Operación Cóndor was a plan in which the intelligence agencies and security forces of the military governments of Chile, Uruguay, Argentina, Paraguay, Brazil, and Bolivia collaborated in the exchange of information and carried out human rights violations, including assassinations and disappearances, against real or perceived opponents of their regimes.

10. The so-called Caravana de la Muerte was a military operation led by General Sergio Arellano Stark in October 1973, in which seventy-two people were murdered in various Chilean cities.

11. Fundación de Ayuda Social de las Iglesias Cristianas. (Social Aid Foundation of the Christian Churches).

12. Corporación de Promoción y Defensa de los Derechos del Pueblo, or Corporation for the Promotion and Defense of the Rights of the People.

13. Amnesty International Spanish-language website, "Chile: Informe en derecho sobre la incompatibilidad del Decreto Ley 2191 de 1978 de Chile con el derecho internacional," index no. AMR 22/002/2001/s, January 2001, http://web.amnesty.org/library/index/ESLAMR220022001.

14. The Plaza de la Constitución is one of the main squares in Santiago in front of La Moneda, the presidential palace.

15. "Viviana Díaz, Queremos que las FF.AA. asuman su responsabilidad," *La Nación* online, January 5, 2001, www.primeralinea.cl Caterine Galaz.

16. The majority of the cited cases had occurred in 1973 and 1974. The report did not include information on the 356 cases of disappeared persons attributed to the Dirección de Inteligencia Nacional (DINA, or National Intelligence Agency). Only twenty-seven of these cases were documented in the report given to President Lagos.

17. "FF.AA entregan destino de 200 desaparecidos," *La Tercera* online, January 6, 2001, www.latercera.cl.

18. "Exclusivo: la introducción de los comandantes en jefe en el informe sobre desaparecidos. El Mensaje de las FF.AA. a Lagos," *La Tercera* online, January 21, 2001, www.latercera.cl.

19. "Codepu rechaza informe de FF.AA.sobre desaparecidos," *La Tercera* online, January 11, 2001, www.latercera.cl.

20. Speech to Chilean Senate, 22nd sess., Wednesday, January 10, 2001, Senado—República de Chile website: www.senado.cl.

21. Julio Oliva García, "Detenidos desaparecidos fueron exhumados e incinerados," *El Siglo* online, November 2000, www.elsiglo.cl.

22. www.primeralinea.cl, December 27, 2000.

23. See Brian Loveman and Elizabeth Lira, *El espejismo de la reconciliación política* (Santiago: Ediciones LOM DIBAM, 2002).

24. Radio Nederland, www.rnw.nl/informarn/html/act020806_tucapeljimenez.html.

25. Revista *Qué Pasa,* www.quepasa.cl/sitios/enfoco/2001/04/27/.

26. Among them were retired army Major Alvaro Corbalán, Major Krantz Bauer Donoso, Police Commander Iván Quiroz, DINA civil servant Jorge Vargas Bories, and Gonzalo Maas del Valle.

27. For details about those involved in the judicial cases see FASIC, "Nómina de miembros de las Fuerzas Armadas, Carabineros, Investigaciones y de Servicios de Seguridad, sometidos a proceso y condenados," www.fasic.org/juri/nomina.htm.

28. OpinionJap, La Trinchera, "El Invitado Mayo 2003,"www.opinionjap.cl/invitado_mayo.htm.

29. Ibid.

30. Francisco Bañados and Gaspar Ramírez, "Ejército toma medidas: problemas por la reclusión en recintos castrenses: ex militares procesados complican doctrina Cheyre," July 30, 2003, www.emol.cl. Among those detained were retired Brigadier General Miguel Krassnoff (accused of fourteen kidnappings); retired Brigadier General Pedro Espinoza (accused of sixteen kidnappings); retired Colonel Germán Barriga (accused of ten kidnappings); Colonel Carlos López (accused of ten kidnappings); Colonel Hugo Cardemil (accused of eight kidnappings and the kidnapping of a minor); Major General Alvaro Corbalán (accused of thirteen first-degree murders, seven charges of depriving liberty, four kidnappings with homicide, and six kidnappings); Lieutenant Colonel Andrés Magaña (accused of nineteen first-degree murders and seventeen kidnappings); General Eugenio Covarrubias (accused of obstruction of justice); Brigadier General Enrique Leddy (charged with one first-degree murder); Major General Jorge Herrera (accused of twelve first-degree murders; and General Raúl Iturriaga (charged in the Prats case). General Carlos Prats, Chile's former commander in chief of the army and vice president of the republic, who had fled Chile after the coup, was murdered on September 30, 1974, by a car bomb in Buenos Aires. This case was part of Operación Cóndor.

31. The government of the Concertación did not recognize militants of left-wing groups who had been detained for so-called terrorist acts or for posing a threat to the state's internal security after 1990 as political prisoners, even though those prisoners argued that their actions had been guided by political motives.

32. *Chacabuco, memorias del silencio* (2001), by Gastón Ancelovici, is a documentary film that narrates the experiences and recollections of a group of former prisoners who return to Chacabuco, a concentration camp in the Antofagasta region, where they had been imprisoned for several months.

33. Both texts may be found online at the *La Nación* website under "El intrincado camino de los derechos humanos," http://www.lanacion.cl/p4_lanacion/site/arctic/20030624/pags/20030624114225.html.

34. *Diputados,* 70th sess., June 17, 2003, 36–37.

35. www.memoriayjusticia.cl/español/sp_derechos_afdd.html.

36. The issue had been discussed in Congress (1991–1998) in relation to proposed legislation to return possessions confiscated by the military junta through decrees. Acknowledging the fait accompli, the legislation sought to repair the consequences, in fact accepting that the confiscations had already taken effect, regardless of the legality of the decrees. Obviously, Senator Sergio Fernández (UDI), who had been the minister of the interior in the military government, considered that those decrees were fully legal and he was against any compensation legislation.

37. "DDHH: Exiliados buscan ser incluidos en propuestas de reparación," *El Mostrador,* June 6, 2003, www.elmostrador.cl.

38. "General Sarabia hace gesto de unidad. FACH reintegra a oficiales exonerados en gobierno militar," *La Tercera* online, June 7, 2003, www.latercera.cl.

39. Raúl Vergara Meneses, "Sobre el reencuentro de la familia aérea." www.elmostrador.cl. Palabras de Raúl Vergara Meneses "Sobre el reencuentro de la familia aérea," June 11, 2003. www.aginadigital.com.ar/articulos/2003/2003cuart/noticias32/1060413-6.asp.

40. Ibid.

41. Ibid.

42. Bachelet's father had been an air force general who was killed under torture in 1974.

43. "FF.AA. y Carabineros harían gesto," *El Mercurio Calama* online, vol. 37, no. 12.223, June 11, 2003, www.mercuriocalama.cl/site/edic/20030610233339/pags/20030611055736.html.

44. Ministerio de Educación de Chile, www.mineduc.cl/cultura/deprov/N2002013017291826558.html#a3; see also, Ricardo Lagos, "Carla Abierta a la comunidad de chilenos en el exterior," Octubre 1999. www.dipres.cl.

45. www.dicoex.net/RegionXIV.htm.

46. See Elizabeth Lira and Brian Loveman, *Políticas de reparación Chile: 1990–2004* (Santiago: Ediciones LOM DIBAM, 2005).

47. *No hay mañana sin ayer: propuesta del presidente Ricardo Lagos en material de derechos humanos* (Santiago: Gobierno de Chile, August 12, 2003), 49.

48. Ibid.

49. There were two components to this proposal: (1) Modifications to the general reparations law (Law 19.123). This bill was approved in November 2004 and enacted as Law 19.980. This law increased pensions by 50 percent and granted a one-time payment to the children of the detained-disappeared or executed in the form of a bond of up to ten million pesos (approximately US$15,000). It also improved the educational benefits provided by the general reparations law and committed to implement legal initiatives to solve patrimonial problems of family members of the detained-disappeared through resolving the lack of legal status of detained-disappeared persons. Law 19.980 also completed the legal framework for medical assistance for victims of human rights violations and their relatives through PRAIS. (2) The removal of criminal records of former political prisoners. This was enacted as Law 19.962 in August 2004.

50. Comisión Nacional sobre Prisión Política y Tortura, Decree 1040, Article 2, www.comisionprisionpoliticaytortura.cl.

2

Inching toward Democracy

President Lagos and the Chilean Armed Forces

GREGORY WEEKS

President Ricardo Lagos assumed office at a key moment in post-authoritarian civil-military relations in Chile. General Augusto Pinochet's apparent invincibility had evaporated; through a series of round table meetings (the Mesa de Diálogo, which is discussed at length in chapter 1, both military and civilian representatives were seeking to establish greater dialogue about the past, and Chilean judges were becoming ever bolder in asserting their legal right to force military officers to appear before them. It seemed a potentially propitious time for scaling back the political power and influence of the armed forces. The purpose of this chapter is to assess President Lagos' success in doing so.

In order to evaluate the administration of President Lagos in the area of civil-military relations, we must first outline the standard to which he will be held. In this chapter I will use a commonly accepted definition of civilian supremacy as a way to gauge Lagos' efforts to democratize civil-military relations. I will argue that although Lagos has only partially effected the structural reforms necessary to advance civilian supremacy over the military, and in some areas has not attempted to do so at all, he has made significant strides, certainly more than his predecessors. Much of that success, in fact, was compressed into several months in the latter half of 2004. Slowly (but thus far surely), Chile is inching toward democracy.

Although disagreement certainly exists about the definition of civilian supremacy over the armed forces, considerable consensus has emerged regarding its central elements, which incorporate several themes. The government must be able to formulate and conduct general policy without interference from the armed forces. It must also be able to define national defense in all respects, including having the final word on what issues merit the most attention, what the country's goals should be, what strategies are most appropriate, and what the military's proper role within that framework should be. In addition, the constitution, national law, and military codes must codify the subordinate position of the armed forces to the civilian government.[1]

I consider the success of the Lagos administration in enacting democratic reforms and facilitating smoother daily interactions between government institutions and the military leadership, while also analyzing the functioning of the most important formal civil-military contact points, namely the executive branch (especially the Ministry of Defense), Congress, and the judiciary.

However, we must also place Lagos in the context of his predecessors. Ricardo Lagos inherited a difficult situation, since former Presidents Patricio Aylwin and Eduardo Frei had left "loose ends" in many areas of civil-military relations. Nearly a decade of civilian rule and democratic elections had not sufficed to solve many pending issues. In addition, Lagos was the first member of the political left to serve as president since Salvador Allende, which made the military leadership even more skeptical of reform efforts. Finally, the resurgent conservative right, led by Joaquín Lavín of the far-right Unión Democrática Independiente (UDI), was eyeing the presidency and was often vocal about blocking presidential initiatives that aimed to reduce the power and influence of the Chilean armed forces.

When President Aylwin took office in 1990, scholars and policy makers alike discussed the primary reforms that required attention and, in fact, Aylwin and the coalition that supported him had made most of them part of his platform. The most prominent included reform of the copper law that guarantees part of the military budget (Article 96 of the Organic Laws of the Armed Forces), elimination of the military-designated senators (Constitutional Article 45), granting the president latitude in firing commanders in chief (Constitutional Article 93), reducing the power and scope of military courts (outlined in the Military Code of Justice), eliminating the military's ability to force a meeting of the National Security Council (Constitutional Article 95), shifting the Carabineros (national police) from the Ministry of Defense to the Interior Ministry (Constitutional Article 90), and increasing civilian oversight of military intelligence (Organic Laws of the Armed Forces).

Space precludes a detailed description and analysis of all these reform goals and failed efforts to enact them, and indeed that has been done elsewhere.[2] Taken together, however, the laws they sought to replace represent a complex and solid foundation of formal military constraints on civilian authority. Some of these reforms were passed in 2005: specifically, eliminating the designated senators, gaining authority to fire commanders in chief, and preventing the military from convoking the National Security Council. Going the opposite direction was intelligence, as the creation of a new National Intelligence Agency included almost complete autonomy for the military to conduct its own intelligence operations, with minimal civilian oversight.

Furthermore, in other areas the Lagos administration has made significant strides toward, at the very least, normalization of civil-military relations. In particular, it has been successful in improving civil-military trust. Although these improvements do not have an immediate impact on long-term civil-military stability, they may lay the groundwork for it.

Fundamental structural changes, of course, require congressional action. Wendy Hunter has argued that in Latin America the electoral incentives of politicians can trump military desires, so that military influence declines even in the face of resistance.[3] In Chile that outcome has only recently—and only partially—occurred. Even the copper law that allocates a share of copper revenue to the armed forces, the proceeds of which can reasonably be considered tempting for politicians, has yet to be put on the table. The Aylwin and Frei administrations found Congress, the press, and the military focused squarely on conflictive attempts at reform, which in turn not only distracted attention from attempts to roll back the military regime's policies in other areas, but also made the UDI and parts of the center-right Renovación Nacional (RN) less willing to compromise on those other issues. By the time Lagos took office, Congress had proved unable to fundamentally change the constitutional foundations of civil-military relations.

President Lagos also took office as the remarkable transformation of General Augusto Pinochet's image was already underway. The self-proclaimed "Cincinnatus"—who harkened back to ancient Rome to explain how he would return if his country needed him, and who over time had been compared to Hitler, Caligula, and myriad other of the most hated personages in history—was gradually being reduced in the public eye to a stooped and decrepit old man facing a number of legal challenges. As such, even his supporters—both military and civilian—coaxed him out of the political world and the limelight.

The Executive Branch and Limits of Power

In Chile, executive authority over the military is embodied primarily in constitutionally granted presidential powers and in the Ministry of Defense, which is the formally established link between the military leadership and the president. However, limitations on executive power have remained a bone of contention for Chilean presidents, who before 1973 had enjoyed much wider latitude.

One incident exemplifies not only the lack of presidential authority, but also the persistent issue of dealing with the past. The air force has widely been considered the least politicized branch of the armed forces. Its commanders in chief had been the most assertive in countering the power and influence of Pinochet, and commander in chief General Fernando Matthei had in fact proclaimed the victory of the "no" vote in the 1988 plebiscite, thus breaking the military regime's silence about the vote's outcome. In the post-authoritarian period, relations between the air force leadership and civilian governments were smooth. Therefore, when reports surfaced about the reemergence of a dictatorship-era organization within the air force, it was clear that civil-military relations were still highly problematic. The case demonstrates that the institutional barriers that existed (at least, perhaps, until 2005), as well as the ways in which civil-military communication has improved since 1990.

The so-called Comando Conjunto (Joint Command) was created in 1975 by air force officers in combination with civilians from Patria y Libertad, an extremist group of the right. Its purpose then was to coordinate repression, and its purpose, beginning in the late 1990s, was to ensure that the Mesa de Diálogo did not receive information relating to the air force's role in detaining, torturing, and killing political enemies.[4] In fact, air force General Patricio Campos, who was allegedly put in charge of collecting information for the round table, had ties to the Comando Conjunto in the 1970s. Air Force Commander in Chief Patricio Ríos officially denied that any such organization continued to exist.

Lagos could do very little as he watched the episode unfold. Publicly, he voiced frustration that as president he could not force the resignation of the air force commander in chief. If the commanders in chief required the president's confidence, he averred, they would act very differently.[5] The problem, of course, is that his reasoning was precisely why the military government specifically forbade such a firing. As Jaime Guzmán—the most influential intellectual force behind the 1980 constitution—argued during meetings of the Constitutional Commission, the idea of *inamovilidad* was insurance against "commotion" or "alteration" as governments changed.[6] The military, with its stated ethos of remaining above politics and politicians, did not wish to be "corrupted" by the whims of presidents. Instead, initially Lagos had to seek satisfaction in firing the civilian subsecretaries of aviation and of the navy as a sign of his displeasure.[7] Ríos resigned on October 13, 2002, after realizing that General Campos had been lying to him, that both a lawsuit and a constitutional accusation were underway against him, and that his support within the ranks was shaky.[8] Two months later he was forced to testify in court, accused of obstruction of justice in a suit brought by the Communist and Socialist Parties, along with the Group of Families of the Detained-Disappeared.

A similar situation had occurred in 1994, when President Frei informed Carabinero Commander in Chief Rodolfo Stange that he expected his resignation, accusing Stange of being derelict because of his failure to properly investigate a particularly egregious case of human rights abuse.[9] Stange refused to resign and remained without government confidence for a year and a half, finally leaving only after Frei informed him that he would not approve any of the promotions Stange recommended for the year. Thus, an administrative sledgehammer finally resolved the issue, but the lack of presidential authority persisted.

Of course, neither Lagos nor Frei can be blamed for such episodes since Chile's constitutional-legal structure effectively hamstrung them. Yet they demonstrate the dilemma for increasing civilian supremacy over the military. The armed forces enjoy considerable autonomy, a situation that can be changed only with significant congressional majorities. These majorities, meanwhile, never materialized because of resistance from the UDI and some sectors of the RN (depending on the issue), the binomial electoral system, and the presence of military-designated senators. Despite near constant rumors that constitutional reform might have a chance of passing (for example, even Joaquín Lavín suggested he might support allowing the president to remove commanders in chief), Concertación presidents and legislators have usually opted to avoid forcing votes on controversial issues when defeat seems assured. Public opinion reflects the same conundrum. According to a 2002 poll, although 74 percent of Chileans support reforming the constitution to allow the president to remove commanders in chief and 82 percent support eliminating designated senators, only 22 percent believe that political parties can reach consensus to achieve these reforms.[10] The 2004 reforms, therefore, constituted a remarkable breakthrough.

Lagos also cannot be blamed for being unable to change the military's views about the past. The air force incident underlines the fact that when faced with challenges to their interpretations of the military regime, the Chilean armed forces are as close to monolithic as large organizations can be.[11] When representatives from each branch came to the Mesa de Diálogo in 1999, they presented monologues that were carefully scripted and almost identical.[12] If civilians on the other side of the *mesa* were hoping to find some inter-service differences, they were to find the military representatives scrupulous in maintaining solidarity.

The only exception, when the army took a different public stance than the other branches, came in the wake of the release of the report of the National Commission on Political Imprisonment and Torture (known as the "Valech" report for the commission's president, Sergio Valech Aldunate). The report, based on more than 28,000 interviews, revealed in excruciating detail the horrors of the dictatorship's prisons.[13]

Commander in Chief Juan Emilio Cheyre gave a speech and then wrote a newspaper article in which the army took responsibility "for all the punishable and morally unacceptable actions of the past."[14] Although Cheyre fell short of admitting that the report was detailing state policy, he did advance from past assertions that all abuses were aberrations committed by rogue individuals. The air force chose not to assume responsibility, but rather to assign blame to those individuals who gave the orders (*los mandos*).[15] The commander in chief of the navy, Miguel Angel Vergara, declared that the navy would analyze the possibility of someday taking institutional responsibility, but since the navy had cooperated with the Valech Commission, "we have a clear conscience."[16] Retired officers, meanwhile, were simply indignant. The Circle of Retired Generals and Admirals issued a statement that the Valech Commission did not employ rigorous standards and that supposed victims were hoping to receive money.[17] The organization would only admit that it was "possible" that some victims did in fact disappear.

The divide over the past, exemplified by the obstructionism within the air force, also found voice in retired General Manuel Contreras, the former head of the Dirección de Inteligencia Nacional (DINA), the notoriously brutal intelligence service under the control of General Pinochet during the first years after the coup. Contreras had written a book entitled *La verdad histórica: el ejército guerrillero,* published in 2000, which purported to prove the existence of a massive rebel army that threatened Chile's existence before the coup and therefore required a vigorous response by the state. In 2001, he went a step further and published *La verdad histórica II ¿desaparecidos?*. As the title suggests, Contreras argues that the Rettig Commission (created in 1990 to investigate human rights abuses) accepted Marxist lies regarding the supposed disappearances of political prisoners. Many if not most of those labeled as "disappeared" in fact not only were released without any mistreatment and after due process had taken its course, he claims, but also are currently alive and well. For these Marxists (who, according to Contreras, still comprise a large percentage of Chileans) "the truth never interests them, and they only live by lies, calumny, and hatred."[18] To provide "historical accuracy," Contreras examines numerous cases from the Rettig Commission and human rights organizations, using documents that he claims are accurate. (Contreras claims that, unlike the Rettig Commission, he has only impartiality as a goal.) Contreras' primary conclusion is that, given the opposition's fervent desire to discredit the armed forces, it should come as no surprise that hundreds of people prefer to be considered "disappeared" than to admit that they have been free for decades.

For obvious reasons, it is very difficult to assess the degree to which such ideas permeate the ranks, but there is no doubt that Contreras is not the only one who believes them. After General Ríos retired, the so-called Plan Babilonia was made public. A product of retired intelligence officials from the military government, the plan's intent was to control the information being provided to the government about the past actions of military officers.[19] This included attempting to ruin the career of anyone providing too much information, counseling anyone who was called to testify, and seeking to ensure that investigations could not be completed.

Very likely, the passage of time is the primary means by which these examples of persistent obstructionism will fade away. Most current generals (of all branches) served in the military government in some capacity or even were involved in fighting in the coup's aftermath. Although there are numerous senior officers viewed as less political and more willing to work closely with civilians (Army Commander in Chief Cheyre being one), only gradually will their number increase as hard-line officers retire.

Civil-Military Relations at Ground Level: The Defense Ministry

President Lagos has been active in attempting to increase the level of civil-military trust at "ground level," meaning the specific contact points where the majority of routine interaction takes place. Most notably, the Ministry of Defense is where strategies, budget needs, and planning are discussed and debated in detail. Before 1973, it was largely ignored by politicians, who felt there were more important issues to deal with and therefore were content to allow the armed forces to make such decisions themselves. After 1990, civilian policy makers realized that the ministry was critical not only in influencing defense policy, but also simply in establishing positive relationships with military officers.

In 1990, President Patricio Aylwin had to reconstruct the Ministry of Defense, which historically had been peripheral to decision making and had been generally ignored during the military government. With regard to naming the defense minister, President Lagos has been shrewder than his predecessors. Aylwin and Frei had shifted between combative personalities who were consequently ignored by the military (such as Patricio Rojas, the first post-authoritarian minister) and ministers whose desire for stability meant granting the military leadership much of what it requested (such as Edmundo Pérez Yoma, who served under Frei). Lagos chose Mario Fernández, a Christian Democrat who had served both as subsecretary of war and also of aviation, and who had never been viewed as caving in to military pressures. The military considered Fernández a moderate who was also experienced in defense matters.

When Fernández left for another cabinet post in early 2002, Lagos named former Minister of Health Michelle Bachelet as his replacement. She was the first female minister of defense in Latin America, was the first defense minister from the Socialist Party in Chile since the Allende administration (she spent parts of the 1973–1990 period in Australia and East Germany), and was the daughter of an air force general assassinated as a result of his opposition to the military government. However, she was also committed to cultivating and maintaining a professional relationship with the armed forces, as well as to avoiding the public rancor that had plagued previous ministers. Although her background is in medicine and health, in the 1990s she had taken courses at the Academia Nacional de Estudios Políticos y Estratégicos, a Defense Ministry-funded think tank at the Inter-American Defense College in the United States, and had obtained a master's degree from the civil-military program at the army war academy. Her success in the position has made her one of the fastest rising stars within the Concertación. She stepped down from her post in 2004 to pursue the Concertación's nomination for president. Her replacement, Jaime Ravinet, has no defense experience, but as a generally noncontroversial career politician he is also unlikely to make waves.

The Lagos administration has also been working to make the ministry itself a more rational and effective institution. It has few full-time employees, and the offices of the subsecretaries (there are a total of five—army, navy, air force, national police, and civilian intelligence) duplicate a number of duties, thus stretching already scarce resources. Lagos therefore initiated a restructuring effort to ensure that the separate offices did not perform the same tasks. Under the auspices of the ministry, the administration also organized meetings to produce a second defense "white book" (the *Libro de Defensa Nacional de Chile*). Like the first, completed in 1998, it resulted from meetings among government officials, officers, and civilian experts to outline the country's strategic situation and needs, especially in light of technological advances and globalization. Although the results have lacked specificity and precision, the meetings have been useful in terms of fostering greater civil-military communication.

Finally, within the executive branch President Lagos has been compelled to listen to the armed forces through the National Security Council (COSENA). Originally intended by the military government to act as a military watchdog over civilian authorities, through the constitutional reform negotiated in 1989 it was reconstituted with an equal balance of commanders in chief and civilians, thus negating the military advantage. In addition, even when a vote takes place, the president is not required to follow its dictates. Any two members can force convocation, but there has been a tacit agreement that even when at least two commanders in chief desire to meet, they will inform the president and allow him to convoke the meeting.[20] Nonetheless, press leaks make clear that the president is doing so only because of military pressure. Lagos found himself in that situation in late 2000, when Pinochet was facing possible arrest. Although he did not want to meet, he had no choice and so scheduled a meeting in January 2001.[21]

It is noteworthy that by early 2003 Lagos had met with COSENA only that single time, since Aylwin was obliged to convoke COSENA five times during his administration and Frei eight times (during the fifteen months Pinochet was in London, the armed forces forced four meetings). In general, Lagos has followed the pattern established by his predecessors, which is to avoid meeting unless the commanders in chief demand it. This, along with the inability of the military to force any action, has meant that COSENA has not been the authoritarian enclave many believed it might be. Nonetheless, it still allows the military leadership to force the president to deal with any issue it believes is important. The 2005 reforms mark an important advance.

The Military and Congress

Other political institutions, however, have yet to evolve significantly in terms of asserting civilian influence. Both the Chamber of Deputies and the Senate have committees for national defense, but they are neither well staffed nor particularly influential. There is no permanent staff anywhere within the congressional structure with expertise on defense issues. Any member of Congress without prior knowledge of such issues must find his or her own resources, and in practice relatively few members do so. Like the Ministry of Defense, Congress could not build on a past history of effective oversight and activism. Prior to 1973, the military had operated not only with little congressional intervention, but also with little interest from a legislature more focused on the many socioeconomic challenges facing the country.

The composition of the Committee on National Defense in the Senate in 2004 demonstrates some of the limitations to expanding democratic oversight. Of its five members, one (Julio Canessa Robert) was a designated senator who was vice commander in chief of the army during the dictatorship and a close friend of Pinochet. Another, Sergio Fernández Fernández (UDI) was, among other things, minister of the interior in the military government. Baldo Prokurica, a conservative member of RN, was a local government official during the dictatorship. The committee was rounded out by Sergio Paez Verdugo, one of the founders of the Christian Democratic Party, who had no previous experience in defense matters (he took the committee position in March 2002) and Fernando Flores Labra from PPD, who had been in several ministerial positions in the Allende government (and was a political prisoner for three years), but whose main interests have been economic and business-related. Given that the majority have close ties to the military government (and the military itself) and the minority have considerably less experience, it is not altogether surprising that the committee is not a vehicle for reform. In fact, it rarely even meets.

The committee convened only eight times in 2000, five times in 2001, and eight times in 2002.[22] Almost all Senate committees meet more often (there are exceptions, such as Public Works, which met only three times in 2001). In comparison, Mining and Energy or Legislation and Justice often meet more than sixty times a year, and even Foreign Relations (which, given its attention to external threats, also relates to the military) usually meets at least twenty times a year.

Notwithstanding the presence of retired commanders in chief in the Senate (and a scattering of elected retired officers) there is relatively little routine interaction between members of Congress and the military. There are several reasons for this. First and most important, Congress has very little influence over military budgets, which are set by the president and the details of which cannot be modified. Congress can reduce the military budget, but by law not below the 1989 level (the last budget under the military government), adjusted for inflation.[23] Without significant power of the purse, Congress is peripheral to defense decision making. Second, it is generally frowned upon for officers and politicians to interact, which means they do not develop relationships.[24] Officers who do so are viewed as becoming politicized, while politicians are seen to be pandering. Third, there is no recent precedent for congressional activism with regard to defense issues in Chile. Since the establishment of a strong executive in the 1925 constitution, presidential power has consistently trumped congressional influence in the area of defense, a situation that was solidly reinforced by the military regime and the 1980 constitution. Last, Congress is located in Valparaíso, and since the executive branch, the army, and the air force are all in Santiago (a ninety-minute drive away), defense decision making has tended to remain concentrated in the capital.

There is another obstacle to structural reform: The structure of the Chilean Congress, with designated senators and the binomial electoral system, has consistently overrepresented the right, which already has a solid one-third (and at times more) of the popular vote. Therefore, for the Concertación to attain even simple majorities often requires wooing members of the RN or to a lesser extent the UDI. Changing organic constitutional laws (such as those governing the military's share of copper revenue) requires a four-sevenths majority in both houses of Congress, which thus far has not been attained.[25] The 2005 constitutional reforms, however, did demonstrate that reform is not impossible.

The Judiciary and the Military

Despite the problems faced by the executive branch, the courts have continued their work of pursuing specific cases of disappearances, using the legal reinterpretation of the 1978 amnesty to continue an investigation until the individual in question was officially declared deceased. The courts, and especially Judge Juan Guzmán Tapia, became more active in 1999 while Pinochet was still detained in Great Britain, and weathered numerous calls by the military to protect what the latter saw as the all-encompassing original intent of the amnesty (including specific mentions of that fact in the Mesa de Diálogo position papers of each service branch). Furthermore, in 2000, the Supreme Court ruled that amnesty could be granted only to specific individuals (as opposed to automatically applying to everyone) after an investigation had been carried out and a judicial decision reached. Such investigations could not be shut down simply because the crime had been committed between 1973 and 1978. This decision led the way for hundreds of officers to be charged with crimes.

The courts in Chile also began proceedings against Pinochet himself. The Supreme Court ruling had stripped him of immunity, and he faced charges related to the Caravan of Death case. In March 2001, the appellate court ruled that the only charges applicable to Pinochet were knowing about the crimes after the fact and not ordering an investigation or sanctioning those responsible.[26] The crimes of murder and kidnapping therefore did not apply. This was obviously a victory for the retired general; although he remained potentially responsible for the crime of covering up the murders (essentially obstruction of justice), he had avoided standing trial for the more serious crimes. Finally, on July 9, 2001, the court closed the case "temporarily" because Pinochet was suffering from dementia and therefore could not be forced to stand trial. Only if he was ruled to have recovered from that dementia could the case be reopened, and on July 1, 2002, the Supreme Court appeared to eliminate that possibility, ruling that Pinochet's physical condition was irreversible.[27] But Pinochet himself changed that by giving a television interview in late 2003 in which he was lucid and defiant, thereby opening up yet another new avenue for Judge Guzmán to prosecute him. As of late 2005, he has yet to stand trial, but the case remains open.

The courts were clearly far more active than ever before in trying human rights cases against officers, and Pinochet's arrest opened the door for *any* officer to be charged or called to testify, regardless of rank. As a result of the *mesa*'s work, and specifically its revelations of continued frustration in locating the remains of those killed during the dictatorship, in 2001 the Supreme Court appointed special judges whose mandate was to focus on investigating the fates of the disappeared.

Although it is difficult to ascribe credit to the Lagos administration for these developments, they represent an important step forward in civilian supremacy over the armed forces, and certainly the president was responsible for the release of the Valech report, which will likely spur on the courts even more. Even though Pinochet has been released, he is no longer untouchable and, in fact, has found it advisable simply to resign from the Senate and from the public eye. It is obviously impossible to claim dementia while retaining an important political post.

The negotiations of the past, whereby the army would extract concessions in return for allowing a limited number of officers to testify, have not been repeated. In Chile respect for the sanctity of the judicial system overrides military concerns, even for the far right. When navy commander in chief Admiral Miguel Angel Vergara called in November 2002 for a two-year limit on human rights investigations and for the courts to interpret the 1978 amnesty in its "original form," whereby investigations would not take place, he received no public support.[28] However, Lagos did hope to conclude human rights cases as quickly as possible (as did, unsuccessfully, both Aylwin and Frei).[29]

What of Pinochet?

A notable difference between President Lagos and his predecessors revolves around the role of Pinochet himself. Pinochet was a constant thorn in the sides of Aylwin and Frei, as he had a tremendous knack for using public statements, appearances, and symbolic gestures to keep the government off balance and on the defensive before the military. He could not be ignored and was usually able either to block unwanted executive or legislative initiatives or at least to extract major concessions on those he could not prevent. He spoke on behalf of the military as a whole and was never contradicted. But by the time of Lagos' election, that situation had begun to change.

After his return to Chile, General Pinochet's public appearances and statements gradually declined, which can only be deemed as positive for civil-military tranquility. The military—but obviously the army in particular—feels compelled to support him. He commands tremendous respect within the ranks, and at least publicly there does not appear to be any dissent. Nonetheless, the army leadership recognizes that the honorary lifetime commander in chief (*benemérito,* the unofficial title granted him by the army upon retirement) rocks the political boat to such a degree that easing him out of public life is a necessity. Even before he became commander in chief in 2002, General Juan Emilio Cheyre was instrumental in convincing Pinochet to stop going to Senate sessions and then, in July 2002, to resign his seat, arguing that it would be the best thing for the army as a whole.[30]

At that time, Senator (and former Navy Commander in Chief) Jorge Martínez Busch called for a general amnesty, which prompted Senate President Andrés Zaldívar to call a press conference in which he flatly rejected the idea:

"It will be a long time before we can have a single vision of our history."[31] The notion of a new amnesty is not new, both active and retired officers have floated it routinely (and unsuccessfully).

In his resignation letter, Pinochet did not launch his customary criticisms of politicians and the left. Instead, he reiterated that the actions initiated on September 11, 1973, were "in defense of the sovereignty, national security, and peace of our country" and that he hoped his "sacrifice as a soldier" would be recognized by future generations.[32] What followed in the congressional debate reflected an exchange that had become very familiar since the return of civilian rule in 1990, though the catcalls, yelling, and commotion had not been seen since Pinochet first entered the Senate in 1998.[33] Senators of the Concertación deplored the fact that Pinochet could never be judged by a court of law, and that human rights abuses remained an open wound for Chileans. They also wondered how, if Pinochet were legally demented, could he write a letter of resignation? On the right, meanwhile, senators lambasted the left for seeking to question the honor and integrity of such a patriotic man, thereby, in the words of one UDI senator, "trying with their words to return to the sowing of hatred and division among Chileans" while a senator from the RN lamented that the resignation would not serve to "satisfy the appetite for vengeance on the part of a minority sector."[34]

Pinochet's image received serious damage in 2004, when investigations revealed that he had upwards of US$8 million in a U.S. bank (Riggs Bank). His supporters found it difficult to account for such a sum, since the presidential salary was scarcely more than US$40,000 a year. Even former DINA chief Manuel Contreras could only note dryly, "The problem with Pinochet is that he got quite a lot."[35] This disclosure punctured a long-held image of probity, and Chile's tradition of avoiding the corruption so ingrained in many Latin American countries will also serve to detract from the heroic Cincinnatus image. Fewer and fewer politicians wish to associate publicly with him.

Conclusion

Democratizing civil-military relations in Chile is a massive undertaking, requiring transformations not only in the country's constitutional and legal framework, but also in the attitudes of military officers, politicians, and civil society. Progress has thus been slow in terms of long-term structural change, but at the same time the Lagos administration has advanced in several important areas. With regard to civilian supremacy, the government clearly does not have the last word on many important issues, since numerous constitutional articles, laws, and military codes serve to limit civilian authority, but some reforms are indeed underway. Those reforms are critical for civilian supremacy over the armed forces in Chile.

Under Aylwin, the courts made their first unsteady steps in the direction of putting officers on trial, culminating in the imprisonment of General Manuel Contreras in 1995 (though only after protracted negotiations that resulted in concessions to the army) and continued more vigorously after Pinochet's arrest in London. The Frei administration (under the initiative of Defense Minister Edmundo Pérez Yoma) also set up the Mesa de Diálogo that, although deemed highly imperfect by all concerned, became a mechanism for civil-military dialogue about the most sensitive topics of the dictatorship, namely the arrest, detention, torture, and deaths of thousands of people.

Lagos has been much more successful than previous presidents in fostering greater civil-military trust, despite his background in the Socialist Party and as a former Allende administration cabinet member. Although still weak, the Ministry of Defense is more relevant and involved than during the 1990s. Lagos' choices to fill ministerial positions have also reassured the military leadership that his administration is both serious about dialogue and technically competent. If this pattern continues, the level of civil-military trust will gradually rise, which in turn can provide the atmosphere necessary for discussions of civilian supremacy to continue advancing.

In sum, it may be said that Lagos is making the best of a difficult situation. Substantial reforms have been made, but much has yet to be accomplished. A combination of constraints, whether constitutional, legal, partisan, or ideological, has yet to be fully overcome. In spite of those obstacles, he has made important strides. By negotiating reform and increasing military confidence in civilian defense institutions, Lagos is setting the stage for a decrease in military resistance to change. Civil-military relations are therefore inching toward democracy.

Notes

I would like to thank Silvia Borzutzky, Brian Loveman, Aldo Vacs, and an anonymous reviewer for their very helpful comments on this chapter.

1. For an excellent discussion of the concept, see Felipe Agüero, *Soldiers, Civilians, and Democracy: Post-Franco Spain in Comparative Perspective* (Baltimore: Johns Hopkins University Press, 1995).

2. For example, see Claudio Fuentes, "After Pinochet: Civilian Policies toward the Military in the 1990s Chilean Democracy," *Journal of Interamerican Studies and World Affairs* 42, no. 3 (Fall 2000): 111–42; Brian Loveman, "Misión Cumplida? Civil-Military Relations and the Chilean Political Transition," *Journal of Interamerican Studies and World Affairs* 33, no. 3 (Fall 1991): 35–74; Patricio Silva, "Searching for Civilian Suprem-

acy: The Concertación Governments and the Military in Chile," *Bulletin of Latin American Research* 21, no. 3 (July 2002): 375–95; Gregory Weeks, *The Military and Politics in Postauthoritarian Chile* (Tuscaloosa: University of Alabama Press, 2003).

3. Wendy Hunter, *Eroding Military Influence in Brazil: Politicians against Soldiers* (Chapel Hill: University of North Carolina Press, 1997).

4. "Los fantasmas que acosan a la FACH," *Qué Pasa,* September 20, 2002.

5. "Lagos: Es hora de que el presidente pueda remover a los comandantes en jefe," *La Tercera,* September 25, 2002.

6. *Actas oficiales de la comisión de estudio de la nueva constitución política de la República,* Sesión 392, June 29, 1978, p. 2994.

7. Nonetheless, one positive aspect of the incident was that, unlike many situations in the 1990s, government-military discussions were held under the auspices of formal institutions (in this case, the Ministry of Defense).

8. "Las 120 horas más intensas de Ríos," *Qué Pasa,* October 18, 2002.

9. See Weeks, *Military and Politics in Postauthoritarian Chile,* chap. 5.

10. The poll was carried out by the think tank Fundación Chile 21 and reported in "74% de chilenos apoya que presidente remueva a jefes castrenses," *La Tercera,* October 1, 2002.

11. These interpretations filter even into language. Should the Pinochet years be referred to as a *dictadura* or simply the *gobierno militar*? When Allende was overthrown, was there a *golpe de estado* or a *pronunciamiento*? In books, articles, interviews, or any other forum, officers of all branches are careful to use what they believe is the proper terminology to describe past events.

12. For a discussion on the military's view of the past, see Felipe Agüero, *Democracy and the Future of Civil-Military Relations in Chile: An Exercise in Historical Comparison,* Dante B. Fascell North-South Center Working Paper No. 6 (Miami: Dante B. Fascell Center, May 2002); Gregory Weeks, "The 'Lessons' of Dictatorship: Political Learning and the Military in Chile," *Bulletin of Latin American Research* 21, no. 3 (July 2002): 396–412.

13. It also recommended providing compensation to victims, and a law to do so sped quickly and successfully through Congress. For the text of the Valech report, see http://www.presidencia.gob.cl/view/viewInformeTortura.htm#1.

14. Ejército de Chile, "Ejército de Chile: el fin de una visión," November 5, 2004, http://www.ejercito.cl/htm-generado/2010.html.

15. "Fach condena tortura y asigna la responsabilidad a los mandos superiores," *La Tercera,* December 2, 2004.

16. Miguel Angel Vergara, "Armada analizará en su mérito reconocimiento institucional," *El Monstrador,* November 10, 2004.

17. "Ex militares deslegitiman testimonios de informe Valech," *El Mostrador,* December 2, 2004.

18. Manuel Contreras Sepúlveda, *La verdad histórica II ¿desparecidos?* (Santiago: Ediciones Encina, 2001), 3.

19. "El misterioso Plan Babilonia," *Primera Línea,* November 11, 2002.

20. An exception occurred in December 1992, when Pinochet, Navy Commander in Chief Jorge Martínez Busch, and Supreme Court Justice Marcos Aburto voted to convene in response to a constitutional accusation against ministers of the Supreme Court and the auditor general of the army.

21. "FFAA piden aplicar amnistía sin investigar," *La Tercera,* January 3, 2001.

22. Senado de Chile, *Boletín Estadístico No. 32, Labor Desarrollada por el Senado, Año 2000*; *Boletín Estadístico No. 35, Labor Desarrollada por el Senado, Año 2001*; and *Boletín Estadístico No. 38, Labor Desarrollada por el Senado, Año 2002.*

23. A clear analysis of the highly complicated process of military budgeting can be found in Guillermo Patillo, "El presupuesto de defensa en Chile: procesos decisionales y propuesta de indicadores de evolución," *Security and Defense Studies Review* 1 (Winter 2001): 125–46.

24. For a military view of this issue (by a retired air force colonel), see Carlos Castro Sauritain, "Asesoría parlamentaria del Ministerio de Defensa," *Política y Estrategia* 80 (January 2000): 137–45. He advocates a special advisory body composed of active-duty officers, retired officers, and qualified civilians, similar to the Brazilian model.

25. Those laws were passed in the last days of the military government and are part of the so-called *leyes de amarre* (literally "mooring laws") that were intended to tie up indefinitely any attempt at legal restructuring.

26. "Fallo rebaja los cargos graves contra Pinochet," *La Tercera,* March 9, 2001.

27. "Definitivo: sobreseen a Pinochet," *La Tercera,* July 1, 2002.

28. "Gobierno rechaza propuesta de DDHH del almirante Vergara," *La Tercera,* November 7, 2002.

29. "Luna de mel entre gobierno y Suprema tendrá prueba de fuego en DD.HH.," *La Tercera,* February 6, 2004.

30. "El último acto de Pinochet en el Senado," *Qué Pasa,* July 5, 2002.

31. Senado de Chile, "Presidente del Senado sostuvo que es evidente que falta tiempo para 'tener una visión única de la historia,'" press release, July 9, 2002.

32. His letter was published in the Chilean Senate; Senado de Chile, *Legislature 347, Sesión 12 Ordinaria,* July 9, 2002.

33. In 1998, for example, Senator Jorge Lavandero and others wore paper vests with the words "¿Dónde están?," referring to the detained-disappeared. In 2002, a member of the Chamber of Deputies attended and held up a sign referring to his father, who had died during the dictatorship. Communist Secretary General Gladys Marín also attended, which prompted yelling (and throwing of coins) by supporters of the right, to the point that the session had to be suspended and the spectators removed by Carabineros.

34. Senado de Chile, *Legislature 347,* July 9, 2002.

35. Timothy O'Brien and Larry Rohter, "The Pinochet Money Trail," *New York Times,* December 12, 2004.

3

Three's Company

Old and New Alignments in Chile's Party System

PATRICIO NAVIA

The political party system in existence in Chile before 1973 is often described as reflecting a three-way division, with a strong left, a pragmatic center, and a conservative but democratic, right.[1] The polarization of the extremes and the radicalization of the center are cited as responsible for the democratic breakdown and the 1973 military coup. After a seventeen-year dictatorship, the new democratic period witnessed the emergence of two party coalitions. The old center and most of the left formed the Concertación alliance, while the old right gave way to a new conservative coalition associated with the Pinochet dictatorship and interested in preserving the authoritarian legacy.[2] After fifteen years of democratic life and consecutive electoral successes by the Concertación, there is some evidence that the two-way division is weakening. The weakening of the Concertación has led some analysts and political actors to pronounce the death of the two-way division and announce the return of the three-way division, known as the three-thirds (*tres tercios*).

In this chapter, I look at both electoral and public opinion data to analyze whether the old three-way division is reemerging or whether the two-way divide that existed before the 1988 plebiscite still survives. I find no conclusive evidence either way, but I do report a decline in electoral loyalty for the two-way divide in recent congressional elections and, based on polling data, a weakening in support for the political center. I also find that the most critical factor in determining the future nature of Chile's political party system is decisions made by the Concertación's political elite and particularly by the Christian Democratic Party (PDC) leaders. If the latter decide to pursue an independent line, they may well lead the way to the return of a three-way division; if they reaffirm the importance of the alliance, then the two-way division will remain in place.

Because the old three-way divide was broadly characterized by each of the political thirds having a similar electoral weight, many automatically assumed that the new two-way divide that emerged in the wake of the 1988 plebiscite would also be reflective of an equally split electorate. But rather than two coalitions with similar electoral support, the new breakdown gave majority electoral support to those who opposed the dictatorship; that is, those who identified with the old center and left. Since the "no" vote passed by 56 percent in the 1988 plebiscite, the center-left Concertación coalition has consistently commanded majority support in all elections held between 1989 and 1997 and has emerged victorious in all elections held in Chile since the restoration of democracy.

Yet, despite the Concertación's electoral success, the consolidation of two large coalitions that together commanded around 90 percent of the vote was the most salient characteristic of the Chilean party system during the 1990s. If Chile enjoyed a multiparty system before the dictatorship, after 1990 the country experienced the formation and consolidation of a stable two-coalition system.

It is true that before 1973 political parties regularly formed legislative coalitions to exercise control of the executive and legislative branches. For example, between 1938 and 1947 the Popular Front was one such coalition, albeit an unstable one. The Radical Party was the only party that continuously remained a part of it, while the Socialist Party (PS) and Communist Party (PC) moved in and out of the coalition at various times. Thus, the formation of party coalitions after 1988 is not new in Chilean democracy. Rather, it is the stability of the government and opposition coalitions that formed after 1988 that distinguishes current Chilean democracy from the pre-1973 experience.

The Concertación has survived since 1988 without any major defection from among its founding members. Only the small Humanist Party (PH) dropped out of the Concertación in 1993. All the other founding parties have stayed in the Concertación or merged into existing coalition parties. Similarly, the conservative coalition—Alianza por Chile—has maintained its primary structure of the National Renovation (RN) and Independent Democratic Union (UDI) parties. Although some smaller centrist and conservative parties have at different times entered the latter coalition for electoral purposes, these two parties have remained the core members of that coalition.[3] Thus, even though there are currently seven parties with congressional representation and nine parties with representation in municipal councils, the defining characteristic of the Chilean party system in the 1990s has been the presence of two large coalitions.

As argued elsewhere in this book, the consolidation of Chilean democracy has been cumbersome and complex. The nature of the electoral system created by the Pinochet regime during the transition period has been central to this process. The binomial electoral system was established to preserve the rights of the right-wing minority, which in turn would preserve the central features of the 1980 constitution created by General Pinochet and his associates. The binomial system has done more than just preserve the rights of the minority, however. As I show in this chapter, it has consolidated a new political party system consisting of two large, stable coalitions that are at the core of the new democracy that has been created in Chile.

While the focus of this chapter is on the preservation or disappearance of the current system of alliances, the larger issue at stake is the impact of the binomial system on the democratic structure. The interactions among these two alliances have been crucial in determining the Chilean road to democracy, and their presence in Chile's future will be equally critical in determining the nature of the system in the years to come.

The Concertación in Power

Many experts on the pre-1973 political party system attribute some if not all of the responsibility for the democratic breakdown to the weakening of the political center.[4] The excessive ideological purity of the Christian Democratic Party and its inability or unwillingness to form stable and enduring alliances with parties from the right or left led to the lack of a consensus-building centrist party, a feature identified as the leading cause of the polarization observed in the late 1960s and early 1970s. After the PDC replaced the Radical Party as the largest centrist party, its inability to form a moderate reformist coalition during the Frei government (1964–1970) and its militant opposition to Allende (1970–1973) made the three-way political division incompatible with the maintenance of a democratic order.

After the 1973 coup, seventeen years of dictatorship seriously damaged human rights and democratic values. But the dictatorship also provided an opportunity for a realignment of the party system. Most studies on Chile's transition to democracy underline the importance of the alliance between the centrist PDC and the moderate left (that is, several socialist factions) in facilitating the formation of the center-left Concertación coalition in the 1980s.[5] Because the opposition was unified and agreed on a common cause, Chile's transition to democracy was possible.[6] The Concertación guaranteed that Pinochet's exit from power would not lead to new political and social confrontations. Chile's transition was successful because the old left and the old center overcame their ideological and tactical divisions and agreed on a common platform to build and consolidate the Concertación. Grounded on common and solid views of democratic governance and the ability to put historical differences aside, the Concertación parties have been able to provide presidents Aylwin (1990–1994), Frei (1994–2000), and Lagos (2000–2006) with enough political support to govern effectively. The center-left alliance scored consecutive electoral victories in all national and local contests between 1988 and 2004.

However, the wear and tear suffered by all coalitions that stay in power for a long time has eroded some of the electoral support for the Concertación. In addition, because it was initially created to put an end to the dictatorship and guarantee a peaceful transition from authoritarianism, once democracy was consolidated (that is, no reversion to authoritarianism was possible), the alliance had fulfilled its founding mission. The coalition has been hard-pressed to find a new unifying cause around which to reinvent itself and remain successful. The 1998 economic crisis and the slow economic recovery that characterized the first four years of the Lagos administration brought about new tensions within the Concertación. Many Concertacionistas who initially opposed the economic model implemented by the Pinochet dictatorship and embraced later by the Concertación governments became disillusioned with the model. Thus, the economic recession, the subsequent difficult economic times, and the persistent high levels of income inequality have fueled their previously muted discontent.

The debate between those who advocated a change in the economic model and those who defended it first emerged in 1997, with two documents produced by different groups within the Concertación. On the one hand, those in favor of the neoliberal economic model produced a document entitled "La fuerza de nuestras ideas," in which they proposed continuing to build on the economic policies adopted by presidents Aylwin and Frei. The so-called complacent group (*auto-complacientes*) advocated deepening the model often referred to as "neoliberalism with a human face," or the socially oriented market economy, as President Aylwin liked to call it. Conversely, those who sought to adopt policies that more aggressively addressed the problem of income and wealth distribution produced a document entitled "La gente tiene razón," in which they criticized the complacent nature of the other group and called for more proactive government involvement in fostering economic development and redistribution of wealth. This group was rapidly identified as self-flagellating.[7] This division led some analysts to identify a profound rift within the Concertación. Others minimized the split by stating that the two documents simply reflected slightly different priorities: While the complacent group sought to prioritize economic growth over redistribution, the self-flagellating group was more immediately interested in distribution policies, provided that the neoliberal economic model was not under attack. The debate was never fully resolved within the Concertación, and many saw it reemerging during the 1999 Lagos presidential campaign. Yet aside from the merits of both arguments, there was a growing perception that the coalition was finding it increasingly difficult to speak with a unified voice and to share a common vision.

Shortly after Lagos' presidential election victory, there was ample talk about the upcoming Lagos six-year term as a "farewell ceremony,"[8] that is, a caretaking wrap-up government that would eventually hand power over to conservative candidate Joaquín Lavín. Lavín, a former advocate of the Pinochet government, had forced Lagos into a runoff election in late 1999 when he obtained the highest electoral vote of any conservative candidate during Chile's history of full enfranchisement. In fact, some within the Concertación even suggested that it would be healthy for democracy if the conservative opposition achieved a victory in the 2005 presidential election. By anticipating and even celebrating a conservative victory in the 2005 presidential election, several Concertación intellectuals were undermining the strength of the very democracy that they claimed to defend. Yet the belief that Lagos' six-year term would constitute the last Concertación government became generally accepted among the political elite soon after Lagos was inaugurated.

Not surprisingly, the talk of a farewell ceremony worried the Concertación parties. Political parties seek to win and stay in power. The farewell ceremony syndrome was correctly perceived as detrimental to the interests of the Concertación. In response, the different Concertación parties began to develop competing approaches and strategies to increase their electoral chances in the 2005 presidential and congressional elections. A good deal of political strategy during Lagos' tenure has focused on finding ways to make the Concertación competitive. From the debate about what policies the Lagos administration should advocate to cabinet appointments, all decisions on policy and politics have been interpreted as reflecting conflicting views about the best strategy to make the Concertación a viable electoral coalition.

One proposal from within the Concertación designed to recover an electoral majority suggested that the Concertación must place emphasis on separately rebuilding the leftist and centrist support bases that originally constituted it. This approach has gained some support and has been widely circulated and discussed in documents and statements. Those who support this view argue that focusing on the growth of the center and left poles of the Concertación can prevent possible erosion in electoral support as a result of the Alianza's effort to cater to moderate voters, as well as efforts by leftist parties outside the Concertación to attract the support of left-leaning voters.

The political strategy undertaken by current PDC president Adolfo Zaldívar since his election in January 2002 reflects the view that the Concertación can only be fortified by first strengthening the individual parties that comprise it. Ironically, Zaldívar's strategy was formally outlined more than a year earlier by two Socialist Party members, Senator Carlos Ominami and political scientist Alfredo Joignant.[9] Although the Joignant-Ominami text was written as a plan to strengthen the Concertación, the strategy under which Adolfo Zaldívar became party president was directly aimed at strengthening the PDC. Yet both strategies seek to reinvigorate the three-way political party alignment that existed before 1973, in order either eventually to increase the Concertación's electoral strength (as argued by Joignant and Ominami) or to prevent further erosion of the PDC. The common goal of both strategies is to fortify the two poles that gave birth to the Concertación. To be sure, Zaldívar has repeatedly stated that a strong Concertación cannot exist without a strong PDC. His opponents believe that Zaldívar cares much more about a strong PDC than about a strong Concertación, but his argument ultimately coincides with the view of the two socialists that the center and left components of the government coalition need to be reinforced.

Proponents of both approaches perceive the Concertación merely as an electoral coalition formed by distinctly different centrist and leftist parties. They reject the argument that the Concertación is the result of the rearrangement of the political party system along the yes-no divide seen in the 1988 plebiscite. In their view, the Concertación does not constitute a unified and stable political force that evolved from a common set of interests and goals among those who opposed the Pinochet dictatorship. Instead, for them, the Concertación simply represents an alliance between the parties of the center and left that happened to oppose the Pinochet dictatorship. The 1988 plebiscite was simply an occasion for the PDC and the Socialist Party to unite, rather than representing the birth of a long-lasting alliance between two groups that share a common ideology. In other words, according to these views, the 1989 election marked the moment in which two of the three thirds formed an alliance to govern the country. Those who adopt this view do not believe that a two-way divide replaced the old three-way split.

Naturally, it is impossible to determine empirically whether the yes-versus-no political divide that emerged in 1988 will survive the passage of time, or if there is a latent three-thirds division based on historical cleavages waiting to reemerge. If one believes that political party systems are long-lasting because societies change very slowly, then one must also believe that the old three-thirds division will not go away easily. In fact, one can argue that the three-way divide will reemerge as soon as General Pinochet is out of the picture. Some might even argue that because Pinochet retired from political life after he was stripped of his congressional immunity in 2000, the time is ripe for the three-way division to resurface. However, as I discuss later, because the current electoral system is designed to reduce the number of political parties, the passing of Pinochet might not be sufficient to resurrect the three-way divide.

On the other hand, if new political alignments have occurred, the Pinochet dictatorship and the 1988 plebiscite might constitute a new divide (or even, according to some, a new social cleavage separating democrats from authoritarians).[10] In that case, the yes-no divide that has characterized Chilean politics in the 1990s will survive Pinochet's passing and will remain the defining division of the Chilean party system. The traumatic experience of the seventeen-year dictatorship and the profound division it caused between Chileans who supported it and those who sought the return of democracy might, in fact, have resulted in the emergence of a new alignment that has replaced the old three-way split. In other words, the realignment produced by the dictatorship might have taken on a life of its own. In fact, it might have become a new defining cleavage. True, social cleavages are long-lasting, deep arrangements that condition the party system of a country and that do not change often. However, the positions that different parties took with regard to the authoritarian-democratic struggle and in response to the protected democracy framework of the 1980 constitution could reflect the formation of a new social cleavage. In any case, aided by the incentives provided by the electoral rules and the recent history of political coalitions, the two-way divide might be here to stay.

To be sure, the preceding is more a theoretical than an empirical debate. As mentioned, cleavages do not appear accidentally. They result from political developments that are not always exogenous to the political party structure. The decision by the old left and center to put aside their differences and form a united front to oppose the dictatorship was not an inevitable result of the authoritarian period. If the new divide appeared in the yes-no 1988 plebiscite, this was partially the result of the strategic and tactical decisions made by the old political center and left. Second, political elites have some influence over how new social cleavages are expressed in the political party arena. In that sense, whether the two-way division will survive beyond Pinochet or the three-thirds alignment will return as the defining characteristic of Chilean politics will depend in part on the decisions of political elites. Given that the status quo is the two-way division, the reemergence of the three-thirds divide in the Chilean party system will occur only through conscious strategizing by leading political parties. In addition, the acquiescence of the electorate to that decision will also be necessary for such a realignment to take place. Neither condition by itself is sufficient for the three-thirds to replace the two-way division. Neither political parties nor the electorate alone can unilaterally alter the two-way status quo.

The conservative parties seem to be satisfied with the two-way division. After the most recent congressional elections in 2001, the UDI celebrated the consolidation of a two-way divide and defined the two coalitions as democratic center-right and democratic center-left. UDI leaders have repeatedly underlined their support for a two-way alignment, and they have openly expressed their intention to drive the PDC out of Chilean politics so that a so-called democratic center-left and democratic center-right could consolidate as the new poles in the Chilean political party system.

The left is unclear about the wisdom of trying to resurrect the old three-way divide. On the one hand, the PS seems relatively enthusiastic about the reemergence of the three-thirds. In fact, reflecting its desire for the reemergence of a strong and unified left, the PS even attempted to generate some mutual understanding with extra-Concertación leftist parties in the 1997 and 2001 congressional elections. On the other hand, the other leftist Concertación party, the PPD (Partido por la Democracia), seems to favor the two-way divide. After all, the PPD was born when that divide was in place. A three-thirds division would force the PPD to define itself as either a centrist or a leftist party. The PS has not actively engaged in attempting to resurrect the three-thirds because of the immediate conflicts with the PPD and the PDC that such a move would generate. Thus, the parties of the left have not moved forward in attempting to resurrect and strengthen the three-thirds, nor have they actively sought to consolidate the post-1988 two-way status quo.

In order to accurately assess the likelihood that the three-thirds division can successfully replace the two-way divide, one must determine whether the current PDC strategy of separating itself from the leftist Concertación parties has a chance of success. Given that the PDC is the only party that can currently attempt to resurrect the three-thirds division, a successful replacement of the two-way divide by the old three-thirds requires that the PDC strategy be successful. In order to test electoral support for the initiative to resurrect the three-thirds division, I considered the electoral results of the 1997 and 2001 congressional elections. The evidence suggests that voters showed more support for the two-way divide in 1997 than in 2001. In the most recent congressional elections, voters were less likely to vote a straight ticket than in 1997. This outcome might be interpreted as reflecting voters' preference for a centrist alternative distinct from the Alianza or the Concertación, or it might represent a weakening of allegiance to either coalition, which facilitates ticket splitting. In addition, the most recent electoral results show significantly increased support for the conservative "third," to use the old terminology. The Alianza has grown, obtaining well over one-third of the votes in the most recent election. Although Pinochet obtained 44 percent of the vote in the 1988 plebiscite, conservative parties have not gained more than 40 percent of the votes in any of the elections held during the 1990s. Yet, in both the 2000 municipal election and the 2001 congressional election, the vote for conservative parties was higher than 40 percent.

The Effect of Low Voter Turnout

The growth in voter support for conservative parties has been widely explained as reflecting a drop in support for the PDC. Yet that explanation is not entirely accurate. The PDC began to lose electoral support in the 1993 congressional elections, years before conservative parties began to gain support. In part, the drop in electoral support for the PDC went unnoticed because that party did not suffer significant losses in congressional seats until the 2001 elections. Despite having fallen from 27 percent to 23 percent of the vote between 1993 and 1997, the PDC actually gained one seat in the Chamber of Deputies, from 37 of 120 seats in 1993 to 38 seats in 1997. In 2001, PDC candidates' share of the vote fell again by 4 percent, from 23 percent to 19 percent. In terms of legislative positions, however, the effect was more dramatic; the PDC lost fourteen seats, going from thirty-eight seats to twenty-four in the Chamber of Deputies. In the Senate, the results were equally dramatic. While the PDC had won ten senate seats in ten senatorial districts in 1997, the party captured only two seats in nine districts in 2001. That dramatic drop took place despite only a moderate decline in electoral support, from 29 percent in 1997 down to 23 percent in 2001.

Table 3.1 shows the results for the 1993, 1997, and 2001 congressional elections. One can easily observe a decline in the number of votes cast.[11] On the other hand, there is an evident growth in voter support for the UDI and a decrease in support for the PDC.[12] Over eight years, there was a 7.5 percent decline in the vote for the Concertación.

In order to study this issue further, I disaggregated the results and conducted a simple test of electoral performance in each of the country's 341 municipalities. Since the rate of electoral participation (valid votes/registered voters) was not uniform across the country, I estimated the change in the abstention rate—that is, the percentage of registered voters who failed to vote—in each municipality between 1993 and 2001. Any deviation from the abstention rate indicates that a political party either did better or worse than expected.[13] I included in the analysis municipalities that were split into two communes after 1993, except in two cases.[14] Table 3.2 shows the expected drop in electoral support for each party in 2001, based on the decline in electoral participation between 1993 and 2001.

As shown in Table 3.2, the actual decline for the PDC was much larger than predicted, at 629,461. The rest of the Concertación parties experienced a slight gain after accounting for the abstention rate effect. This is particularly relevant because the PDC had candidates in forty-eight districts in 1993 and fifty-four districts in 2001. Thus, while the PDC lost votes, the other Concertación parties improved their performance, despite having fewer candidates.

le 3.1. Congressional Election Results, 1993–2001

ty	1993	%	1997	%	2001	%
ón Demócrata Independiente (UDI)	816,104	12.1	837,736	14.5	1,538,835	25.2
novación Nacional (RN)	1,098,852	16.3	971,903	16.8	840,568	13.8
er Alianza (Unión) por Chile	556,833	8.3	291,753	5.0	327,751	5.4
al Alianza por Chile	2,471,789	36.7	2,101,392	36.3	2,707,154	44.3
tido Demócrata Cristiano (PDC)	1,827,373	27.1	1,331,745	23.0	1,155,597	18.9
tido Radical de Chile (PR)	200,837	3.0	181,538	3.1	247,576	4.1
tido Socialdemocracia Chilena (PSD)	53,377	0.8				
tido Socialista de Chile (PS)	803,719	11.9	640,397	11.1	611,305	10.0
tido por la Democracia (PPD)	798,206	11.8	727,293	12.6	777,278	12.7
er Concertación	49,764	0.7	46,719	0.8	134,044	2.2
ncertación Total	3,733,276	55.4	2,927,692	50.5	2,925,800	47.9
tido Comunista de Chile (PC)	430,495	6.4	434,148	7.5	318,638	5.2
tido Humanista (PH)	96,195	1.4	168,597	2.9	69,265	1.1
ependents and others	7,104	0.1	163,944	2.8	86,283	1.4
al valid votes	6,738,859	100.0	5,795,773	100.00	6,107,140	100.0

rce: Data from Ministerio del Interior, "Información Histórico Electoral," http://www.elecciones.gov.cl.

The big winners were the conservative parties. The Alianza por Chile increased its share of the vote, after accounting for the abstention rate effect, by 437,633 votes, or 7 percent of the valid votes in 2001. The UDI gained significantly more than the RN. In fact, while the UDI observed a net increase, adjusted for the abstention rate effect, of more than 789,000 votes, the rest of the Alianza experienced a drop of nearly 353,000 votes. Thus, we can safely speak of a new alignment within the Alianza. The UDI has grown at the expense of independent conservatives and the RN. It is also true that, overall, the Alianza increased its percentage of the vote between 1993 and 2001, after adjusting for the abstention rate effect, by more than 437,000 votes.

If we follow the logic of the three-way divide, the growth in electoral support for the right represents an enormous challenge to the monolithic control of the political center exercised by the PDC during the 1990s. With the Lagos presidential nomination, the Concertación seemed to have moved, however slightly, toward the left. After Lagos' victory, the PDC chose to actively seek to recover the political center. Yet, even though in the 1999 presidential election leftist Ricardo Lagos faced conservative Joaquín Lavín, thus depriving voters of a centrist candidate, the electoral results of the 2000 municipal elections and 2001 congressional elections seem to indicate that the electorate was not thrilled

Table 3.2. Vote Tallies Adjusted for Abstention Rate Effect, 1993–2001

Party/Coalition	1993 Deputies	2001 Deputies	Net Vote Loss 1993–2001	Estimated Vote Loss 1993–2001	Difference (Net – Est.)
PDC	1,827,373	1,197,912	629,461	147,513	–481,948
Other Concertación	1,905,903	1,814,986	90,917	149,560	58,643
Total Concertación	3,733,276	3,012,898	720,378	297,072	–423,306
UDI	816,104	1,534,847	–718,743	70,989	789,732
Other Alianza	1,655,685	1,166,624	489,061	136,962	–352,099
Total Alianza	2,471,789	2,701,471	–229,682	207,951	437,633
Concertación and Alianza	6,205,065	5,714,369	490,696	505,023	–14,327
Left	2,432,593	2,171,112	261,481	191,729	–69,752
Total Valid Votes	6,738,859	6,091,776*	647,083	647,083	0

Source: http://www.elecciones.gov.cl/

* The 2001 total is lower than the official 6,107,140 because I omitted the 11,565 votes of Padre Hurtado (District 31) and the 3,799 votes of San Rafael (District 38) since those municipalities were created after 1993 by merging parts of different municipalities.

about supporting centrist candidates. In both elections the UDI increased its share of seats and votes within the right-wing alliance, and within the Concertación, the PPD-PS-PRSD parties increased their share of seats in Congress.

The Effect of the Electoral System

In part, the decline in electoral support for the PDC results from the distortional effects of the electoral system. The so-called binominal system, a two-seat proportional representation arrangement, has built-in incentives that lead to polarization rather than to convergence toward the median voter.[15] These are centrifugal incentives of the system—using the same d'Hondt seat allocation formula utilized before 1973—as compared to the centripetal incentives of a single-member district with runoff. Whereas under a two-seat proportional representation system a candidate can secure a seat with one vote more than a third of the total vote, under a single-member district with majority runoff, 50 percent plus one vote is required to secure a seat. Incentives to polarization—that is, the lower electoral thresholds that allow minority parties to achieve representation—were entrenched in the electoral law adopted by the Pinochet dictatorship. Conceived as an insurance mechanism against an electoral defeat of the right, a proportional representation system with two seats per district allows a party to secure 50 percent of the seats with slightly more than one-third of the votes. Although candidates for Congress need obtain only one-third of the vote to secure 50 percent of the seats, presidential candidates need to secure an absolute majority to win the election. Yet, when congressional and presidential elections are not held concurrently, as happened in Chile in 1997 and 2001, the centrifugal effect is not present.

Public Opinion and the Three-Thirds Divide

Despite the fact that the structural incentives generated by the electoral rules were already in place before 2001, the PDC managed to capture the support of a significant share of the electorate to become the party with the largest plurality of votes and seats. In recent elections, however, the electorate seems to have fallen out of love with the PDC and, thus, the political center has weakened. There is no reason to expect that this trend will be reversed in the near future. The PDC's embrace in 2002 of the Zaldívar doctrine, which advocates stressing the party's differences with the Lagos government, ultimately reflected its desire to resurrect the three-way divide.

Polling data from the highly respected Centro de Estudios Públicos (CEP) biannual poll reveals voters' self-identification with the traditional three sectors of Chilean politics. While there has been a clear increase in those who identify with the right between 1990 and 2004, there has been a simultaneous drop in those who identify with the center. The number of voters who self-identify with the left has fluctuated over time, although this group has been the most consistent throughout.

The CEP polls also asked respondents to self-identify with either the Concertación or the Alianza. Their findings show that self-identification with the right-wing coalition has remained constant, while self-identification with the Concertación has decreased over time. The decrease among those who identify with the Concertación results from a decrease among those who identify with the center.

Although there is some evidence to suggest that the center has in fact weakened since the return of democracy, it would be unfounded to suggest that the current two-way divide has replaced the old three-way alignment of the Chilean electorate.

Ticket Splitting in Congressional Elections

In the 2001 congressional elections, voters from nine senatorial districts went to the polls to elect senators and Chamber of Deputies members concurrently.[16] The rest of Chilean voters cast ballots only for the Chamber of Deputies, since they had concurrently voted for Senatorial and Chamber of Deputies candidates in 1997. It is often argued that sophisticated voters go beyond party identification and split their ticket; that is, they vote for candidates of different parties. Thus, a divided government results from low levels of party identification and high levels of sophistication among voters.[17] Simply put, more sophisticated voters are more likely to split their tickets and vote for a candidate from one party for the presidency and a candidate from a different party for the legislature. Some have claimed that voter sophistication is a result of greater social and economic development, while others believe that voter sophistication tends to occur in countries with well-established democracies.

Traditionally, polling data have been used to test these propositions.[18] For example, survey data show that split-ticket voting rates in the United States are higher now than in previous decades.[19] Some researchers have argued that voters intentionally split tickets to produce a certain mix of policies or to create checks among parties.[20] Other accounts include as explanatory factors the decreasing ideological differences between political parties,[21] the competitiveness of congressional elections,[22] and the incentives offered by certain ballot mechanisms.[23] But the most widely accepted view is that ticket splitting results from shrinking party identification by voters and the growth of personalized campaigns. People vote for candidates rather than for parties.[24] Naturally, in parliamentary systems and in presidential systems with closed lists, it is more difficult to move away from the party vote to the personalized vote. Chile is a country with a presidential system and open-list provisions for congressional elections. In other words, voters have to cast votes for candidates rather than for parties.

Recent survey data from Chile have also indicated lower levels of political party identification among voters,[25] and recent publications have underlined shrinking party loyalty among Chilean voters.[26] Others have argued that candidates also are campaigning more on their personalities and have weaker party identifications.[27] Thus, the phenomena observed in the United States and other industrialized nations seem to have reached Chile as well.

By studying ticket splitting, we can determine if voters align along the two-way or the three-way divide. If voters split their tickets among candidates within one of the two large coalitions but not across coalitions, this evidence would support the argument that a two-way divide exists. If, however, voters split their votes both within and across coalitions, we can argue that perhaps a significant number of centrist voters alternate between supporting Concertación and Alianza centrist candidates. Thus, the more inter-coalition ticket splitting that exists, the more evidence that voters prefer the three-way divide. Conversely, the more intra-coalition ticket splitting that exists, the more likely it is that voters still identify with the yes-no cleavage that manifested itself in 1988.

le 3.3. Santiago Western Senatorial District Vote, 1997

	PC	(PPD-PS-PRSD) candidates	Total Concertación	RN-UDI	PH	Chile 2000	Total*
outies	119,977	294,784	554,411	362,340	39,773	21,280	1,097,781
ators	174,780	177,965	487,335	382,286	26,794	42,771	1,113,966
ference p – Sen)	–54,803	116,819	67,076	–19,946	12,979	–21,491	–16,185

rce: Calculated using data from Ministerio del Interior, "Información Histórico Electoral," http://www.ciones.gov.cl.

e numbers do not total across the table because there are omitted candidates and because column 3 al concertación) incorporates the values from column 2 (PPD-PS-PRSD).

Intra-Coalition Ticket Splitting in 1997

In the 1997 congressional elections, the aggregate figures provide little evidence of ticket splitting in either direction. While the Concertación obtained 49.8 percent of the vote in the Senatorial election (in ten senatorial districts), it won 50.5 percent in the Chamber of Deputies election (in sixty districts, comprising the entire country). The right-wing RN-UDI coalition obtained 36.3 and 36.6 percent in the Senatorial and Chamber elections, respectively. However, if one looks at each of the ten senatorial districts by party, there is clear evidence of a limited but significant amount of intra-coalition ticket splitting, particularly in Santiago's Western Senatorial District (see table 3.3).[28] The Senate and Chamber of Deputies vote for the PDC varied considerably across senatorial districts in 1997. The PDC consistently got more votes for its Senatorial candidates than for its Chamber of Deputies candidates.[29]

Conversely, the other Concertación parties did better in Chamber of Deputies than in the Senatorial elections. For example, the combined vote for Chamber of Deputies candidates from the PPD-PS-PRSD was consistently better than that of the Senatorial candidates from those parties.[30]

Altogether the Concertación vote in the Chamber and Senatorial elections ended up being very similar in most districts. This outcome seems to contradict the arguments of a number of analysts who have pointed to the continuities of the Chilean party system.[31] The evidence seems instead to indicate that the old three-way split of the Chilean party system might be giving way to a new two-way divide of Concertación versus Alianza.

The Survival of the Yes-No Divide in the 1999 Presidential Election

The 1999 presidential election results have also been used as evidence of the consolidation of a Concertación vote (rather than distinct centrist and leftist votes) among the electorate. In the 1999 election most centrists had the option of voting for a left-wing Concertación presidential candidate. The poor electoral support obtained by self-proclaimed centrist Arturo Frei in the 1999 election shows that, when faced with an admittedly mediocre alternative, voters preferred the two-way divide over the old three-way split.

Lavín's strong 47.5 percent showing, higher than that obtained by Pinochet in the 1988 plebiscite, fuels speculation that many centrist voters deserted the Concertación. On the other hand, it is also true that the left-wing candidate obtained a larger share of the vote than any previous leftist candidate in Chilean history. In the runoff election, Lagos surpassed the 1971 municipal election tally obtained by the Popular Unity government. Thus, just as a considerable number of centrist voters must have opted to vote for Lavín in the 1999 presidential contest, an even larger number evidently opted to support Lagos. Analysis shows that the Concertación vote has remained stable over the years and that even in 1999 the Concertación vote did not depart significantly from the pattern observed in previous elections. We can safely argue that the 1988 yes-no cleavage remained strong throughout the 1990s, including in the 1999 presidential election.

2001 Inter-Coalition Ticket Splitting

In 1997, ticket splitting appears to have occurred within both the Concertación and Alianza parties but generally not across political coalitions. The 2001 congressional election results, however, seem to show a different pattern and have fueled the argument that Chilean voters do indeed cross party and coalition lines to exercise their ticket-splitting option and vote for Chamber of Deputies candidates from one coalition and Senatorial candidates from the other coalition. Because there was no centrist alternative in this election, voters could have been choosing centrist candidates from the slates offered by the leftist Concertación and the rightist Alianza.

The PDC Senatorial candidates again performed better than did PDC Chamber of Deputies candidates in most regions, with the notable exception of northern Chile (Regions I and III).[32] The same can be said for the PPD-PS-PRSD. How can it be that both the PDC and the PPD-PS-PRSD Senatorial candidates did better than their Chamber of Deputies colleagues? I infer from voting data that the government coalition consistently did better in the Senatorial election than in the Chamber of Deputies contest, thus providing evidence of ticket splitting.

This evidence of inter-coalition ticket splitting calls into question the preliminary conclusion from the 1997 results. In the most recent congressional election, Chileans split their tickets within and across political coalitions. To be sure, one could argue that inter-coalition ticket splitting does not reflect the strength of the three-thirds divide, but rather shows the weakness of party loyalty observed in Chile today. In that sense, the thesis advanced by Tironi and Halpern identifying a new Chilean voter who can no longer be appropriately portrayed using the pre-1973 political alignment would be supported by this evidence. Yet even if that were the case, the claim that Chileans remain distinctly split along the yes-no divide first demonstrated in the 1988 plebiscite is also called into question.

The phenomenon of inter-coalition ticket splitting observed in 2001 may be due in part to the electoral strategies devised by the different political coalitions. Whereas the Concertación continued to field two candidates in every senatorial and Chamber of Deputies district, the Alianza negotiated a slate that presented only one Alianza Senatorial candidate in seven of the nine districts up for election.[33] That transformed the Senatorial election into a de facto closed list for Alianza voters. Rather than having a choice of two Alianza Senatorial candidates, voters who preferred the conservative opposition were forced to accept the candidate selected by the Alianza elite. Because an unopposed Senatorial candidate has more limited opportunities to campaign than do two competing candidates, a coalition with only one candidate will likely have a lower vote tally than a coalition that is presenting two candidates. That was the case in the 2001 congressional elections. One of the unintended effects of the Alianza's strategic choice to reduce the intra-coalition confrontation between UDI and RN candidates might have been to foster inter-coalition ticket splitting.

The 2005 presidential and congressional elections will be voters' first chance in twelve years to cast presidential and congressional ballots concurrently. In the ten Senatorial districts up for election in 2005, voters will cast three ballots: one (1 vote) for the president, one (2 votes) for two senators, and one (2 votes) for two deputies. That election will provide an excellent opportunity to test the assertion that centrist voters are choosing between moderate candidates from the Concertación and the Alianza.

Conclusion

Since 1988 Chile has witnessed the formation and consolidation of two large blocks formed out of the challenges posed by the transition to democracy. On the one side, those who opposed the dictatorship formed the Concertación, while on the other, those who supported the dictatorship formed the Alianza. During the 1990s the two blocks effectively replaced the old three-thirds Chilean party system. As the cleavage that emerged at the end of the dictatorship begins to disappear, however, some have begun to speculate about a resurrection, or reemergence, of the three-way division that existed before 1973. With

Pinochet gone from the political scene, the motives that brought the centrist PDC and the parties of the left together to form the Concertación coalition are rapidly disappearing.

When the Concertación was initially formed, most analysts understood it to be a temporary electoral coalition formed by centrist and leftist parties. Yet, seventeen years after its creation, one can legitimately speculate that the Concertación might have permanently bonded the old left and center into a new center-left alliance. If the Concertación has already evolved into more than a temporary coalition, the existence of that party in formation will necessarily render the three-thirds division impossible. It is indeed possible that the goals that brought together the Concertación parties in 1988—that is, peaceful restoration of democracy and economic growth with equity—have already evolved into lasting common objectives that will eventually transform the Concertación into a party of parties. After three consecutive presidential election victories and fifteen years in power, it should not be surprising to see evidence that the Concertación has acquired a life of its own so strong that the parties that comprise it have no electoral alternative but to remain part of it.

Yet it might also be possible that after fifteen years of Concertación rule, the three-thirds division is still latent underneath the surface of a two-coalition system that is destined to die together with Pinochet. In fact, those who advocate against changes in the binominal electoral system often invoke the fear that the three-thirds division is a latent possibility in the Chilean party system. If a more proportional representation system is adopted, they argue, the three-thirds will immediately make a comeback. That argument presupposes that the three-thirds is the true underlying alignment of the Chilean political party system and that the binomial electoral system is the main obstacle preventing its reemergence.

The polling data presented in this chapter highlight a weakening of the political center. In addition, while the 1997 congressional election results seem to indicate a clear two-way divide, the 2001 results provide some evidence for the possible reemergence of a three-thirds alignment. On the other hand, the concentration of electoral support for Lagos and Lavín in the 1999 first round presidential election provides limited support for the thesis that the two-way divide has replaced the old three-way division. As I argued previously, however, even when the electorate might tend to favor, or accept, a three-thirds alignment, the decisions of the political elites will ultimately determine whether voters have a choice between a two-way or a three-way party system. If the Concertación parties remain united and enter the election as a coalition with a single presidential candidate, voters will not be provided with a clear option of resurrecting the three-thirds divisions. If, on the other hand, the Concertación breaks down, with the PDC further strengthening its centrist strategy and the PS-PPD seeking to create an electoral alliance with the extra-Concertación left, then voters will have the choice of going along with the reemergence of the three-thirds or massively supporting one of the two former Concertación factions.

Although the 2005 elections will help us identify whether the three-thirds is reemerging, the decisions of the leadership of existing political parties might prevent voters from being able to make that choice. If the leaders of the existing political parties remain loyal to the two-coalition system, the three-thirds division will likely not reemerge. If, on the other hand, the leaders of the political parties choose to offer three distinct alternatives to voters, left-center-right, then voters might indeed opt to revive the three-thirds party system that characterized Chilean politics before 1973.

The strategy of resurrecting the three-thirds system can be justified under the premise that the centrist third can guarantee stability and governability. It is also grounded in the belief that the Concertación is just a temporary electoral coalition and that it could easily be ended. The three-thirds—right, center, and left—is symbolic of the period that ended tragically with the 1973 military coup. During the 1950s and 1960s, every time the center joined in coalition with either the left or the right, the country enjoyed political stability. When the center was not able to form a coalition, periods of political instability followed. Thus, the effort by any one of the three thirds to govern without forming a strong coalition systematically failed in Chile's past. According to this hypothesis, the success of the Concertación in the 1990s has resulted from the center's ability to co-govern with the left.

The reemergence of the three-way divide in the Chilean political system might threaten the political stability the country experienced during the 1990s. Most scholars attribute the 1973 breakdown of democracy in large part to the center's inability to form a government coalition with either the right or the left. True, political instability is not an inevitable result of the three-thirds divide. Chile went through long periods of political stability under a three-thirds arrangement. Yet the chances that instability will reemerge are greater under a three-thirds arrangement than under the present two-way divide. If the three thirds reemerge and the difficulties in forming electoral and legislative majorities return, Chileans will be reminded that insofar as politics is concerned, three's company.

Notes

1. This article was originally prepared for delivery at the 2003 meeting of the Latin American Studies Association, Dallas, Texas, March 27–29, 2003. I am grateful to Francisco Javier Díaz, Alfredo Joignant, Miguel Angel López, and an anonymous reviewer for comments provided, and to Cristóbal Aninat for useful discussions on the subject. I am grateful to Fondecyt (Project #1020684 "Ser competente en política") and Instituto de Ciencias Sociales (ICSO) of the Universidad Diego Portales for funding.

2. Alan Angell, "Chile since 1958" in *Chile since Independence,* ed. Leslie Bethell (Cambridge: Cambridge University Press, 1993); César Caviedes, *The Politics of Chile: A Sociographical Assessment* (Boulder, Colo.: Westview Press, 1979); Julio Faúndez, "In Defense of Presidentialism: The Case of Chile 1932–1970," in *Presidentialism and Democracy in Latin America,* ed. Scott Mainwaring and Matthew Soberg Shugart (Cambridge: Cambridge University Press, 1997); Manuel Antonio Garretón and Tomás Moulián, *La unidad popular y el conflicto político en Chile* (Santiago: Ediciones Minga, 1983); Federico Gil, *The Political System of Chile* (Boston: Houghton Mifflin, 1966); Timothy Scully, *Rethinking the Center: Party Politics in Nineteenth- and Twentieth-Century Chile* (Stanford: Stanford University Press, 1992); Paul Sigmund, *The Overthrow of Allende and the Politics of Chile, 1964–1976* (Pittsburgh: University of Pittsburgh Press, 1977); Arturo Valenzuela and J. Samuel Valenzuela, eds., *Chile: Politics and Society* (New Brunswick: Transaction Books, 1976); J. Samuel Valenzuela, "The Origins and Transformations of the Chilean Party System," Working Paper No. 215, Helen Kellogg Institute for International Studies at Notre Dame University, South Bend, Ind., 1995.

3. The coalition has changed names over time: Democracia y Progreso (1989), Participación y Progreso (1992), Unión por el Progreso de Chile (1993), Unión por Chile (1996–1997), and Alianza por Chile (1999–2005).

4. Scully, *Rethinking the Center*; Valenzuela and Valenzuela, *Chile: Politics and Society*; Paul Drake, "Chile: 1930–1958" in *Chile since Independence*; Sigmund, *Overthrow of Allende.*

5. J. Samuel Valenzuela and Timothy Scully, "Electoral Choices and the Party System in Chile," *Comparative Politics* 29, no. 4 (1997): 511–27; Eugenio Tironi and Felipe Agüero, "Sobrevivirá el nuevo paisaje político chileno?" *Estudios Públicos* 74 (1999): 151–68; J. Samuel Valenzuela, "Respuesta a Eugenio Tironi y Felipe Agüero: reflexiones sobre el presente y futuro del paisaje político chileno a la luz del pasado," *Estudios Públicos* 75 (1999): 273–90; Eugenio Tironi, Felipe Agüero, and Eduardo Valenzuela "Clívajes políticos en Chile: perfil sociológico de los electores de Lagos y Lavín, *Revista Perspectivas* 5, no. 1 (May 2001): 73–87; Peter Siavelis, *The President and Congress in Post-Authoritarian Chile: Institutional Constraints to Democratic Consolidation* (State College: Penn State University Press, 2000); J. Esteban Montes, Scott Mainwaring, and Eugenio Ortega, "Rethinking the Chilean Party System," *Journal of Latin American Studies* 32 (2000): 795–824.

6. Edgardo Boeninger, *Democracia en Chile: lecciones para la gobernabilidad* (Santiago: Editorial Andrés Bello, 1997); Genaro Arriagada, *¿Hacia un big-bang del sistema de partidos?* (Santiago: Editorial Los Andes, 1997).

7. Lois Hecht Oppenheim discusses this group's position in more detail in chapter 5.

8. The phrase *ceremonia del adiós* was coined by socialist analyst Antonio Cortés Terzi in a paper with limited circulation. Yet newspaper reports in 2000 made the phrase more widely known and used in the media.

9. Alfredo Joignant and Carlos Ominami, "Notas para refundir la coalición: la hora de la verdad, *Rocinante* 26 (December 2000): 37–40.

10. For a complete debate on this issue, see J. S. Valenzuela, "Respuesta a Eugenito Tironi y Felipe Agüero; and Tironi and Agüero, "Sobrevivirá el nuevo paisaje político chileno?"

11. This was widely discussed in the 1997 congressional election when turnout reached an all-time low of 5,795,000 votes.

12. The electoral advantage of the Concertación over the Alianza shrank dramatically between 1993 and 2001. Although the 1993 congressional elections were held concurrently with presidential elections—where the popular Concertación candidate obtained more than twice as many votes as the conservative candidate—a comparison between the two elections clearly shows significant fluctuations.

13. Assuming that the decline in electoral participation hurt all political parties proportionally (that is, no party suffered more than others from higher abstention) the *abstention rate effect* is the predicted decline in votes for each party between 1993 and 2001. Thus, if the decline in electoral participation in a given municipality was 13 percent (70 percent of the registered population cast valid votes in 1993 but only 57 percent did so in 2001), I assumed that each party should have experienced a 13 percent drop in its total number of votes due to lower participation. Because this estimate is constructed for each municipality, the abstention rate effect indicator varies widely across the municipalities.

14. Concón was included in Viña del Mar; Chillán Viejo was included in Chillán; Chiguayante and San Pedro de la Paz were included in Concepción; and Padre Las Casas was included in Temuco. Because Padre Hurtado and San Rafael were created by taking territories from several municipalities, I omitted those two municipalities for the 2001 election. For that reason, my totals are different from official tallies published in Ministerio del Interior, "Información Histórico Electoral," http://www.elecciones.gov.cl/.

15. Eric Magar, Marc R. Rosenblum, and David J. Samuels, "On the Absence of Centripetal Incentives in Double-Member Districts—The Case of Chile," *Comparative Political Studies* 31, no. 6 (December 1998): 714–39.

16. Those districts were Tarápaca (I), Atacama (III), Valparaíso-Coast (V), Valparaíso-Interior (V), Maule-North (VII), Maule-South (VII), Araucanía-North (IX), Araucanía South (IX), and Aysén (XI).

17. Alberto Alesina and Howard Rosenthal, *Partisan Politics: Divided Government and the Economy* (New York: Cambridge University Press, 1995).

18. Christopher H. Achen and Phillips Shively, *Cross-level Inference* (Chicago: University of Chicago Press, 1995).

19. Barry C. Burden and David C. Kimball, "A New Approach to the Study of Ticket Splitting," *American Political Science Review* 92, no. 3 (September 1998): 533–44.

20. Alesina and Rosenthal, *Partisan Politics*; Morris P. Fiorina, *Divided Government*, 2nd ed. (Needham Heights, Mass.: Allyn and Bacon, 1996).

21. Richard Born, "Split-Ticket Voters, Divided Government, and Fiorina's Policy-Balancing Model," *Legislative Studies Quarterly* 18 (February 1994): 95–115; Joe Soss and David T. Canon, "Partisan Divisions and Voting Decisions: U.S. Senators, Governors, and the Rise of a Divided Federal Government," *Political Research Quarterly* 48 (June 1995): 253–74.

22. Gary C. Jacobson, *The Politics of Congressional Elections*, 4th ed. (New York: Longman, 1997).

23. Paul Allen Beck, *Party Politics in America*, 8th ed. (New York, Longman, 1997; Gary Cox, *Making Votes Count* (New York: Cambridge University Press, 1997).

24. Bruce E. Cain, John Ferejohn, and Morris P. Fiorina, *The Personal Vote: Constituency Service and Electoral Independence* (Cambridge, Cambridge University Press, 1987).

25. See Miguel Angel López and Gustavo Martínez, "Opinión pública y democracia: las encuestas en la redemocratización chilena," in *La caja de Pándora: el retorno de la transición chilena*, ed. Amparo Menéndez and Alfredo Joignant (Santiago: Editorial Planeta, 1999); CEP (1990), Centro de Estudios de la Realidad Contemporánea, Informe de prensa, Encuesta Nacional, Santiago, October 1993; and Informe de prensa, Encuesta Nacional, Santiago, April 1994; Ximena Hinzpeter and Carla Lehmann, "Dime por quién votas . . . y te diré quien eres. Perfil de los votantes de Lagos, Lavín, Zaldívar e indecisos en base a encuesta CEP, abril–mayo," *Estudios Públicos* 3, no. 210 (May 1999) 199, and "El fin de los tres tercios tradicionales? La irrupción de una nueva fuerza política," *Estudios Públicos* 3, no. 217 (August 1999); and most recently the CEP poll databank, http://www.cepchile.cl/cgi-dms/procesa.pl?plantilla=/base.html&contenido=categoria&id_cat=44 3.

26. See Felipe Agüero, Eugenio Tironi, Eduardo Valenzuela, and Guillermo Sunkel, "Votantes, partidos e información política: la frágil intermediación política en el Chile post-autoritario, *Revista de Ciencia Política* 19, no. 2 (1998); and Tironi, Agüero and Valenzuela, "Clívajes políticos en Chile."

27. Eugenio Tironi, *La irrupción de las masas y el malestar de las elites* (Santiago: Editorial Grijalbo, 1999); Pablo Halpern, *Los nuevos chilenos* (Santiago: Editorial Planeta, 2002).

28. The combined vote for the PPD-PS-PRSD candidates for the Chamber of Deputies in this district, RM-West, was about 60 percent higher than the votes obtained by the PS senatorial candidate. The presence of Communist Party leader Gladys Marín as a senatorial candidate might have led many PPD-PS-PRSD sympathizers to cast their senatorial vote for that extra-Concertación leftist candidate. After all, the likelihood of having both Concertación candidates elected was minimal, and so was the chance of having the opposition get twice as many votes as the Concertación. Thus, because their vote would have had no effect either way, many voters might have chosen to cast a vote

for the communist candidate to make a statement, knowing that the Concertación and the Alianza would still end up getting one senate seat each.

29. True, the PDC had candidates for the Senate in each of the ten senatorial districts up for election, but it failed to sponsor a candidate in five of the sixty Chamber of Deputies districts. Regardless, even in regions where the party had Chamber of Deputies candidates in all districts, the senatorial candidates performed consistently better than the candidates for the lower house.

30. Again, in five Chamber of Deputies districts, both Concertación candidates belonged to the PPD-PS-PRSD, but even in regions where the two Concertación candidates were split between the PPD-PS-PRSD and the PDC, the Chamber candidates of the left-wing Concertación parties did better than the Senatorial candidates from those parties.

31. See Valenzuela and Scully, "Electoral Choices and the Party System in Chile"; Montes, Mainwaring, and Ortega, "Rethinking the Chilean Party System"; Siavelis, *President and Congress in Post-Authoritarian Chile.*

32. Although those expecting to see a repetition of the pattern observed in 1997 would have expected the opposite for the PPD-PS-PRSD vote, the Senatorial candidates from those parties often did better than the Chamber of Deputies candidates. In six of the nine Senatorial districts where elections were held, the Senatorial candidates from the PPD-PS-PRSD obtained more votes than their Chamber of Deputies counterparts.

33. Those districts were Regions III, V-Coast, V-Interior, VII-North, VII-South, IX-North, and XI. Although there were two candidates on the Alianza ticket in Valparaíso-Interior, Maule- North, and Manuel-South, the Alianza made it clear that there was only one privileged candidate, and Alianza voters successfully coalesced behind that candidate to prevent intra-coalition competition.

4

A Clash of Values

Church-State Relations in Democratic Chile

WILLIAM M. LIES, C.S.C.

In 1997, Chilean President Eduardo Frei Ruiz-Tagle concluded a speech that outlined his administration's program initiatives this way:

> Chile will not be fully modern if it does not confront with courage and honesty the problems that people confront in their everyday lives. . . . We cannot expect the material and spiritual progress of our society if we are afraid of liberty and freedom or the good judgment of our people. . . . The question is not whether we protect or do not protect the values of the society and the family, but the question is how we support those values while we confront our problems without hypocrisy and without cynicism.[1]

With respect to this policy agenda, Frei announced, among other initiatives, the continuation of the government-sponsored sex education program in schools and a legislative proposal to legalize divorce.

For the bishops of Chile, this sort of discourse and the policy initiatives that follow from it have seemed to confirm some of their earlier fears. At their conference at Santo Domingo in 1992, the Latin American bishops had warned of "a cultural crisis of unsuspected proportions" and of a time when the moral order desired by God in Creation and in Redemption would be called into question, leaving human culture disassociated from all transcendental authority.[2] With that concern, the bishops made a clear call for "a new evangelization that must be able to awaken a new missionary spirit."[3] It was their hope that this new evangelization would succeed in inculturating the Gospel; that is, returning to the roots of culture the Christian values that are present there but have been repressed or forgotten. A range of government policy initiatives since the return to democracy and the popular support for them must surely have them doubting whether their new evangelization is working.

In this chapter I discuss the Catholic Church's role in post-dictatorship Chilean politics and its current role in the Chilean public policy discourse. Toward that end, I outline and characterize the shape and direction the Catholic bishops' evangelization has taken, particularly with respect to their pastoral emphasis as it bears on Chilean public policy. By framing issues to emphasize one policy goal over another, the bishops have tried to affect the balance citizens strike between competing values. As I explore how the bishops have framed these issues, I consider the effectiveness of their campaign both among the masses and in the legislative realm. In so doing, I argue that there is growing tension within the Chilean church due in large measure to the bishops' lack of success in effectively persuading their constituents to follow their lead in the area of personal values and family morality. The church, like so many other Chilean institutions having to adapt to the democratic environment, has been compelled to intervene more assertively in the legislative process in its efforts to achieve its goals. This analysis outlines the Catholic Church's struggle to adapt to democracy and succeed in the new political environment. The church has lost both public support and important legislative struggles in its efforts to press its personal values and family morality agenda.

The Chilean Church and Public Policy Discourse

Although the Chilean Catholic bishops largely welcomed the military coup in 1973, their support for it waned as repression and violence intensified. Indeed, from the mid-1970s through the 1980s, the Catholic Church played a key role in opposing the Pinochet dictatorship. Its involvement throughout that period caused many, especially on the right, to question the appropriate role of the church in the political arena. The end of the Pinochet regime found the church confronting this nagging question of its appropriate involvement once again. The Vatican's wishes were unambiguous, however.

Early on in his papacy, John Paul II made it clear he would follow a more conservative line than his recent predecessors. With regard to Latin America, he expressed strong concern that due in part to the political involvement of pastoral agents during the dictatorship, local Catholic leaders had betrayed some of their primary pastoral responsibilities.[4] John Paul II and the Vatican now desired to disentangle the church from its intense political involvement, in part by encouraging a return to matters of spiritual and moral concern. It was in this context, aided by the appointment of more conservative bishops, that the church's highly political focus began to take a much more spiritual tone. Shifting from an earlier concern about a "preferential option for the poor," the Chilean hierarchy—following the Vatican lead—now emphasized a renewed "evangelization of culture."

The Latin American bishops took up this new emphasis more stridently than did many of their counterparts in other regions of the world. Although encouraged by the Vatican and espoused by most bishops, this pastoral emphasis has not found wide support among rank-and-file Catholics. With earlier worries about human rights, civil liberties, and social justice somewhat lessened with the passing of the dictatorship, the bishops' primary concerns now involved a newly opened culture and society, one that seemed to be turning away from its religious values and even the religious tradition in which it was rooted. The bishops of Latin America were also confronted with a new challenge from the growth of Pentecostalism.[5] Some scholars have argued that efforts to compete with the pastoral line of these growing Pentecostal communities led the bishops to accentuate their more conservative agenda even more.[6] So, just as surely as the church came to enunciate its role in society throughout the turbulent years following Vatican II, it annunciated its post-authoritarian role throughout the 1990s. And the stance of the bishops is clear: The systematic campaign of the Catholic hierarchy on issues of the defense of life and of the family has been the centerpiece of its agenda.

Framing the Issues

Democracy relies on competent citizen evaluation of political issues. To come to an opinion, citizens need information that will help them bring their values and interests into interplay with the choices available in the political world. The greatest challenge for democracy, according to some, is providing reliable information so citizens may develop "authentic" political opinions.[7] The literature on issue framing argues that public opinion on contentious political issues is partially shaped by how elites construct or define policy problems and solutions. Moreover, the function of political communication is to provide reliable information that enables citizens to foresee the results of their political actions.

The Chilean bishops, like so many other political communicators, have taken their role seriously as they have worked hard to be a part of the public discourse around a range of political issues, particularly in the area of personal values and family morality. In addressing these issues, the bishops have not only offered their constituents crucial information, but have also attempted to paint a picture of the potential results of their political choices.

The Chilean bishops' initial articulation of their new agenda began on the very eve of democracy's return. In November 1989, in "Certainty, Coherence, and Confidence: A Message to Chilean Catholics in an Hour of Transition," the bishops clarified the church's stand on various issues with regard to the transition.[8] The document touches on many of the progressive themes that had concerned the church during the dictatorship, such as economic justice, dignity of the worker, and concern for human rights. Alongside these, the bishops voiced their concern for the culture and its moral values: the crisis of modernity, the crisis of the family and youth, consumerism, permissiveness, and secular positivism. Referring to secular society as "atheistic,"[9] the bishops took an aggressive stance in which they pitted the values of modern society against the values of the church.[10]

Most of the document is dedicated to a clarification of the church's position on this range of issues. Then its emphasis turns to the importance of political participation, calling on the faithful to participate in the electoral process and in political life more generally. It is in this context that the bishops stress that unity of belief among Catholics is essential. Acknowledging that there is room for "a legitimate diversity of opinions on debatable topics," they warn against division.[11] They go so far as to say that the reconciliation and unity of the Chilean people lie in the balance. The bishops have a particular message for public officials, as they encourage Catholic lawmakers to avoid taking part in any efforts to formulate or pass laws that oppose church teachings. Through this document the bishops insist that there is an objective moral norm not only for Christians, but for society as a whole, and by extension, that society should conform to church teachings.

The posture of the church in this regard is based on its long tradition of appealing to natural law. A universal law considered above human law, *natural law* is one "that man does not dictate for himself but which he discovers in the deepest part of his conscience, a law written by God in nature with universal characteristics."[12] Through natural law, the church can insist on the absolute nature of morality. It is a belief in a moral "order which regulates all of human conduct, the idea that life has a meaning and a purpose, and that there is a path for achieving them."[13] The Chilean bishops have appealed to natural law ever more frequently in their opposition to government policy.[14] It is to the hierarchy's stand on several specific policy concerns that I now turn.

Policy Concerns of the Church and the State

Through the mid-1900s, the Latin American Catholic hierarchy was generally classified as a conservative ally of the right. With the rise of the dictatorship, the church began to be seen as a friend to the left.[15] Both then and now, however, a simple characterization of its political alliances is impossible. Even with a careful look at its present priorities, pinning one all-encompassing political label on the Catholic hierarchy's issue stance is impractical. Its "pro-life" stance, described as the "seamless garment" approach (a reference to the cloak stripped from Jesus at the time of the crucifixion), has the church supporting issues across the entire political continuum. On the one hand, its support for labor unions, concern for the environment, opposition to capital punishment, and support for social welfare place it left of the political center. On the other hand, its support of traditional gender roles and its corresponding opposition to abortion, birth control, and divorce place it more in line with the political right.

The Catholic Church's stand on the latter issues took shape very early in the church's formation.[16] In contrast, the church's more liberal position regarding the defense of the worker evolved over the last century and a half.[17] Since the end of the dictatorship, with the perceived moral confusion of these democratic times and the potential liberalization of abortion, contraception, and divorce laws, the Chilean Catholic hierarchy has dedicated increasing energy to these issues. The papacy of John Paul II (1978–2005) has seen a great emphasis placed on personal values and family morality. This shift in the church's pastoral emphasis—coupled with changes in organizational structure and personnel geared toward reinforcing the Vatican's message—have served to unify the church hierarchy's position.[18]

This new emphasis has been of particular concern for the bishops during the Lagos presidency, from the beginning of which the church has appeared to be preparing for a fight regarding issues of moral values and reproductive rights. The battleground was surveyed in a series of articles published in the newspaper *La Tercera* beginning on June 4, 2000. The first of these was by Marcarena Lescornez entitled "Iglesia católica prepara batalla valórica contra Lagos: Conferencia episcopal crea comité asesor especial" (The Catholic Church Prepares Battle on Values against Lagos: Episcopal Conference Creates Special Committee). So, just as the defense of human rights warranted the establishment of the Vicaría de la Solidaridad, so now the defense of human life warranted the more recent establishment of the Vicaría de la Familia (1997). The latter office was created to promote church doctrine on the family, particularly around issues such as divorce, sex education, and abortion.

The Issues

I turn now to a more careful consideration of the range of issues that has been a focus for the church, particularly as they relate to the church's public policy interests. In doing so, I look at the policy stance of the Catholic hierarchy, the way it frames each issue, and the corresponding attitudes of Chilean Catholics. The issues of particular concern are those that constitute the current emphasis of the bishops: divorce, abortion, contraception, and sex education. I will also consider the hierarchy's continuing concern about social justice and human rights.

Divorce

Marriage, according to the Catholic Church's Code of Canon Law, has two essential properties: "unity and indissolubility." Further, the bond that arises is "permanent and exclusive"; that is, "it cannot be dissolved by any human power, nor by any cause outside of death." To say that marriage is a sacrament of the church means that it is a sign and means "by which faith is expressed and strengthened, worship is offered to God and our sanctification is brought about."[19] The Vatican has seen the legalization of divorce as a serious threat to the sanctity of marriage. For the Roman Catholic Church, not only is sacramental marriage between baptized Catholics indissoluble, but because of the church's appeal to natural law, the very institution of marriage is thought to be a permanent enterprise. In this way, justified through natural law, the indissolubility of marriage (along with many other moral teachings of the church) is seen as a universal good to be espoused by all.[20] Since the return to democracy, the Chilean hierarchy has not been shy about preaching and writing against divorce, nor about putting pressure on its adherents and on Catholic politicians to ward against the passage of legislation allowing it.[21]

In the earliest days of transition, then Cardinal-Archbishop of Santiago Carlos Oviedo released a statement promoting morality in politics, both among the citizenry and among politicians. In "Los católicos y la política," Oviedo makes clear that this public morality is to be understood as "dictated by the law of God and reflected in the natural law."[22] The document maintains that the Catholic politician, following his or her principles, must reject corruption, populism, and totalitarianism. Further, the Catholic lawmaker must reject all forms of secular temptations, such as abortion and divorce. Arguing that the mature democracies of the world have a certain minimal consensus on cultural and ethical order, the cardinal insists that the Catholic politician cannot leave his or her religion at the door of the government or of the party. In this regard, he announces that "for grave ethical and social reasons—and not exclusively religious—Catholics should exclude themselves from participation in any sort of attempt to legalize civil divorce."[23]

A more recent statement from the bishop of San Bernardo, Orozimbo Fuenzalida, addressed even more directly the responsibility of rank-and-file Catholics. Referring to the then-pending national congressional elections of 2001, Fuenzalida prepared a document for the Chilean Bishops' Conference entitled "Responsabilidad moral y las elecciones próximas" (Moral Responsibility and the Next Elections), in which he calls on all Catholics to consider carefully their vote choice, encouraging them not to vote for candidates who support legislation that would legalize divorce. The text itself reads: "Knowing that a certain candidate, if elected, would vote for a marriage law that would introduce the legalization of divorce, the Catholic voter and all who believe in the indissolubility of marriage should exclude that candidate from their preferences."[24]

The Chilean Episcopal Conference defended and further clarified this statement, saying that all Catholics should vote for those candidates who best represent Catholic values. In his response, Cardinal-Archbishop Francisco Javier Errázuriz of Santiago maintained that it is "a duty of all citizens to give their vote to the persons who promote the values that we want for Chile."[25] For the church, pronouncements such as these are not seen as interventions in the electoral process, but simply as a part of their duty to call the faithful to consistency and unity.

Until recently, the bishops' message would seem to have hit home, for with respect to divorce in Latin America, Chile has been an outlier. Moreover, Chilean society, in spite of its level of development and the impressive participation of women professionals in the workforce, has remained quite conservative. Whereas the legalization of divorce came to Brazil and Argentina in the late 1970s and 1980s, for instance, divorce legislation only recently moved through the Chilean Congress. While several factors bear on this conservatism in Chile, some scholars have argued that it is a result of the cultural and political constraints of the country's long dictatorship. Others argue that it is due to the effective lobbying of the Catholic Church in the public policy arena.

Whatever the reason for this persistent conservatism, attitudes of Chileans have surely shifted over time. Indeed, in spite of the bishops' calls for unity, a majority of Catholics today, and well over half of all Chileans, favor enacting a law that would legalize divorce. As early as 1991, a survey conducted by the Centro de Estudios Públicos (CEP) revealed that more than half of all Chileans (approximately 56 percent) favored some sort of divorce legislation. Among those who identified themselves as practicing Catholics, however, only 39.5 percent favored such legislation. Data have also shown that support for divorce legislation has been growing steadily in Chile during the period of consolidation.[26] And a recent Facultad Latinoamericana de Ciencias Sociales (FLACSO) survey reveals that 72 percent of those interviewed were to some degree in favor of the legalization of divorce (see table 4.1). Yet another survey, conducted by CEP in 1998, records similar findings, showing that 79 percent of Chileans support a law that would legalize divorce.[27] Further, dividing the sample by religious preference reveals that support for some sort of divorce law among practicing Catholics has increased by nearly 60 percent since the 1991 survey. In 1998 CEP found that 66 percent of practicing Catholics felt that divorce ought to be legal in some instances, while 34 percent felt it should not be legalized at all. Among

Table 4.1. Chilean Public Opinion on Divorce

"Do you believe that divorce should be legalized?"

Response	Agreement (%)
No, absolutely not	27
Agree	33
Strongly agree	23
Very strongly agree	16

Source: Facultad Latinoamericana de Ciencias Sociales (FLACSO), as reported in Parker, "Religión y cultura," in *Chile en los noventa,* ed. Cristian Toloza and Eugenio Lahara (Santiago: Dolmen Ediciones 1998).

practicing Evangelicals, on the other hand, 60 percent felt that divorce ought to be legal in some instances, and 40 percent opposed it under any circumstances. Attitudes among the Protestant sample (which is dominated by the growing number of Pentecostals) are marginally closer to the position of the Catholic hierarchy than those of the Catholic respondents. Yet, in spite of its generally strong popular support, legislation on divorce has moved forward very slowly.

After nearly a decade-long debate, Chile recently legalized divorce. Before this legalization, Chilean law permitted marital separation under certain conditions, but did not allow for the termination of the conjugal bond. The only means of severing that bond was through a surrogate and well-institutionalized civil annulment process. The annulment could be obtained, primarily by citizens of wealth, through the help of lawyers who convinced judges that there was some procedural error in the original civil marriage process. Passage of a divorce law in Chile was delayed not only because of the church's strong opposition, but also because separated couples could annul their marriage using this procedure.[28] As a result, the political pressure to enact a divorce law was muted. Nonetheless, support for legislation legalizing divorce in Chile was finally strong enough to lead to its passage by the Chamber of Deputies in 1997.[29] Until very recently, however, Senate debate on the measure was blocked and delayed. Finally, in January 2002, the Constitutional Commission of the Senate approved for Senate debate a marriage law that, if passed, would include the legalization of civil divorce in Chile. Proposals during the commission's debate reflected the diverse political sectors invested in the discussion.[30] The success in bringing this debate to the Senate floor marked a significant victory for those who sought to legalize divorce in Chile. The Senate successfully passed the legislation in August 2003, and it was signed into law by Ricardo Lagos in May 2004.

Amid their efforts to unite Catholics and Catholic legislators behind their agenda, the bishops released a statement in 2001 about their position with regard to the then-pending legislation. In this document, they made their strongest efforts to frame the issue and its consequences, intensifying their argument that the loosening of some fundamental morals could lead to cultural chaos and even societal collapse. This social deterioration argument of the bishops, articulated by Haas, borrows from Christian ethics the notion of the slippery slope:

> Central to Church opposition to specific policies is the belief that allowing even a minor relaxation of existing norms risks opening the door to eventual moral chaos. The possibility of the future legalization of abortion in Chile is one of the Church's greatest concerns, intensified by calls from sectors of the women's movement and the political center-left for public debate on the topic. . . . Abortion is seen as a probable eventual consequence both of sex education and the legalization of divorce.[31]

In their declaration, the bishops reiterated their objections to divorce and furthered this argument.[32] They asserted that countries with divorce laws progressively denigrated the notion of marriage. Divorce, the bishops argued, weakened the family union and the resolve to remain faithful to one's spouse, causing the disintegration of family. They went on to imply that a rise in the divorce rate, as families were less likely to stay together, would undoubtedly bring a rise in delinquency and drug addiction. This line of reasoning was at the heart of their recent campaign against the passage of the divorce legislation.

Abortion

The Catholic Church's stand on abortion has been consistent and clear: "Since the first century the Church has affirmed the moral evil of every procured abortion. This teaching has not changed and remains unchangeable."[33] "From the first moment of his existence, a human being must be recognized as having the rights of a person—among which is the inviolable right of every innocent being to life."[34] For the church, direct abortion, that is to say, abortion willed either as an end or a means, is contrary to moral law. In a recent effort to contextualize the evil of abortion for all Chileans, Cardinal-Archbishop Errázuriz argued that abortion is a violation of human rights.[35] The cardinal maintained that with the same force that the church intervened in the past on the side of victims of the dictatorship's human rights abuses, now is "the time to . . . defend the right of every human from its very beginning."[36]

Whereas Chilean public opinion widely supports divorce legislation, there is not similar broad support for the liberalization of abortion law. When speaking of the legislation on abortion in Chile, it is generally understood that the only procedure legalized would be therapeutic abortion, performed only when the life of the mother is in danger. Although first allowed in Chile in 1931, thera-

Table 4.2. Chilean Public Opinion on Abortion

"Do you believe that some form of abortion should be legalized?"

Response	Agreement (%)
No, absolutely not	51
Agree	25
Strongly agree	18
Very strongly agree	5

<ts>*Source*: Facultad Latinoamerica de Ciencias Sociales (FLASCO), as reported in Parker "Religion y cultura."

peutic abortion was banned by the passage of a comprehensive abortion law in 1989. This legislation, signed just before the end of the Pinochet regime, prohibits abortion under any circumstances.

Although support for abortion legislation is not high, it has increased over the last decade of consolidation. According to a survey done by the Centro de Estudios de la Realidad Contemporánea (CERC), support for the legalization of abortion was at 22.4 percent in 1991, the first full year of democratic governance. According to a more recent FLACSO survey undertaken in the metropolitan region of Santiago, public opinion was divided nearly down the middle on whether abortion should be legalized—a substantial increase in support (see table 4.2). The recent data reveal a fairly even divide among the Chilean public between those who would support the legalization of abortion (48 percent) and those who would not (51 percent).

While the FLACSO survey does not consider religious affiliation, an earlier one conducted by CEP does. These CEP survey results mirror the FLACSO results, with 49.7 percent in favor of abortion legislation and 49.2 opposed in all circumstances. When the sample was divided by religious affiliation, 51 percent of Catholics agreed that some form of abortion legislation should be passed, which is higher than overall public support. That percentage dropped when considering only practicing Catholics, among whom 42 percent supported legislation. Protestants (mainly Pentecostals), on the other hand, have more restrictive views, as 69 percent rejected abortion outright while approximately 30 percent accepted some form of it. Although illegal, abortions are commonly performed in Chile, where the per capita number of abortions is the highest in Latin America.[37]

One reason support for abortion legislation is growing among Chileans may be because of the high social cost of the present abortion policy. When abortion was outlawed in 1989 under Pinochet, the Chilean abortion laws became among the most restrictive in the world. Other than El Salvador, Chile is the only Latin American country that outlaws abortion under any circumstance, yet it is thought to have the highest abortion-to-birth ratio in all of Latin America. Estimates put the number of abortions in Chile at 160,000 per year, which means that there are four abortions for every ten live births in Chile.[38] In addition, researchers and health professionals estimate that one in five abortion patients requires hospitalization, and that nearly a third of all maternal deaths are directly related to complications from abortion.[39] One reason death rates are high is that the Chilean criminal code prohibits all abortions, even when a woman's life is in danger, and it penalizes women who consent to abortion and the providers who perform it. Because of their hesitation to seek medical care, numerous Chilean women suffer complications, costing the Chilean public health system an estimated US$15 million per year.[40]

Despite these high abortion rates, high social costs, and increasing public support, passage in Chile of even the most limited abortion legislation (that is, therapeutic abortion to save the life of the mother) seems unlikely. Prior to 1989, lawmakers from the political left had spoken in favor of liberalizing abortion laws, and by the early 1990s, the Socialist Party had assumed an official position in favor of therapeutic abortion. But when a bill was introduced in Congress in 1991, it met strong opposition from the Catholic hierarchy. It also had opposition from the parties and organizations of the right and from many Christian Democrats, whose members tend to be socially conservative on moral issues and more progressive on economic issues. The abortion bill was never approved for congressional debate and has not been seriously proposed since. In their study of legislative initiatives relating to women's rights, Blofield and Haas comment that since the 1991 abortion debacle, "the left in general began to distance itself from what it saw as a dangerously contentious bill, and which would not only fail but also succeed in creating tension within the coalition."[41]

Contraception

The Catholic Church's position on contraception is most clearly spelled out in the 1968 encyclical of Paul VI, *Humanae Vitae,* and the more recent encyclical of John Paul II, *Evangelium Vitae* (1995). Affirming that every sexual act must be unitive and procreative, the former states, "Every action which, whether in anticipation of the conjugal act, or in its accomplishment, or in the development of its natural consequences, proposes, whether as an end or as a means, to render procreation impossible" is intrinsically evil.[42] For their part, the Chilean bishops in 1994 released a statement warning the faithful that they should "not be taken in by the campaigns against natural birth, which do not respect the dignity of man or woman."[43] Along with abortion, the bishops went on to denounce all artificial methods of birth control, arguing that they "violate the very nature of the human person."[44]

A recent ethical debate in the area of reproductive health has prompted a further clarification of the Chilean hierarchy's stance on contraception and, by extension, abortion. The Catholic Church worldwide has summarily rejected the use of the "morning- after pill," a contraceptive recently introduced by the Chilean government through its Ministry of Health. Making reference to then Minister of Health Michelle Bachelet, Cardinal Errázuriz expressed reservations that one person should make a decision that affects the entire society. "This process questions our entire judicial process, to leave a question of such gravity regarding the right to life and the culture of a country in the hands of one person, however capable and well intentioned she may be."[45]

Articulating the bishops' concerns in an earlier statement, Cristian Caro, an auxiliary bishop of Santiago, accused powerful political forces—namely the World Health Organization, the United States, and other industrialized nations—of manipulating Chile and other Latin American countries. "They want to promote the sale of contraceptives . . . [so they] send their leftover condoms and birth control. There is a powerful economic and political campaign to diminish the family in our countries, because the First World countries, which no longer have children, see that our countries have more children and thus continue to grow, and they are going to lose their political hegemony."[46] Various conservative groups have supported the church's efforts to block the use of the morning-after drug. These groups include the World Movement of Mothers–Chile, the Coalition for Life and Action, the International Center on the Study of Human Life, and the Research, Formation, and Study of Women center, directed by Ismini Anastassiou. Largely successful in their lobbying efforts, the church and its allies have succeeded in blocking the release of the morning-after pill, for although the Chilean government had initially granted approval, Congress eventually voted it down.

In spite of the church's opposition to contraception, however, its use is widely accepted among the Chilean populace. According to 2001 data collected by the Catholic University of Chile, 82.4 percent of all Chileans approve of the use of contraceptives. Even among practicing Catholics, 75.9 percent find artificial contraception acceptable, according to a survey done by the Instituto de Sociología in 2001. National health programs have facilitated access to birth control since the 1960s, and the use of contraceptives is widespread. Because these programs are mainly geared to provide prenatal and postpartum primary care, they generally provide birth control to women who have already had at least one child. Birth control is therefore more difficult to obtain for childless women, especially younger and poorer women.

Sex Education

The Catholic Church's teaching on sex education has been laid down by the Vatican in two important documents. *Familiaris Consortio* is a 1981 apostolic exhortation of Pope John Paul II on "the Mission of the Family"; and "Truth and Meaning of Human Sexuality," issued in 1995 by the Pontifical Council for the Family, is a set of guidelines for education within the family. The former calls on Christian parents to give to their children clear and delicate sex education. It decries a contemporary culture "that largely reduces human sexuality to the level of something commonplace, since it interprets and lives it in a reductive and impoverished way by linking it solely with the body and with selfish pleasure."[47] *Familiaris Consortio* goes on to say that, in view of the close links between the sexual dimension of the person and his or her ethical values,

> education must bring the children to a knowledge of and respect for the moral norms as the necessary and highly valuable guarantee for responsible personal growth in human sexuality. . . . For this reason the Church is firmly opposed to an often-widespread form of imparting sex information dissociated from moral principles. That would merely be an introduction to the experience of pleasure and a stimulus leading to the loss of serenity—while still in the years of innocence—by opening the way to vice.[48]

Given this premise, government-sponsored sex education in secondary schools has been of deep concern for the hierarchy of the church in recent years. In the firm belief that sex education must be taught in the context of values, the Chilean bishops are particularly concerned about a sex education program that was piloted for use in schools in 1995.

The government maintains that the program, called Jornadas de Conversación en Afectividad y Sexualidad (Conversation Sessions on Affection and Sexuality, or JOCAS), is a means of facilitating the discussion of sexual issues among parents, teachers, and high school students. It is a voluntary, three-stage program. The first stage is a three-day session during which youth express their concerns about sexuality. In the second stage, experts come in to answer questions. And finally, parents and students meet together to discuss the issues and engage in educational activities. Among the program's stated goals are to curb the rate of teenage pregnancy (which is at 40,000 annually), reduce the rate of abortions (estimated at 160,000 annually), and limit the spread of HIV/AIDS. The JOCAS program is a joint effort of the Ministries of Education and Health, the National Women's Service (SERNAM), and the National Youth Institute, among other partners. First implemented in several regions of Chile in 1995, under the Frei administration, JOCAS has been expanded since. It is now in use in nearly every region of the country.

The major criticism of JOCAS comes from conservative groups and the Catholic hierarchy, who accuse the program of promoting immorality by discussing sexuality in clinical rather than moral terms and by subverting parental rights. In his defense of the program, President Frei implicitly accused its critics of being out of touch and hypocritical, and defended the state's obligation to work with parents in the sex education effort. Frei's statements provoked a strong reaction from the church. Auxiliary Bishop Cristian Caro of Santiago said the church does not close its eyes to the reality of the nation's youth, but nor does it want them receiving "fallacious and immoral" information about "safe sex."[49] He said sexual activity could not be separated from greater values such as love, respect for and dignity of the human body, fidelity, and the importance of raising a family.

This debate between the government and the church mirrors the wider debate within Chilean society.[50] Defenders of the JOCAS program claim that erroneous reports by *El Mercurio*, the leading newspaper in Santiago, led to considerable and unfair criticism of the program.[51] Despite the bad publicity, however, a majority of Chileans support some form of sex education in the schools.[52] And the implementation of the JOCAS program has continued.

Social Justice

The Chilean bishops' agenda since the return of democracy has not focused exclusively on personal morality and family values. Other issues that have occupied their attention include the environment; consumerism; and diverse social problems associated with teachers, farmworkers, miners, health, drugs, and HIV/AIDS.[53] Their strongest calls in this issue area, however, have been around their concern for the continuing injustices of poverty and inequality, and for truth with respect to the crimes committed under the Pinochet regime. Despite being eclipsed by new priorities, the bishops' "preferential option for the poor" has not been abandoned. While it has been subject to wide interpretation and has generated much debate within the church and beyond, this preferential attention to the world of the poor has also been part of the motivation behind the action and mission of the Catholic Church since the return of democracy.

Over the last decade, the bishops have expressed in various ways their concern about social welfare issues. These concerns center on, among other things, the continuing struggle to overcome underdevelopment and the need to elevate the quality of life of all Chileans. The bishops have also been attentive to the issues of poverty and extreme inequality. In 1992, Cardinal Oviedo released the document "Los pobres no pueden esperar" (The Poor Cannot Wait), in which he expressed the hope that democracy would bring justice for the masses of Chilean poor. For its part, the Chilean Episcopal Conference released "Superación de la pobreza en Chile" (Overcoming Poverty in Chile) in 1994, and a year later, an Easter message with a similar theme called "Cristo nuestra esperanza" (Christ Our Hope).

In their campaign against poverty, many of the bishops have not been afraid to criticize the free market economics of neoliberalism.[54] In their meeting in 1994, attended by the recently elected President Frei, the bishops insisted on their concern for the poor, social problems, and the need to move toward an economy of solidarity. In November 1996, the bishops furthered their critique: "More and more we are configuring a new style of development, where the logic and the categories of a market economy, open and competitive, require strong consideration, beyond strictly the economic ramifications . . . they constitute an immense challenge for renewed evangelization."[55]

In this document, the bishops go on to denounce the disloyal, illegal, stressful, and dehumanizing effects of economic competition; the problems of the environment, poverty, and misery that persist; as well as the intolerable inequality and social exclusion of many. They challenge all Chileans to work together in overcoming poverty. They also call on the state to collaborate with the private sector to support social programs. They mention the need for greater attention to education, job training for workers, and greater participation for all in the advance of the Chilean economy.[56]

The bishops reiterated their concern on this front in December 2001. Meeting with President Lagos, the permanent committee of the Chilean Bishops' Conference expressed their concern about the economic situation of Chile, the problems of unemployment, and the hardships they cause all Chileans. They addressed too the need to resolve the socioeconomic problems of the Mapuche Indians. Avoided were several issues that have caused particular tension between the Lagos administration and the church (namely the morning-after pill and divorce). The participants did discuss, however, the effects that cultural changes and individualism are having on the family and the institution of marriage.[57]

Human Rights

The Catholic hierarchy has also demonstrated a deep concern for the victims of the dictatorship's repression and for other human rights abuses. The most important defense against that repression was its own human rights organization, the Vicaría de la Solidaridad.[58] Although the Vicaría has been eliminated, the bishops have continued to voice their concerns in this realm. Statements and documents from the earliest days of the transition have called for both reconciliation and justice in matters related to human rights. Indeed, the bishops have on various occasions expounded on the need for truth on the road to reconciliation and healing for Chile.[59]

One of the church's recent efforts in this regard came through its participation in the Mesa de Diálogo Sobre los Derechos Humanos. This series of talks, convened by then Minister of Defense Edmundo Pérez Yoma, brought together human rights attorneys, representatives of the military and uniformed police, members of civil society, and church leaders. The church played a key role in bringing these groups together, and Santiago Auxiliary Bishop Sergio Valech chaired the Mesa de Diálogo for a time. The commission came to an agreement in June 2000 that required all parties to turn over any and all documents and information regarding the thousands who disappeared, were tortured, or were murdered during the dictatorship. The Chilean Congress one week later passed legislation that made this agreement law. Designed to reveal information that for decades had been concealed by those responsible, this agreement offered the first hope for many that they might obtain information on the fate of relatives who disappeared during military rule.

This agreement fell far short of moving along the process of reconciliation in Chilean society and democracy.[60] Its success rested in large measure on the cooperation of the armed forces and the police in complying and providing the fullest information possible. Ultimately, the military failed to cooperate in handing over documents. Nonetheless, many feel that the commission, which delivered its report to Lagos in January 2001, was a success in that through this dialogue, the armed forces and the police for the first time acknowledged some part in the excessive repression of the dictatorship. More recently, in November 2004, the Comisión Nacional Sobre Prisión Política y Tortura (the National Commission on Political Imprisonment and Torture), of which Auxiliary Bishop Sergio Valech was head, delivered its conclusions to President Lagos, clearing the way for compensation of victims.

In the end, there can be little doubt of the instrumental role the Catholic Church has played in helping to give credibility to dialogues like these—much as it did to other negotiations during the transition.[61] Some scholars have argued that the Chilean transition to democracy will remain incomplete if the fate of the detained-disappeared is not fully known and legally investigated.[62] To the extent that the church's mediation between the military and the families of the victims has helped this process, it has also aided in strengthening democracy in Chile.

The Collective Effect of the Bishops' Agenda

The Roman Catholic Church in Chile, through its bishops, has spoken out forcefully in defense of the pastoral agenda and its translation to public policy. The church's appeal to natural law has allowed it to proclaim and defend certain moral precepts as absolute. Further, the church contends that "when there is doubt or disagreement as to the content of these principles or their application, it (alone) has the authority (from God) to resolve ambiguities."[63] The church's priorities in the realm of personal morality and family values are quite clear. As we have seen, however, support for them is declining. But in a liberal democracy, tension between a church's agenda and that of the state and the masses is not unusual, nor need it be all that problematic. Indeed, in many ways it is to be expected. But in Chile and in Latin America more generally, where the church's influence has remained strong, this confrontation between the hierarchy and the members of the church is somewhat more surprising, and the conflict with the state more troublesome. This tension has two particular characteristics that bear on the consolidation of democracy in the region. First, the center of this conflict generally resides within a category of personal morality and family values issues, which has found particular support from the political right. And second, because of the confluence of issues being discussed and the way they have been framed and categorized by the bishops, the agenda is having a powerful collective impact that is causing moderate societal discord.

Despite the present conflict around a range of moral and family issues, a similar tension has not emerged around social justice issues.[64] Torcal and Mainwaring argue that calls to radically address redistributive and class issues in democratic Chile were muted by a general consensus that the government should rely on rapid growth to improve Chile's standard of living and, further, that the success of such a strategy would make economic redistribution unnecessary.[65] While the Catholic Church and several other groups in civil society have voiced their concern in these areas, these calls have not generated broader societal debate, for there is wide agreement that something must be done. Indeed, a deliberate and sustained strategy of "growth with equity" on the part of the governments of the Concertación has attempted to address social inequality. But whether due to the reduced intensity of these issues, a greater societal consensus, or the government's willingness to address them, the issues of social justice and human rights, with which the church has also attempted to contend, have not caused division similar to the issues of personal morality and family values.

It is also the case that the issues around social justice and human rights have not been categorized in the same collective way as the moral issues. Because the family values issues disproportionately affect women, they are linked together by efforts of women's rights and health groups, which offer their own set of competing issue frames against those of the church. In their framing, women's groups and many others articulate these family morality issues as a matter of rights (described by some as fundamental human rights) that bear on gender equality and the advancement of women. The same issues are also explicitly connected as life issues by the church. In issue framing, it is not unusual for a communicator to rank preferred goals over others, but in the case of morality and family values, the church does not prioritize. Indeed, in speaking of a consistent ethic of life, the church serves to bring together what others might perceive as unrelated issues. While this sort of categorization is helpful to the public as a cognitive tool for coping with the informational demands of our social and political worlds,[66] it may not be serving the bishops' purposes very well. While it is traditional for the church to connect these concerns as life issues in the public policy realm, there is a danger when the church fails to set priorities among them. The risk is that because of this issue-connectedness, the implementation of the government's sex education program is placed on a moral par with the legislation of abortion rights. Also, while any one of these issues might by itself attract some attention, their collective nature coupled with the hierarchy's opposition has caused quite a commotion in the Chilean media and in society more generally. While perhaps internally consistent, the hierarchy's broad opposition to a range of policy concerns is perceived by many to be elitist, uncompromising, and disconnected from the Chilean reality. As a result, the bishops' attempts to connect these issues so closely may be working against their ultimate legislative goals.

The tension around these issues is further heightened by the policy agenda of the Lagos government. Although all came from the center-left coalition of the Concertación, each of the three democratic administrations since the end of dictatorship (of Aylwin, Frei, and Lagos) has been viewed by the church as moving increasingly to the left. From the moment democracy dawned, the hierarchy voiced its concern around these issues, but it has expressed a particular concern about the present administration of Ricardo Lagos. In anticipation of his administration's policy initiatives, the Chilean Bishops' Conference created a special committee to prepare a strategy to counter several of the initiatives Lagos had articulated during his presidential campaign.[67] The hierarchy has been vocal in this effort and has solicited the help of an array of organizations, politicians, and parties. Their campaign and the ensuing conflict have exposed some of the divisions that exist within the organization of the church.

Indeed, collectively, the bishops' stance and their opposition to current government policy initiatives have created a situation that has the church's hierarchy on the defensive even with respect to its democratic commitment.[68] Its recent and vocal opposition to the policy areas outlined in this chapter has played a divisive role in society in general. Most indications are that the bishops' public rhetoric has largely failed to persuade their constituents and, further, has offended their competitors. This point is illustrated through two recent conflicts. The first is a recent struggle between the Catholic Church and several women's rights groups; the second is between the Catholic Church and several other religious denominations within Chile.

At the core of the church's struggle with several women's rights groups lies legislation brought before the Chilean Congress in late 2001 that takes its origins from a United Nations Committee resolution of 1979. *El protocolo facultativo para la eliminación de toda forma de discriminación de la mujer* (The Convention on the Elimination of All Forms of Discrimination against Women, or CEDAW) sets out, in legally binding form, internationally accepted principles regarding the rights of women that are applicable to all women in all fields. The rights of particular concern to the Catholic Church are those around reproduction and abortion.

While CEDAW's original proposal came to the military government in 1989, its adoption has come through a number of legislative reforms since then, including the Domestic Violence Act and reforms to improve access to employment and training, working hours, and social benefits for female workers. More recently, the Lagos administration has advanced further legislative reforms in the name of CEDAW. Upon the introduction of these reforms Cardinal Errázuriz of Santiago released a statement condemning the convention as failing to defend the family or life. Appealing to the sovereignty of Chile, the cardinal argued that "Chile is a state that is capable of respecting, enriching, and developing its own culture and the road to human progress, vigorously promoting among us a legislation that respects the human rights of all, and a way of living together in solidarity, fraternity, and justice, while at the same time Chilean."[69] Within a week, the legislature pulled back from ratifying the convention.[70] Reaction to the cardinal's statement and the decision of the Congress was very strong and very public. And the church found itself having to defend itself against a barrage of criticism that labeled it as opposing the rights of women.[71]

The second illustrative conflict pits several religious denominations against the Catholic Church. It results from the increasing tendency of bishops to call on Catholic citizens and legislators to vote in particular ways, especially as the December 2001 elections neared. Throughout the fall of 2001, Cardinal Errázuriz and others called upon Catholics to vote according to their Catholic values. This call was stated most succinctly by Chilean Cardinal Jorge Medina, the Vatican prefect for the Congregation for Divine Worship and the Discipline of the Sacraments. Visiting from Rome shortly before the December 2001 elections, Medina declared "a Catholic cannot vote in the next legislative elections for any candidate that contradicts the values of the church with respect to divorce, abortion, euthanasia, and the morning-after pill."[72]

The Catholic Church's stance on these and other like issues prompted a strong response from Chilean citizens, legislators, and above all other churches. In an ironic twist that was missed by few, the Catholic bishops found themselves accused by several other churches of *fundamentalism*, a term traditionally used by the Catholic Church to describe its present accusers. Among these critics were the Masons, whose Chilean grand master, Jorge Carvajal, released a declaration on his adherents' behalf. The pronouncement criticized the Catholic Church for the pressure it was putting on the Chilean legislature. It also expressed suspicions regarding the Catholic hierarchy's charge to its rank and file: "Religious pressure has always existed in Chile, but never have we seen such open interventionism as we do now. The call to not vote for certain candidate exceeds the moral limits of any religious creed: attempting to impose a particular value choice on the entire country."[73] He added that the Order of Masons sees in this attitude toward divorce and the use of contraception a "renewed fundamentalism that echoes the intolerance" that in another age had people being "burned at the stake."[74]

Evangelical Protestants entered the fray as well, as several days later the president of the Consejo de Unidades Pastorales Evangélicas (Council of Evangelical Pastors), Bishop Emiliano Soto, voiced his criticism. Soto accused the Catholic bishops of using "fundamentalist" criteria in their efforts against divorce, the morning-after pill, and abortion. He said the Catholic Church was wrong in trying to impose its own particular vision on the entire society and in putting pressure on Deputies and Senators not to pass the divorce law.[75] The response of the Chilean Episcopal Conference was immediate. Through its spokesman, Enrique Palet, it declared that "the Catholic Church is not imposing anything," and that "it is only completing its mission" to orient, suggest, and invite people to reflect on these issues. Nonetheless, even among Chilean Catholics there are many who feel that the church has overstepped its bounds in its campaign on behalf of these issues. While there are many who agree with the hierarchy's stand, there are an increasing number of people who dissent from the church's position on several of these personal morality and family values issues.

Presenting credible evidence that a policy change will bring about a beneficial outcome is the task of the communicator who seeks to persuade the public.[76] While a more systematic analysis of the direct effect of the bishops' rhetoric on their public is beyond the scope of this study, it is clear that their more recent efforts have not proven very successful. Indeed, conflicts on these issues and the attitudes they engender have Chileans reassessing the role religion is playing in society. In a recent CEP survey, Chileans were asked whether they agreed or disagreed with the following statement: "Looking at the world, in general do you think that religions bring more conflict than peace?" Forty-nine percent of Chileans either agreed or strongly agreed that religion brings more conflict.[77] Similarly, respondents were asked whether people with very strong religious beliefs were usually very intolerant of others. Among the Chilean respondents, 70 percent agreed or strongly agreed, placing Chile among the countries with the highest level of agreement. Finally, when asked whether Chile would be a better country if religion had less influence, 50 percent of the Chileans interviewed agreed.[78] This percentage places Chile directly on par with the respondents of Ireland (49 percent) and Israel (51 percent) and fourth in its percentage of agreement among all thirty-one countries where the survey was conducted. These findings reveal that many Chileans are finding the role of religion in society more divisive than constructive. While the data do not allow us to ascertain whether it is the Catholic, Pentecostal, or other churches—or a mix of them—that primarily elicit such a response, it is not difficult to see that Chileans are deeply concerned about the present involvement of religion in politics.

Conclusion

The Vatican and bishops' call for unity has gone largely unheeded by rank-and-file Catholics throughout Latin America. In actual fact, as several trends outlined in this chapter show, the cleavage between the hierarchy of the Catholic Church and the Chilean masses is increasing, not diminishing. On fundamental moral issues that have important implications for public policy, Chilean Catholics increasingly dissent from the bishops' teachings. Up to now, arguing that the Catholic Church has always been able to embrace a wide range of theological positions has been sufficient to explain away this divide. Indeed, Catholicism, even through the Middle Ages, has tolerated a great deal of diversity of belief and practice and, in turn, through its monasteries and orders has offered a fair amount of variance to the faithful as well. This wide theological diversity has traditionally represented a minimal threat to the church's teaching authority. But as the firestorm around these current issues grows, so does the threat. There is only so much difference of opinion the church can tolerate before certain sectors are in schism.[79] But the ramifications go beyond ecclesial concerns about church unity, for such an internal rift threatens the church's potential power in every arena, particularly the political.[80] How effective can its political influence be if the church is unable to mobilize even its own members around the beliefs that define its socioreligious and political agenda for society? Worse still, for some bishops, is that their very own Catholic lawmakers are the ones proposing the legislation contrary to Catholic teachings, specifically, divorce legislation.[81] With seemingly little success at persuading their public and, thus, unable to claim the support of even their own members, the bishops have felt obliged to intensify their involvement in the policy-making process. As political party alignments shift and change, this effort of the bishops has serious implications for political party structures as well. The tension within the church's organization has important implications for democratic politics and the church's involvement therein, particularly in light of the political cleavage that it may be intensifying.[82]

As this chapter reveals, while the church succeeded in organizing the opposition to the Pinochet regime, it has not been very successful in influencing the policies of the Concertación, which was born under its protection. In fact, the church not only is struggling in its efforts to have influence in the legislative realm, but in the process may actually be creating a rift between the church and society. The church's participation in the public policy discourse, which has failed to generate positive results, is at the heart of the matter. Catholics are setting out on their own with regard to moral decision making, and there is a growing rift between the hierarchy and the masses within the Catholic Church. Further research must carefully consider the sources of this tension, the interplay of public rhetoric and political attitudes, and the role various players may have in influencing these trends. On the local level, for instance, the priest's role in explaining this growing divide must be considered. The increasing competition from evangelical Protestantism and its impact on the message of the bishops, and further, the clarity of that message as it is being delivered to the masses will also be an important focus for future research.

Notes

1. Eduardo Frei, Speech Temuco, quoted in Cristian Parker, "Religión y cultura," in *Chile en los noventa,* ed. Cristian Toloza and Eugenio Lahara (Santiago: Dolmen Ediciones 1998), 658.

2. CELAM #230. CELAM stands for Conferencia Episcopal Latinoamericana and represents 22 bishops from Latin America and the Caribbean area. It was created in 1955 and provides a permanent forum for Latin American bishops.

3. CELAM #124.

4. Brian Smith, *Religious Politics in Latin America: Pentecostal vs. Catholic* (South Bend, Ind.: Notre Dame University Press, 1998).

5. Ibid.

6. Michael Fleet and Brian Smith, *The Catholic Church and Democracy in Chile and Peru* (South Bend, Ind.: Notre Dame University Press, 1997); Edward Cleary and Juan Sepulveda, "Chilean Pentecostalism: Coming of Age," in *Power, Politics, and Pentecostal-*

ism in Latin America, ed. Edward Cleary and Hannah Stewart Gambino (Boulder: Lynne Rienner Publishers, 1992); Joshua Prokopy and Christian Smith, introduction to *Latin American Religion in Motion*, ed. Christian Smith and Joshua Prokopy (New York: Routledge, 1999); Frans Kamsteeg, "Pentecostalism and Political Awakening in Pinochet's Chile and Beyond," in Smith and Prokopy, *Latin American Religion in Motion*.

7. Thomas E. Nelson, "Group Affect and Attribution in Social Policy Opinion," *Journal of Politics* 61, no. 2 (May 1999): 331.

8. CECH 1989. CECH stands for Conferencia Episcopal de Chile.

9. CECH 1989, 47.

10. Parker, "Religión y cultura"; Liesel Haas, "The Catholic Church in Chile: New Political Alliances," in Smith and Prokopy, *Latin American Religion in Motion*.

11. CECH 1989, 48.

12. Carlos Oviedo, "Los católicos y la político" in Carlos Oviedo, *Los documentos pastorales*, Tomo 1, Santiago, Arzobispodo de Santiago 1998.

13. *Humanae Vitae* 1968. This is a papal encyclical, which is a pastoral letter that is usually addressed by a pope to the bishops of the Catholic Church or the hierarchy of a particular country.

14. Haas, "Catholic Church in Chile."

15. Brian Smith, *The Church and Politics in Chile: Challenges to Modern Catholicism* (Princeton: Princeton University Press, 1982); Scott Mainwaring and Timothy Scully, *Building Democratic Institutions: Party Systems in Latin America* (Stanford: Stanford University Press, 1986).

16. This is one of the principal reasons why, in 1968, Pope Paul VI found it so difficult to change the church's teaching on contraception. Contrary to the advice of a commission he drew together, the pope released *Humanae Vitae* (Human Life: On the Regulation of Birth, 1968), reaffirming the church's longstanding position on reproductive concerns. Pope John Paul II's more recent *Evangelium Vitae* (The Gospel of Life: On the Value and Inviolability of Human Life, 1995) further clarifies the church's long-held stance on these issues.

17. The progression of the church's teaching in the area of workers' rights and the like came through several important encyclicals, including *Rerum Novarum* (On the Condition of the Working Classes, 1891), *Quadragesimo Anno* (On the Fortieth Anniversary of *Rerum Novarum*, 1931), *Populorum Progressio* (On the Development of Peoples, 1967), and *Centesimus Annus* (On the One Hundredth Anniversary of *Rerum Novarum*, 1991).

18. Merike Blofield, *The Politics of "Moral Sin": A Study of Abortion and Divorces in Catholic Chile since 1990* (Santiago: FLACSO-Chile, 2001).

19. Catholic Church Code of Canon Law #1056, #1134, #1141, #840.

20. CECH, 2001a and 2001b.

21. A series of documents attest to this, including *Los católicos y la política* (September 24, 1990) and *Responsabilidad moral y las elecciones próximas*. Not all bishops are in agreement with this sort of hard-sell campaign. Bishop Tomás González of Punta Are-

nas, for example, has voiced his feeling that "the church should promote, not impose, its doctrine." See *El Mercurio*, July 7, 1994.

22. Oviedo, "Los católicos y la política," statement, 1990, 28.

23. Ibid.

24. CECH, 2001b, 4.

25. *El Mercurio*, July 7, 1994.

26. Merike Blofield, *Politics of "Moral Sin": A Study of Abortion and Divorce in Catholic Chile Since 1990*. Santiago, Chile: Facultad Latinoamericana de Ciencias Sociales, 2001.

27. Unlike the FLACSO survey, the CEP survey question did not inquire about the intensity of the respondents' agreement. Instead, the question was simply whether the respondent agreed or disagreed that there should be a law authorizing divorce (CEP 1998).

28. Maureen Meehan, "Annulment Used as Divorce Loophole in Chile," *Latinamerica Press*, July 11, 1991.

29. This bill was originally proposed in 1995 and was distinct from three failed divorce bills that preceded it. It was passed on for congressional debate largely because of the concessions made by the left, who proposed it. For example, it includes a mandatory five-year waiting period for a divorce, and judges are given wide powers to deny petitions for divorce. Blofield and Haas discuss this bill and argue that it makes divorce even more difficult than annulment is under the current system, which led the Christian Democrats to endorse it; see Merike Blofield and Liesel Haas, "Legislative Dynamics in Chile: Exploring Left Influences on Policy, 1990–1998," paper presented at the Latin American Studies Association Meeting, Miami, March 16–18, 2000.

30. By and large, support for the legislation has come from the left, whereas those who stand with the church in opposition to it have generally been from the right. A brief look at the committee's debate and proposals will suffice to make this point: The original proposal, passed by the Chamber of Deputies in 1997, implied that the marriage bond was null and void when one of the parties abandoned his or her duties. Included in the more recent proposal by two members of the PDC, Andrés Zaldívar and Juan Hamilton, was an amendment that authorized the dissolution of a marriage with the simple consent of both parties. In contrast, a proposal by right-wing lawmakers Sergio Romero and Sergio Díaz of the RN and Andrés Chadwick of the UDI, essentially rejects divorce in any form. For more information, see *La Tercera*, January 17, 2002.

31. Haas, "Catholic Church in Chile," 49.

32. CECH 2001.

33. Catechism of the Catholic Church, 2000, #2271.

34. Ibid., #2270.

35. This issue is framed in opposite terms in *Women behind Bars: Chile's Abortion Laws: A Human Rights Analysis* (New York: Center for Reproductive Law and Policy; Santiago: Open Forum on Reproductive Health and Rights, 1998). This book addresses abortion laws in relation to human rights, arguing that control over reproductive decisions is appropriately classified as a human right, not the violation of such.

36. *La Tercera*, October 2, 2001.

37. Viviana Erazo, "Aborto: proponen aumentar la penalidad," *Fempress* 203 (September 1998), 4; Verónica Matus, Carmen Anthony, and Josefina Hurtado, *Women's Rights in Chile: A Shadow Report* (New York: Center for Reproductive Law and Policy, 1999); Blofield, *Politics of "Moral Sin."*

38. Center for Reproductive Law and Policy, *Women behind Bars.*

39. Ibid.; Matus, Anthony, and Hurtado, *Women's Rights in Chile.*

40. Blofield, *Politics of "Moral Sin."*

41. Blofield and Haas, "Legislative Dynamics in Chile."

42. *Humanae Vitae* #14.

43. CECH 1994b.

44. Ibid.

45. *La Tercera*, March 15, 2001.

46. *La Epoca*, September 26, 1996. "Frei supports JOCAS sex-ed program. Calls policy of avoidance immoral."

47. *Familiaris Consortio* #37.

48. Ibid., #3.

49. *La Epoca*, September 26, 1996.

50. Haas, "Catholic Church in Chile"; Mala Htun, *Sex and the State: Abortion, Divorce, and the Family under Latin American Dictatorships and Democracies* (New York: Cambridge University Press, 2003).

51. *La Epoca*, September 16, 1996.

52. Cristian Bofill and Pedro Ramírez, "Sexo, SIDA, divorcio, censura e hipocresía, según Lavín," *Qué Pasa*, May 3, 1997, 4–8; Haas, "Catholic Church in Chile."

53. Parker, Religión y cultura"; Smith, *Religious Politics in Latin America.*

54. CECH 1995a; CECH 1995c; CECH 1996b.

55. CECH 1996a, 14.

56. CECH 1996a.

57. *El Mercurio*, December 13, 2001.

58. Cynthia Brown, *The Vicaría de la Solidaridad in Chile* (New York: America's Watch Committee, 1987); Cristian Precht, *A Sign of Hope: The Past and Present of the Vicaría de la Solidaridad* (Notre Dame: Notre Dame Law School, Center for Civil and Human Rights, 1993); Pamela Lowden, *Moral Opposition to Authoritarian Rule in Chile: 1973–1990* (New York: St. Martin's Press 1996).

59. CECH 1989; CECH 1995b; CECH 1995c.

60. Elizabeth Lira 2000. "Mesa del "Diálogo de Derechos Humanos en Chile, 21 Agosto 1999–13 Junio 2000." In Francisco Rojos Aravena, ed., *Chile y las Américas*. Santiago: FLACSO, 2000.

61. Thomas Bruneau, *The Political Transformation of the Brazilian Catholic Church* (Cambridge: Cambridge University Press, 1974); Bruneau, *The Church in Brazil: The Politics of Religion* (Austin: University of Texas Press, 1982); Daniel Levine, *Popular Voices in Latin American Catholicism* (Princeton: Princeton University Press, 1992); Smith,

Church and Politics in Chile and *Religious Politics in Latin America*; Mainwaring and Scully, *Building Democratic Institutions.*

62. Mario Aguilar, "The Disappeared and the Mesa de Diálogo in Chile: Searching for Those Who Never Grew Old," *Bulletin of Latin American Research* 21, no. 3 (July 2002): 422–23.

63. Fleet and Smith, *Catholic Church and Democracy in Chile and Peru,* 287.

64. Edward Cleary and Hannah Stewart Gambino note, "The political role of the Church has become far less crucial as a defender of human rights and constitutional processes than it was in much of Latin America from the early 1970s through the mid-1980s" (*Power, Politics, and Pentecostalism in Latin America,* 9–10). In *The Catholic Church and Democracy in Chile and Peru,* Michael Fleet and Brian Smith, for their part, have argued that moral and religious issues are more likely to precipitate internal problems for the church in the years to come than are disagreements relating to the church's social mission. And finally, Brian Smith states that while church involvement has continued in areas of poverty alleviation and social justice, "open confrontations between local church leaders and bishops have become less frequent since the return to democracy, and some of the more extreme aspects of liberation theology widely discussed a generation ago are now quite rare" (*Religious Politics in Latin America,* 66).

65. Mariano Torcal and Scott Mainwaring, "The Political Recrafting of Social Bases of Party Competition: Chile in the 1990s." Working paper #278, University of Notre Dame, Kellogg Institute for International Studies, p. 32.

66. Keith Holyoak and Paul Thagard, *Mental Leaps: Analogy in Creative Thought* (Cambridge, Mass.: MIT Press, 1995); George Lakoff and Mark Johnson, *Philosophy in the Flesh* (New York: Basic Books, 1999); Nelson, "Group Affect and Attribution."

67. *La Tercera,* June 4, 2000.

68. Jean Daudelin and W. E. Hewitt, "Churches and Politics in Latin America: Catholicism Confronts Contemporary Challenges," in *Religion, Globalization and Political Culture in the Third World,* ed. Jeff Haynes (Chippenham: Anthony Rowe, 1999); Haas, "Catholic Church in Chile."

69. Monsignor Errázuriz, statement, 2002, 4. Cardinal Francisco Javier Errázuriz, "U.N. Pressuring Nations to Undermine the Family, Chilean Cardinal Condemns 'Cultural Colonialism,'" Zenit News Agency, January 26, 2002.

70. For the vote on this measure 107 deputies were present, 42 of whom voted in favor of the convention, 20 against, with 2 abstaining. The remaining 43 recorded no electronic vote whatsoever. Cardinal Errázuriz expressed his dismay at the position of the Christian Democrats who supported the measure (adding that the decision of the leftist PS and PPD parties did not surprise him). See "Gobierno mantiene oposición al aborto," *El Mercurio*, August 20, 2001.

71. *El Mercurio*, January 18, 2002.

72. *El Mercurio*, November 18, 2001.

73. *El Mercurio* November 13, 2001.

74. *El Mercurio* November 13, 2001.

75. *El Mercurio*, November 24, 2001.

76. Arthur Lupia and Matthew D. McCubbins, *The Democratic Dilemma: Can Citizens Learn What They Need to Know?* (New York: Cambridge University Press, 1998).

77. Carla Lehmann, "¿Cuan religiosos somos los chilenos?: mapa de la religiosidad en 31 países," *Estudios Públicos* 85 (Summer 2002).

78. Ibid.

79. Smith, *Religious Politics in Latin America.*

80. T. Scully, *Rethinking the Center: Party Politics in Nineteenth and Twentieth Century Chile.* Stanford: Stanford University Press, 1992; Genaro Arriagada, *¿Hacia un "big-bang" del sistema de partidos?* Santiago: Editorial Los Andes, 1997.

81. See, for example, Mariana Aylwin and Ignacio Walker, *Familia y divorcio: razones de una posición* (Santiago: Editorial Los Andes, 1996). In this book Aylwin and Walker, two prominent Catholic Christian Democrats, give their reasons for supporting divorce legislation in the Chilean Congress.

82. J. Samuel Valenzuela, "Class Relations and Democratization: A Reassessment of Barrington Moore's Model," Working Paper 265, South Bend, Ind., University of Notre Dame Kellogg Institute for International Studies, 1999. Valenzuela argues that too much of the literature on democratization neglects consideration of political cleavages along divisions other than class, and this becomes a significant limitation when analyzing political developments in cases where other cleavages are important—such as in the church-state conflict that has had a major impact on Chilean party politics.

PART II

The Consolidation of the Market

5

Chilean Economic Policy under the Concertación

The Triumph of the Market?

LOIS HECHT OPPENHEIM

Chile today is considered one of the few economic success stories in the region, a Latin American "jaguar." One of the remarkable aspects of this success story is that the country's economic transformation into a model of the free market approach is touted as a triumph by both proponents and opponents of the Pinochet military government. Today, the market approach is accepted by virtually all of Chilean society as the only viable framework for economic development.

Despite what appears to be a general consensus about the market approach, key political differences remain with regard to interpreting the manner in which the economic model was first imposed on Chile by the Pinochet regime, as well as understanding the neoliberal model's impact on Chilean society. This is especially the case with regard to the social cost of the model; that is, the dramatic increase in the rate of poverty, as well as greater inequalities of income and wealth. Looming above these disagreements are more fundamental questions: Is the neoliberal model that the Pinochet regime introduced into Chile in the years after the 1973 coup still in force, or has the Concertación, in power since 1990, fundamentally altered it? In other words, has the Concertación simply managed the military's neoliberal model, or has it been able to carve out a distinct economic policy within the framework of the market approach? And is this economic model, which largely depends on the exportation of primary products, sustainable over the long run?

This chapter presents an overview of Chile's economic policies since 1990 and analyzes one of the key elements of the Concertación's economic policy: Chile's trade policy initiatives. Trade policy is a key component of the Concertación economic policy because the export sector has been an engine for Chile's economic growth over the past two decades. In essence, Chile's current economic policy is anchored in its international trade policy. As a result, international trade policy provides an interesting case study of the manner in which neoliberal market ideas have penetrated into Chile, and it may also help us address the questions about the nature of the economic model and its sustainability.

Trade policy is not the same under the Concertación as it was under the military regime, however. Pinochet's economic policies served to expand Chile's export-driven economy by unilaterally facilitating an opening of the economy to foreign trade and capital flows. The Concertación's trade policy, while rooted in this transformation, is designed to facilitate the growth of Chile's export-driven economy by preserving and expanding the country's access to foreign markets and by establishing clear rules and protocols through a series of trade agreements. In one sense, this policy reinforces Chile's prior mode of insertion into the global economy. Unlike the Pinochet regime's unilateral trade policies, however, trade liberalization and the opening of Chile's economy to the global arena under the Concertación are based on achieving a series of trade negotiations with external actors. These have taken the form of bilateral, plurilateral (or regional), and multilateral agreements. Thus, it is fair to say that although the Concertación has not challenged the concept of the free market, it has attempted, through trade negotiations, to have some input into global trading rules and even gain some control over the rules by which it participates in international trade.

Ultimately, this analysis of Concertación trade policy allows us to understand the extent to which market economic principles have penetrated Chilean society, as well as the ways in which they set parameters for the future evolution of the country's economy. This chapter also complements Joaquín Fermandois' chapter on foreign policy. While Fermandois focuses his analysis on the foreign policy dimensions of trade policy, I examine the domestic dynamics that are behind those policy decisions.

The Economic Revolution of Augusto Pinochet

The story of Chile's economic transformation by the "Chicago Boys" is by now well known. When the military took power in Chile, they were determined to "cut out the cancer of Marxism" from Chile.[1] On the economic front, this strategy involved undoing the actions of the Allende government, which had been elected on a platform designed to begin the transition to socialism. A peaceful transition to socialism had meant, in large part, creating a large social sector of the economy through nationalization of key industries. In addition, worker activism, especially in the 1972–1973 period, had led to state intervention in numerous factories, essentially placing several hundred of them under state control. Last, Allende had also fully implemented the 1967 land reform law, such that all farms of more than eighty hectares had been redistributed by the time of the 1973 coup.

Pinochet found a ready-made economic approach that gave him a rationale to undo this economic restructuring. Under the strict free market philosophy of the Chicago Boys, all lands and factories that had been occupied by workers and peasants were returned to private hands, and peasants who had legally acquired lands and worked them collectively were given title to individual plots. By the end of the 1970s, only a few industries remained under state control, the most important being the large copper mines. Moreover, under the guidance of the Chicago Boys, the principle of a strong, interventionist state was jettisoned; instead, the state seemingly withdrew from overseeing the economy in favor of allowing market forces to operate unfettered. In reality, however, this lack of state regulation aided powerful domestic and foreign economic forces[2] and favored the upper sectors of society.

This strategy had its ups and downs. After an initial shock to the economy there was a short-lived boom in the late 1970s, fueled in part by land speculation and dominated by a few powerful economic conglomerates. It was followed in the early 1980s by a severe economic crisis. In 1982 the gross domestic product (GDP) shrank by 14 percent, unemployment climbed to more than 20 percent by official statistics,[3] and bankruptcies numbered in the hundreds. A slow recovery took place during the mid-1980s. It was during the period of economic crisis that began in late 1981 that political opposition to Pinochet's rule mobilized. In an effort to save the system—and his regime—Pinochet replaced one of the more doctrinaire Chicago Boys, Finance Minister Sergio de Castro, in early 1982. Under his successors the state temporarily took a more activist posture, including the takeover of banks. Slowly the economy pulled out of the doldrums, aided in early 1985 by Pinochet's naming of a new finance minister, Hernán Büchi.

Under Büchi's more flexible guidance the economic recovery advanced, leading to a second economic boom by the latter half of the 1980s. This boom was also facilitated by the increased flow of foreign capital into Chile, under Decree Law (DL) 600. Although DL600 had been implemented in 1974 as a way for the military government to woo foreign capital, it had a very limited impact on the rate of capital flows into Chile during the first decade of military rule due to the country's pariah status in the international arena.[4]

By the mid-1980s, not only was an economic recovery in process, but the concept of the market had begun to penetrate Chilean society and its psyche. The Pinochet regime had by then extended the concept of the unfettered market to many areas of social policy, through the Seven Modernizations program. This program included reforms in the areas of labor, health, education, social security, and pensions. In short, the central idea of the Seven Modernizations was to apply the concept of the free market to social policy by encouraging competition and privatization. The first area to be "modernized" was labor, through the 1979 Labor Code. The new code not only permitted the formation of competing unions, it prohibited closed shops, industry-wide unions, and open-ended worker strikes.[5] The same concepts of competition and privatization were then extended to other areas of social policy, so that private entities began either to replace or to compete with the state's delivery of education, health care, and pensions.

In terms of trade policy, the Pinochet government opened Chile's economy unilaterally to foreign trade and investment. Tariff levels were unilaterally dropped, reaching a low of 10 percent by 1978, which converted Chile into a virtually open economy. As a result, foreign goods flooded into the country, providing heavy competition with domestic industries, many of which went bankrupt by the early 1980s.[6] Although the commitment to an open economy remained in place, the application of low tariffs was not linear. During the 1980s economic crisis, the government felt forced to raise tariffs, which reached a high of 35 percent by the beginning of 1985, before starting a downward trend again.[7] Attracting foreign investment was initially a slower process. However, there was increasing foreign investment in the export copper mining sector, and new, privately owned copper mines were developed. During the mid-1980s, after the economic crisis, there were also efforts to develop new export products, beginning with fruit, especially table grapes. Other export products included fish, wine, and wood products. This emphasis on trade, including foreign investment in the export sector, was an important part of the economic model under the military. The Concertación, as we will see, later built on this foundation.

During the 1980s there was also burgeoning political opposition to the military regime. The economic crisis of 1981–1982 had opened the door to grassroots opposition to military rule, but even after three years of marches and protests, the Pinochet government refused to negotiate a political transition to democracy. Opposition political parties remained clandestine and underwent dramatic transformations of their own. The most important change, in terms of its impact in the 1990s, took place within the Socialist Party. A large segment of the party underwent a process of "renovation," whereby they disavowed Marxism and embraced the ideas of a liberal, democratic state and of the market. It was in part this change of philosophy that allowed the Socialists to join with Christian Democrats in opposition to military rule.[8]

Eventually Pinochet had to face the electorate,[9] and despite his efforts to stack the political deck in his favor, he was defeated in a plebiscite in October 1988. A little more than a year later, in December 1989, Patricio Aylwin, the nominee of the Concertación Democrática de los Partidos Políticos, or the Concertación, won the presidential election.

Legacy of the Military: Constraints on Concertación Economic Policy Making

The early market conversion in Chile during military rule created both constraints and opportunities for the civilian Concertación governments that followed. On the one hand, the restructuring of Chile's economy, which included the privatization of state-owned enterprises and banks, the termination of land reform, the deregulation of the market and the flow of foreign investment, and the unilateral lowering of tariff barriers, created a new set of economic and political realities. The international financial community's approval of these changes, along with Chile's recuperation by the mid-1980s from the dramatic economic downturn in the early part of the decade, severely constrained post-military governmental economic policy choices.

On the other hand, the fact that Chile's early economic transformation had, by the late 1980s, resulted in macroeconomic stability and high levels of growth presented the post-1990 civilian leaders with certain opportunities. The most difficult period of structural adjustment had already taken place under the military regime. Chile could take advantage of the fact that it was the first country in the region to carry out far-reaching market reforms and reap some benefits from these economic changes, particularly in a global economy that had by then accepted the market approach. The Concertación was aided by the fact that theirs was a democratically elected government that had been given a friendly reception in the international arena, something that the Pinochet dictatorship, long treated as an international pariah, could never attain.

The Concertación and Economic Policy

Patricio Aylwin took office in March 1990 as the first civilian, elected president of Chile since 1970. He promised to reinstitute democracy and the rule of law. What President Aylwin did not promise, however, was to change the fundamental free market economic thrust. By 1990 the Concertación had accepted the fact that the market approach was the only economic strategy available to them. Aylwin publicly acknowledged in his first message to the nation, in May 1990, that the "motor" of economic growth in Chile was the private sector. The context for continued economic growth was political and economic stability, both of which were necessary to sustain private-sector economic vitality. The economic framework for any development strategy in Chile, then, was premised on a general market strategy, in terms of both domestic and international economic policy.

President Aylwin and the Concertación coalition also realized that they faced a number of thorny challenges, even without attempting to change the economic approach. These political challenges included the dilemma of how to eliminate numerous undemocratic features of the political system inherited from the military, such as nonelected senators who tipped the balance of the senate to the right and an electoral system biased toward the minority (that is, the right) to name just a few. In addition, Pinochet had not returned to the barracks cowed; quite the contrary, in fact. Declaring that he had completed the mission that had been laid out for him in 1973, Pinochet left office stating that he and his military government had saved Chile. He made clear that he did not expect anyone to tamper with the institutions he had created and the policies that he had enacted. Moreover, Pinochet and his military colleagues in the junta had made it very difficult to enact changes to their system. They did this by approving a series of laws—dubbed *leyes de amarre,* or laws that tie (one's hands)—which were designed to cement in place the military's political and economic systems. The Concertación also faced the challenge of finding a way to deal with the serious violations of human rights that had taken place during the seventeen years of military rule. They knew that this would ruffle military feathers; in fact, military-civilian relations and military subordination to civilian authority were key issues for the Concertación; they were at the heart of any effort to reestablish a full democracy and the rule of law in Chile.

A final reason for leaving economic policy alone was the fact that the economy was doing well. There was a consensus within the Concertación that it would not be prudent to embark on a new economic path that might endanger Chile's economic well-being. In fact, if there was a challenge on the economic front, it was to demonstrate that a center-left civilian government could manage the economy well. The memory of economic difficulties under Salvador Allende's 1970–1973 government, including hyperinflation and scarcity of goods by 1973, stayed in the minds of center-left politicians and, to them, left a mark to be erased.

This is not to say that the Concertación has not made changes to the free market economic approach it inherited. When Patricio Aylwin donned the presidential sash on March 11, 1990, he promised not only a democratic government, but changes in social policy to eliminate the social cost of the neoliberal model. Social spending has increased dramatically under the Concertación. There have been changes to foreign investment policy, as well as state regulation of private enterprises, especially monopoly ones, which have the effect of greater regulation of private capital. For example, the Concertación imposed the *encaje,* a deposit for all short-term capital flows to Chile. The idea behind the *encaje* was to prevent sudden and destabilizing outflows of short-term capital. The government has also created programs to help small and medium-sized enterprises. This said, it is also evident that these differences refer more to modalities within the free market model than to any kind of fundamental change or shift away from the market.

Macroeconomic Policy under the Concertación

President Aylwin selected Alejandro Foxley to head his economic team. Foxley was a respected Christian Democratic economist who made clear from the outset that although he had criticisms of the neoliberal model, especially the high poverty rates it created, he accepted the basic market approach. This included the concept of an economy oriented toward exports and a rejection of the old dependency arguments that export-oriented economies were disadvantaged and dependent on core capitalist countries. Economic growth was both steady and significant during this period: Under President Aylwin the economy grew at an average annual rate of 7.7 percent.[10]

Attention to macroeconomic stability was not central only to Foxley; it continued to be so under the second Concertación government of Eduardo Frei Ruiz-Tagle. Economic growth during the first three years of the Frei administration (1994–1997) averaged 7.8 percent, and inflation continued to decline, averaging 7.4 percent during those years.[11] The dramatic decline in the rate of inflation was exemplary, both in terms of Chilean historical experience and in comparison with Chile's neighbors. In addition, Chile's currency did not suffer from the kinds of sudden and deep devaluations that occurred in fellow Latin American currencies; if there was any currency issue during this period, it was an overvaluation of the Chilean peso, which drove up the cost of Chilean exports on the international marketplace.

The economy continued to grow steadily until 1998, when the country began to feel the effects of the 1997 Asian currency crisis. Beginning in 1998 the economy stalled, and economic growth for the last two years of the Frei presidency averaged a meager 1.1 percent.[12] What had happened was that despite its diversification of export destinations, Chile's export-oriented economy found itself vulnerable because one-third of the country's exports were sold to Asia. Although it was inevitable that the country would be affected by an economic downturn in Asia, Chile's economy was cushioned somewhat by the fact that two-thirds of its trade was with other regions. The 2000 Argentine economic crisis also had an impact on Chile. As an associate member of the Common Market of the South (MERCOSUR), Chile had been increasing trade with both

Brazil and Argentina, and the latter was a destination for a variety of Chilean manufactured goods. As a result, President Lagos inherited a stagnant economy when he took office in March 2000.

If there was a central theme to Frei's presidency, it was modernization of the state. This modernization involved reforms not only of the judicial system, especially Chile's Supreme Court, but also of the educational system. The latter reform had an impact on the budget, as did continuing anti-poverty programs.

Concertación Trade Policy: Ensuring the Growth of the Export Economy

The most innovative aspect of economic policy since 1990, which has run through all three Concertación administrations, has to do with trade policy. Under the Concertación, Chile has distinguished itself among its Latin American neighbors not only by following an activist trade policy, but by developing a multifaceted trade policy that has permitted a "multiple and flexible"[13] insertion into the global economy. Instead of simply relying on a unilateral opening of the national economy, as the Pinochet regime did, the Concertación governments developed a conscious policy of negotiating trade agreements that would give them access to important world markets.

The current policy developed over time. It began as an extension of the military's open economy strategy and was created in response to changes in the global economy in the early 1990s. Today, it has become a coordinated program involving negotiated trade; that is, the negotiation of numerous bilateral and plurilateral trade agreements that complement both the unilateral and multilateral components of Chile's trade policy.

It is reasonable to ask why, if unilateral economic opening under the military had been considered successful, the Concertación decided to undertake a major shift of emphasis away from sole reliance on unilateral opening to an emphasis on trade agreements. A principal reason for this change in trade policy has to do with the context of the global economy in the early 1990s. As a small country with an export-oriented economy, Chile had—and continues to have—very little economic and political leverage in the international arena. Soon after the country's transition to civilian rule in early 1990, it appeared as if the world might divide up into competing regional trade blocs. The creation of the North American Free Trade Agreement (NAFTA), MERCOSUR, the Asian Pacific Economic Cooperation (APEC), and European agreement on the Maastricht Treaty that aimed to create an economic, political, and monetary European Union (EU) all took place during the early 1990s. During the same years the Uruguay Round negotiations continued past the 1990 deadline, creating worries that a larger framework to facilitate global free trade might not emerge soon.

The end of the Cold War was also a factor that facilitated the shift toward a multipolar global economy.[14]

The regional situation had also changed. By the 1990s many Latin American countries had stabilized or were in the process of stabilizing their currencies and carrying out structural economic reforms similar to those Chile had already undergone. This was a double-edged sword for Chile. On the one hand, it made the region a more hospitable arena for expanded trade and economic integration. However, it also meant increased competition in the global economy, undercutting Chile's previous advantage as the first Latin American country to have transformed its economy and inserted itself in new ways into the global economy.

For Chilean economic policy makers, the conclusion was clear. It was necessary to protect Chile's export economy by forging bilateral trade agreements and joining in regional trade associations. This strategy, which evolved over time as opportunities presented themselves, has become a hallmark of Chile's post-1990 trade policy. The change in emphasis from a unilateral opening to a more nuanced approach emphasizing a negotiated trade strategy was not enacted without dissent, however.[15] Although a virtual consensus existed in Chile regarding the importance of expanding free trade, there were differences over how to achieve it. The political right and private entrepreneurial sectors argued that Chile should maintain its policy of unilateral opening, and there was special concern from traditional agricultural sectors, such as wheat, dairy, and cattle, about an agreement with MERCOSUR. Negotiating some of these trade agreements and regulating foreign capital flows—as occurred with the Concertación policy of regulating short-term capital flows through an *encaje*—were contested because they were seen as unnecessary obstacles to market forces.

The Concertación bases its trade policy on several basic principles. The first principle, carried over from the military period, has been to maintain Chile's open economy by being amenable to trade with any country in the world. The aim here is to diversify the country's export trading partners. As a small country with an export-oriented economy, Chile can best protect itself from becoming overly dependent on any trading partner or region by an open, global trading posture. In line with this, the Concertación has maintained the military's policy of a unilateral, low, uniform tariff. Over the past few years Concertación governments decided to lower even further the tariff, reducing it from 11[16] to 6 percent over a five-year period, which ended in 2003.[17]

The success of this strategy is borne out by examining the extent to which Chile has diversified its trading partners. Under the Concertación, Chile has achieved a much more balanced export trade among Latin America, North

Table 5.1. Chilean Exports by Destination, 1997–2003 (in percentages)

Destination	1997	1998	2003
European Union	24.4	28.1	24.2
United States	15.9	17.7	18.0
Latin America	20.2	23.0	18.2*
Asia	33.1	25.0	29.8**
Japan	15.7	13.3	11.1
China	2.5	3.1	9.0
Canada	0.8	1.0	2.0
Australia, New Zealand	0.4	0.4	0.6
Others	5.2	4.8	7.2
Total	100.0	100.0	100.0

Source: Data compiled from Appendix 2a, p. A4, of DIRECON, "Comercio exterior de Chile, cuarto trimester, 2003," February 2004.

*The drop in exports within Latin America is due principally to a steep decline in exports to Argentina, from 4.6 percent in 1997 to 1.6 percent by 2003.

**The recuperation of trade to Asia is due in part to an increase in demand from China, which helped to counter a decline in demand for Chilean goods by Japan.

America, Europe, and Asia. Its trade diversification contrasts with the situation of its South American neighbors. As table 5.1 demonstrates, there is a broad diversification of destinations for Chilean exports, and this process has continued from the 1990s into the present. One can also see in the data in table 5.1 the impact of the Asian economic crisis on Chilean exports by comparing 1997 to later years. The impact of the Brazilian currency crisis and Argentina's ensuing economic crisis after 2000 are also factors in the decline of Chilean exports to other Latin American countries. Overall, Chile has been quite successful in diversifying trade around the globe, and its record stands in contrast to that of the region as a whole. In contrast to Chile, the Latin American region directed almost one-third of its exports to the United States in 2000, 17 percent to the EU, and only 10 percent to Asia.[18] As a result, it is clear that Chile has lessened its historic dependence on trading with any one nation or region, particularly the United States and western Europe.[19]

Another critical part of the export economy strategy has been to diversify the basket of products that Chile exports. In this regard, Chile has also achieved some level of success. Copper accounts for less than half of the value of Chile's exports today, with other important exports being fruit, wood products, fish and fish products, and wine, as well as some manufactured goods. However, most of Chile's exports, especially those exported to countries outside of the region, are still classified as primary products. In 2000, for example, fully 87 percent of Chile's exports to countries outside of Latin America were primary products, principally copper and foods, which accounted for 56 percent of these exports.[20]

A second Concertación principle regarding trade policy has been to facilitate global free trade through support for multilateral trade agreements. A prime Concertación objective has been to expand the World Trade Organization (WTO) framework to include other areas, such as services, and to overcome non-tariff barriers to trade, such as anti-dumping mechanisms. The Concertación governments have viewed the WTO agreement as important to their project because it sets the global rules of the game; that is, it provides the framework for international trade.[21] Chile does not share the concerns of other Third World countries, including many of its Latin American neighbors, who see the WTO as helping the advanced, industrialized nations at their expense. Instead, the Concertación believes that such multilateral trade agreements provide Chile with important support by setting clear and fair rules for all trading partners and by establishing a process for recourse and redress if these norms are violated.[22] The Chilean government believes that transparent and consistent rules and processes are extremely important for a small, internationally vulnerable country like Chile.

Such adherence to free trade at the global level has resulted in Chile being an exceptional case in the region, but Chile's hopes for quick WTO action in new areas were dashed after the Seattle WTO meeting debacle in 1999. Thus, although the Chilean government still believes that the WTO arena is a useful one, it began to focus attention on other tactics.

The third Concertación principle regarding trade involves negotiated trade through forging bilateral and plurilateral trade agreements. This has been an area on which Chile has placed increasing attention. The Concertación governments see this strategy as an innovation to trade policy that complements and completes the previous goals of achieving multilateral arrangements and maintaining a unilaterally open economy. The Concertación's view today is that these trade agreements are in line with Chile's policy of "open regionalism," which assumes that Chile can maintain a global access strategy even while joining regional trade associations that function within the guidelines established by the WTO framework. Through the bilateral and regional trade arrangements that now make up an integral part of trade policy, Chile hopes to achieve a number of goals. The first is to open more markets to Chilean goods. Since trade agreements require commitments from both sides, they necessarily open markets, something unilateral opening does not necessarily achieve. In addition, these agreements can help guarantee Chile's access to important trading partners, something especially important in Latin America, where trade conditions have historically not been very stable. They also protect the terms of Chile's access to markets, which is crucial in an era when other regional trade arrangements might affect the conditions under which Chile has trade access. Last, trade agreements could also help to eliminate non-tariff barriers to trade that might otherwise be difficult for a small country like Chile to negotiate successfully, for example, the use of anti-dumping mechanisms.[23]

An important aspect of this strategy during the latter part of the 1990s was the regional effort to forge a hemispheric-wide free trade area, the Free Trade Area of the Americas (FTAA, or ALCA in Spanish), initially supported by the United States. A complex series of meetings was designed to lead up to the formation of ALCA. Despite Chile's active participation in these meetings, changes in regional dynamics, especially increasing wariness on the part of two major players, the United States and Brazil, have put this regionwide project on hold.

In summary, under the Concertación, Chile has developed a multifaceted trade strategy that involves a unilateral component, complemented by support for multilateral agreements that set the rules for open global trading, along with a policy of negotiated trade. The latter has become increasingly important over the course of the Concertación governments and today constitutes a central place in its trade strategy.

The Evolution of a Negotiated Trade Strategy

Although Chile's negotiated trade strategy today looks like a well-articulated and coordinated program, it evolved over the course of the 1990s. Initial efforts were oriented toward a trade agreement with the United States and, to a lesser extent, toward bilateral agreements with its Latin American counterparts. In the early 1990s, there was uncertainty about the extent to which a regional agreement would be compatible with a trade agreement with the United States.[24] In the second phase, there was more emphasis on negotiations with regional trade associations, but without setting clear priorities among regions or coordinating the negotiations. Only in the third phase did a more coordinated and coherent strategy of trade negotiations emerge.

Under the first Concertación government of President Aylwin (1990–1994), the initial emphasis was on reaching a trade agreement with the United States, as well as signing bilateral trade agreements with other nations in the hemisphere, thereby taking advantage of the welcome a redemocratized Chile received in the international arena. Chile signed its first complementary trade agreement with Mexico in 1991, followed within a few years by others, including ones with Venezuela in 1993 and Colombia in 1994. Chile also joined APEC in December 1993.

Under the second Concertación government of Eduardo Frei Ruiz-Tagle (1994–2000), Chile continued to sign bilateral trade agreements. For example, in 1996 it signed a free trade agreement with Canada that followed the NAFTA framework and included labor and environmental issues. This accord was also Chile's first free trade pact, and other free trade agreements were soon finalized, including one with Mexico in 1998.

The Frei government also began a more intensive process of negotiating with regional associations, including NAFTA and MERCOSUR. By the time of his presidency the latter organization had been established as a customs union. In addition, the Frei government negotiated with the EU and joined in regional negotiations for the FTAA. By the end of the Frei administration Chile had signed some kind of trade agreement with virtually all the countries in the hemisphere, including an October 1999 free trade agreement with the governments of Central America. The only exceptions were the United States and the Caribbean countries.[25] In 1996 Chile also signed treaties establishing associate status with MERCOSUR[26] and a framework agreement for associate status with the EU.

During the first three years of Frei's government, however, trade negotiations with the different regional trade associations were carried out almost as an extension of Chile's policy of global openness and competition, only this time there was competition among government ministries.[27] Despite the president's stated emphasis on joining NAFTA, in terms of actions, his government did not initially set priorities among the three regional associations of NAFTA, EU, and MERCOSUR. Instead, the government followed a decentralized process in which domestic politics played a significant role. For example, the government did not carry out any studies of the pros and cons of association with each of the three organizations. Instead, ministerial interests and the personality and political ability of each minister played major roles in the evolution of these trade agreement negotiations.[28] For three years three different negotiating teams, working independently under three distinct ministries, each of which was headed by a politician from one of the three principal Concertación political parties,[29] held talks with NAFTA, EU, and MERCOSUR representatives. The Ministry of Finance, headed by a Christian Democrat, negotiated for inclusion in NAFTA (and, when that stalled, with the Canadians). Separately, the Socialist minister of foreign affairs had his own negotiating team, who met with representatives of the EU. Under the aegis of the Ministry of the Economy, headed by a member of the PPD, a third negotiating team undertook the MERCOSUR integration efforts.[30]

International politics also played a role in setting negotiating priorities. A major case in point involved negotiations with the United States for entry into

NAFTA. In December 1994 Chile had been invited by the three NAFTA nations to enter into negotiations to join the trade association. Although President Frei quickly stated that NAFTA was his highest priority, success depended less on domestic politics than on the vagaries of U.S. politics and the ability of Chilean diplomats to navigate the U.S. political landscape. It was only after Chile tired of the continuing difficulties with the United States over entry into NAFTA that it shifted its focus toward MERCOSUR, the EU, and talks for a hemisphere-wide free trade agreement. In the end, it was almost a decade later, under President Lagos, that a free trade agreement was finalized with the United States.

In 1997 President Frei decided to rationalize the trade agreement policy process by centralizing trade negotiations under the Ministry of Foreign Relations. Frei built on an earlier effort in 1992, under Aylwin, to create a coordinating mechanism for negotiations.[31] A number of factors led to this institutional effort. The inability of the Chilean government to gain entry into NAFTA was one factor, as were the political skills of the foreign minister, who had successfully negotiated a framework agreement with the EU. There were larger issues at play, however. This change represents an enhanced appreciation of the role of economic policy in foreign affairs and a new understanding of the need to integrate the economic and political dimensions of foreign policy. Not only have all trade negotiations been centralized under the Ministry of Foreign Relations, but also more professional negotiating teams, especially in the Dirección General de Relaciones Económicas Internacionales (General Office for International Economic Relations, or DIRECON) have developed.

Given the increasing importance of trade agreements, these groups are in almost continuous negotiations with different regional organizations, making greater coordination and communication important. Coordination takes place in a variety of ways. Inter-ministerial meetings have enhanced communication and efficacy. The thematic as well as territorial division of labor helps enable Chilean negotiators to take the same position in distinct negotiating venues. There are regular meetings of DIRECON staff, but in the end, much depends on the goodwill of the staff members who, through regular communication, strive to keep Chile's trade positions consistent and coherent, whatever the international setting.[32]

Thus, institutional changes have taken place as a result of Chile's new trade policy. In addition to new institutional arrangements within the Ministry of Foreign Relations and inter-ministerial communication linkages deemed necessary for advancing trade negotiations, the significance of private-sector groups acting as partners with government in facilitating the growth of exports is now an accepted fact. New forms of communication and links between these private groups and the state will continue to be created. To some extent, other civil society actors are being brought into the process, including labor and environmental interests. These changes will continue, supported by President Lagos, who has already demonstrated the will to modify existing institutional arrangements.[33]

The Chilean Jaguar and Lagos' Dilemma: How to Reactivate the Economy

Despite the general success of the Concertación economic approach, including its innovative trade strategy, Ricardo Lagos faced a series of challenges when he took office in March 2000. In fact, Lagos began his administration under a set of disadvantages with which neither of his predecessors had had to contend. First, the economy had been in a slump for several years, averaging a mere 1.1 percent growth during the last two years of Frei's presidency, in 1998–1999. President Lagos' first order of business was to try to reactivate the economy. Simply managing the macroeconomy would not be enough. It is worth noting that most Chilean economists thought that the economy would revive during 2000; that is, right after the presidential elections. These expectations seemed at first justified, because economic growth in Chile reached 4 percent in 2000. Growth faltered again, however, declining to a low of 2 percent in 2002. Although Chile's rate of economic growth was far better than that for the region, Chileans had grown used to high levels of economic growth, and 2 percent seemed puny indeed. In addition, unemployment began to rise during the same period. The question of how to rev up economic growth quickly became a high-priority issue.

Second, Lagos was not only the candidate of the Concertación coalition, he was also a Socialist. This party affiliation, along with his reputation as someone who had not been afraid to be confrontational during the military dictatorship, raised popular expectations that he might be able to make some substantial changes to the free market model. Such hopes, given the various constraints under which Lagos had to operate, were perhaps unrealistic.

These popular expectations were heightened by the third factor: that Lagos was elected president with a very slim margin of victory. The vote had been so close in December 1999, in fact, that a runoff election in January 2000 had been necessary, as neither presidential candidate had received an absolute majority of the vote. The margin of victory in the second round was also just a few percentage points. There were several consequences of this election outcome. To begin with, the political opposition, led by its presidential contender, Joaquín Lavín, felt quite heartened by this showing. This was the first time that any right-wing candidate had broken out of the low 40s in terms of percentage of the vote. The results of the 1999–2000 presidential election implied that the political right could well emerge victorious in the next presidential contest. Lavín, who easily bested the Concertación candidate for the mayoralty of Santiago in the municipal elections that followed soon after,[34] remained the right's presidential candidate. From his position as mayor of Santiago, he maintained a high profile. In addition, the lack of economic revitalization allowed the right to question the Concertación's management of the economy. Whatever the popular expectations held for Lagos, he faced a feisty opposition, as well as a sluggish economy, when he took office.[35]

The slow recuperation of the economy only served to heighten the debate about the sustainability of Chile's growth that had been going on among Concertación economists since the mid-1990s. So the debate about how to achieve economic reactivation was in a sense part of a larger debate about the sustainability of Chile's free market, primary product export model. Although economists at the time tried to answer the twin questions of what was the cause of the continuing stagnation of the economy and what was the best strategy for reactivating the economy, they were also asking whether or not the economic model needed to be changed.

In analyzing Chile's economic situation, one of the central issues that emerged was the question of why Chile had not been able to move beyond the exportation of primary products. True, Chile's open economy had allowed it to export an increasingly diverse set of products to a broadening array of countries. Exports included fruits, such as summer fruit and kiwis; farmed salmon; and natural resources, such as copper and wood pulp or chips. The hope was that Chile would be able to jump from the export of these primary products to higher value-added products; that is, that the economy would enter the second phase of the export model.

While some of the hopes for export diversification have been fulfilled with the export of more semi-processed goods, the change has not been to the extent initially anticipated. At one point, when the export markets were booming, some economists claimed that it did not matter much what Chile exported, as long as the country continued to grow her exports. Some economists took the position, which became the position of the Lagos government, that Chile needed the assistance of free trade agreements with advanced industrialized nations, such as the United States and the EU, in order to get around the higher tariff barriers these nations had put in place for high value-added products. Others talked about jumping over the second phase and going directly to the export of services.

Analysis of the economic situation focused not only on what had happened to the second export phase, which was a long-term issue, but more immediately on how to restart the economy. It is important to keep the context of the debate in mind, however. During this period exports continued to grow in terms of volume, although not always in terms of value, due to a drop in the price of copper.

The economy began to recuperate in 2003, however, reaching more than 3 percent growth, and by 2004 the period of stagnation seemed over. Growth for 2004 topped 5 percent. In addition, the price for some of Chile's main exports, including copper and wood products, increased substantially. The world price for copper, in fact, doubled.[36] Of course, this change in the price of copper underscores what continues to be a structural problem for Chile: its dependence on the price of primary products in the international marketplace.

Although the debate about how to reactivate the economy, which was more active during 2002 when the economy was very sluggish, may now seem moot, it is not. Reviewing the issues is still instructive because the underlying debate is about the sustainability of the model. In the next section I review the main arguments of the debate around reactivating Chile's economy. What is crucial here is to understand the points of departure of these different perspectives and their implications for the viability of the Chilean economic model. There were basically three positions about the economy, and what underlies them is either an acceptance or a criticism of the free market, open economy model of growth.

One group of economists within the Concertación took a neoliberal position.[37] This group claimed that the economy could be reactivated by stimulating internal demand and supply. The way to do this was to deepen the neoliberal model by providing incentives for private enterprise to invest and produce, and extending privatization even further, including to the state-owned copper mines.[38] Some of these people constituted the group that had been called the *auto-complacientes*, or complacent ones. Their view, in sum, was that the neoliberal model was the correct one, but that it needed to be deepened not modified.

A second group, consisting of what could be called the *auto-flagelante* (self-flagellating) group, claimed that state action was necessary to pull the Chilean economy out of the doldrums. They believed that the neoliberal model had already been modified by the Concertación, and that these modifications, including social spending to help the poor and regulation of private enterprise and of short-term foreign investment, were necessary. Yet further modifications were called for, given the economic situation. In effect, this group called for a more activist state, one that would enact policies to help reactivate demand by helping the poor, as well as small and medium-sized businesses. Economists in this group also criticized the government's insistence on holding down the deficit to no more than 1 percent of the GDP, believing that in times of economic recession, the government could afford to increase the deficit up to 1.5 or even 2 percent of the GDP.[39] The policy of limiting the deficit to 1 percent had been in place for a number of years, and Lagos' finance minister believed that it was a prudent measure to ensure macroeconomic stability over the long term.[40]

A third, more critical group disavowed the free market model altogether. These individuals were generally leery of the capitalist approach to development.[41] The fact that there were continuing differences over how to "adjust" the model indicated to them that the sustainability of the current free trade, free market growth model was questionable.

President Lagos, however, did not take sides in this debate. Instead, he continued on the path that the Concertación had followed for a number of years, assuming that enhancing free trade would stimulate growth. The Lagos government's position was that the economic recession in Chile was caused by external downturns, and that Chile would recuperate along with these other countries. The analysis went like this: First had come the Asian crisis, then a slowdown in the U.S. economy, a stubborn economic slowdown in Japan, the currency crisis in Brazil, and finally, the economic crisis in neighboring Argentina. Chile had both to wait for changes externally and also to use trade negotiations to gain more access to important markets, especially those of the United States and Europe. Thus, the Lagos government continued to focus on strengthening the export model, principally by signing free trade agreements. Under Lagos, Chile was able—at long last—to finalize its negotiations with the United States, as well as to conclude agreements with the European Union and with South Korea, all during the 2002–2003 period.

The Lagos administration met with much success in its efforts to forge new trade agreements. In 2002 Chile signed the Economic Association Pact with the EU. In February 2003 it also signed a free trade agreement with South Korea (the first free trade agreement ever signed by this Asian country). It was followed by a free trade agreement with the European Association of Free Trade[42] in June of the same year. During the same period, the Lagos government began discussions with China toward negotiating a free trade pact.

In general, the Lagos government has been paying more attention to the Asian Pacific region, evidenced by its hosting of the APEC talks in November 2004. Trilateral talks are currently underway for a Chile–Singapore–New Zealand trade agreement, and negotiations with India for a partial trade agreement are in the offing. Although Chile remains committed to the FTAA, favorable political conditions for it do not exist at the moment, despite years of continent-wide meetings. In addition, as Joaquín Fermandois notes in chapter 6, the country finds itself in a somewhat more complicated relationship in its region today, given territorial disputes with Bolivia, a natural gas crisis with Argentina, and philosophical differences with other regional leaders over the utility of the free market model for driving development. This is likely one reason why Chile has decided to look more toward Asia as the next fruitful region for trade agreements.

Last, it is interesting to note that both South Korea and China decided, for several tactical reasons, to negotiate their first free trade agreements with Chile. First, Chile has much experience in trade negotiations, and second as a small economy, it does not constitute much of a threat to either country's economic interests.[43]

The Lagos government has also been cognizant of the social impact of free market policies internally. It proposed and has continued to make a top priority a health program called Plan AUGE, as Silvia Borzutzky notes in chapter 7. Under this plan, a set of specific common ailments would be covered under a universal health-care plan. The Lagos plan has met with much resistance; despite this, Lagos continues to push it as a concrete manifestation of his sensitivity to fundamental issues of equity.[44]

President Lagos has also tried to ensure that Chile's economy will continue to prosper even when its supply of copper declines. In April 2004 Lagos proposed the institution of a royalty fee on all mining operations. Despite strong negative reaction from privately owned mining enterprises, which are foreign controlled, Lagos has held firm to this position, and his government reintroduced the bill in early 2005. It is one way, he has stated, for Chile to use current resources to invest in its future.

Evaluations of the Economic Model: Challenges for the Future

Although economic trends during the second half of 2003 and in 2004 seemed to bear out Lagos' patience, the underlying central questions remain: is the economic model sustainable, and is it the same as the military's neoliberal model? In terms of the sustainability of the model, some of the issues facing Chile include the following:

1. Part of Chile's advantage in international trade comes from its having been the first country in the region to adopt the free market, trade liberalization model. As other nations sign trade agreements, this advantage will lessen.
2. Chile still depends on the export of primary products, many of which are finite. There is already a scarcity of some of Chile's fish and its native wood. As a result, there are continuing questions about the sustainability of the export model, if it remains based on primary products.
3. Much Concertación emphasis has been placed on ensuring access to global markets through trade negotiations. Other areas, such as improving the

quality of education and educational access for its population, still have room for improvement. One recent study found that Chile is still a highly classist nation,[45] and other studies analyze the impact of the highly unequal distribution of income and wealth.[46]

4. Although the Concertación sees finalizing a free trade agreement with the United States as a major political and economic victory, there are important criticisms of some aspects of the agreement. Some have argued that the government of Chile would have achieved more favorable results if it had negotiated together with other countries in the region, especially Brazil. Among the most cited problematic areas in the free trade agreement with the United States are the virtual elimination of Chile's ability to regulate short-term capital flows[47] and the lack of any agreement by the United States regarding its use of anti-dumping mechanisms against Chilean products. In addition, now that Chile has signed this agreement, it fixes the rules of the game for the indefinite future.
5. In the area of technology and assistance to small and medium-sized enterprises, there is also much room for improvement. The economy is still dominated by large economic groups, both foreign and domestic. The recent initiative by President Lagos to impose a tax on mining, the royalty fee proposal, met with strong public opposition from those interests.
6. Chile's status in the region has become more complicated, as Joaquín Fermandois outlines in chapter 6. The conflict with Argentina over providing natural gas to fuel Chile's electrical power plants, which began in April 2004, and the continuing conflict with Bolivia over its desire for an outlet to the sea are indications of political and economic problems with Chile's neighbors. Moreover, can Chile remain an economic free market star in a region that has serious economic issues and is increasingly critical of the free market approach?

What about the nature of the economic approach under the Concertación? Is it the same as the neoliberal model of the military? The economic model extant in Chile today is not the same neoliberal model as under the military; changes made by the Concertación, however, are within the parameters of a market- and export-oriented economy. Although many criticisms can be leveled against the model—from environmental insensitivity to the inequalities it generates—it is clear that this model is not going to change, at least not in the foreseeable future. Moreover, this approach, as applied by the Concertación, has generated significant economic growth in Chile and has given many Chileans a better life. Poverty rates have decreased from 40 percent of the population in 1990 to around 18 percent today. Chile today experiences many of the ills that more advanced, industrialized nations complain about—the "mallization" of society, galloping consumerism, and consumer debt. But these are conditions that are seen around the globe.

Perhaps the question of whether the current economic approach is the same neoliberal model or not is not the right question to ask; perhaps the question to ask is what changes have been made within this basic free market framework? In other words, given the general market approach, what is the development strategy?[48] One way of answering this question is to look at the current Chilean model through different time-period lenses. If one compares the Chilean approach today against that of the pre-1973 period, then one is more likely to see the last thirty years as comprising one economic model; however, if the time frame begins post the 1973 coup, then one can more easily assert that today's model is different from that of the military. These differences include an emphasis on social policy designed to eliminate poverty and greater government regulation, including a willingness to regulate short-term capital flows. It is especially in the area of trade policy that we see clear differences between today's policy and that of the military regime. The Concertación's policy is marked by a coordinated approach of negotiated trade agreements. This makes the Concertación approach quite distinct from that of the 1970s–1980s neoliberal model, which was based on a unilateral opening to trade.

As I have demonstrated, the larger question of the long-term sustainability of Chile's export model remains unanswered. What is clear is that the Concertación's policy of forging trade agreements at the bilateral, plurilateral, and multilateral levels has been an important factor in Chile's quest for economic stability, given the economy's dependence on its export sector. Thus, domestic economic policy, based on the market model, is intrinsically linked to Chile's foreign policy, as the creation of the office of DIRECON within the Ministry of Foreign Affairs demonstrates. Not only are these domestic economic and foreign economic policies inextricably linked, but the success of the former depends on the success of the latter. In the final analysis, the success of these policies will in large part determine the viability of Chile's free market economic approach; as a result, they constitute a crucial element for the future electoral success of the Concertación.

Notes

1. This statement was made by one of the members of the original military junta in a televised address to the country the day after the coup. The "Chicago Boys" were a group of Chilean economists who played a leading role in the economic transformation of Chile under the military. They had received their postgraduate training at the University

of Chicago. Studying under notables such as Arnold Harberger and Milton Friedman, they adopted the Chicago School's philosophy of strict adherence to the free market, know as neoliberalism.

2. These included powerful domestic economic groups, as well as large foreign investors.

3. Data from the Banco Central, reprinted in Berta Teitelboim, *Serie de indicadores económicos sociales*, 1960–1989 (Santiago: Programa de Economía del Trabajo, 1990), 13.

4. Alvaro Calderón, and Stephany Griffith-Jones, *Los flujos de capital extranjero en la economía chilena: renovado acceso y nuevos usos,* Working Document No. 37 (Santiago: CEPAL, 1995).

5. Under the Concertación, however, reforms were made to the labor code, which, among other things, allowed for the revival of the pre-1973 labor union, the CUT.

6. The mounting bankruptcies were part of the genesis of the 1981–1982 economic crisis in Chile. The Chicago Boys believed in a kind of economic Darwinism, whereby strong enterprises would survive and weak ones die. Unfortunately, many of the "weak" businesses were Chilean. In addition, the Chicago Boys held to a fixed-exchange-rate policy for far too long; the result was to overvalue the Chilean peso, thereby making Chilean exports more expensive and imports more affordable.

7. See Alicia Frohmann, "Political and Institutional Context of Trade Policy in Chile," unpublished paper, March 2004.

8. The Communist Party went in the other direction, advocating an armed strategy to end the dictatorship and complete opposition to the idea of a market economy.

9. Pinochet was required to hold a plebiscite; that is, a yes-no vote on his presidential candidacy, with a yes vote allowing him to hold office until 1998. When Pinochet lost the vote, the military was then required to hold open elections for president and Congress the following year.

10. Ricardo French-Davis and Oscar Muñoz Goma, "Las políticas económicas y sus efectos," in *El período del Presidente Frei Ruiz-Tagle* (Santiago: Editorial Universitaria–FLACSO–Chile, 2002), 247.

11. Ibid.

12. Ibid.

13. Gobierno de Chile, Ministerio de Relaciones Exteriores, Dirección General de Relaciones Económicas Internacionales (DIRECON), http://www.direcon.cl/acuerdos/presentacion/home.htm.

14. See Alberto van Klaveren, "Inserción internacional de Chile," in *Chile en los noventa*, ed. Cristian Toloza and Eugenio Lahara (Santiago: Dolmen Ediciones 1998); and Sebastián Sáenz, Juan Salazar, and Ricardo Vicuna, "Antecedentes y resultados de la estrategia comercial del gobierno Aylwin," *Colección de Estudios CIEPLAN* 41 (December 1995): 41–66.

15. See, for example, Sebastián Sáenz and Juan Gabriel Valdés S., "Chile y su política comercial 'lateral,'" *Revista de la CEPAL*, 67 (April 1999): 81–94.

16. When the Concertación took power, the tariff rate was 15 percent. During its first year the Aylwin government sent a bill to Congress that lowered the rate to 11 percent.

17. In October 1998 a law was approved lowering tariff rates, so that beginning in January 1999, they would decline by 1 percent a year until they reached 6 percent in 2003.

18. *Panorama de la inserción internacional de América Latina y el Caribe en 2000–2001* (Santiago: United Nations and CEPAL, 2002), 82. These data exclude Mexico, because that country trades heavily with the United States. If Mexico were included in the calculation, the region's trade with the United States in 2000 would increase to 60 percent, that with the EU would decline to 10 percent, and that with Asia to a mere 5 percent.

19. In 1960 37 percent of Chile's exports went to the United States and in 1970 western Europe bought almost 61 percent of her exports.

20. *Panorama de la inserción internacional,* 82.

21. Sáenz and Valdés S., "Chile y su política comercial 'lateral,'"; interview by the author with Alicia Frohmann, DIRECON, December 1999.

22. Sáenz and Valdés S., "Chile y su política comercial 'lateral,'"; Frohmann, "Political and Institutional Context of Trade Policy in Chile"; Sáenz, Salazar, and Vicuna, "Antecedentes y resultados de la estrategia comercial."

23. Sáenz and Valdes S., "Chile y su política comercial 'lateral'"; Frohmann, "Political and Institutional Context."

24. Van Klaveren, "Inserción internacional de Chile."

25. Interview with Alicia Frohmann.

26. The agreement was signed on June 25, 1996, was approved by the Congress after some debate, and came into force on October 1 of that year.

27. This process had begun under Aylwin's presidency. See, for example, van Klaveren, "Inserción internacional de Chile," 122–27.

28. Interview with Patricio Meller, Professor of Industry Engineering, University of Chile, Santiago, January 1996.

29. These are the Christian Democratic Party (PDC), the Socialist Party (PS), and the Party for Democracy (PPD).

30. Interview with Patricio Meller, professor of industry engineering, University of Chile.

31. Interview with Verónica Silva, Division of International Commerce and Integration, CEPAL, January 2005.

32. Interview with Alicia Frohmann; van Klaveren, "Inserción internacional de Chile."

33. For example, Lagos named three "superministers" to his first cabinet, each of whom presided over two or three ministries.

34. The candidate was former President Frei's wife.

35. Lagos was not entirely responsible for the close election result. In many ways, the seeds of this close race had been planted years before. The vote for the Concertación had dropped in the 1997 congressional elections, but there had not been a commensurate change of policy by the Frei government. It was perhaps inevitable that the Concertación

vote would drop again in 1999. There was significant frustration with the Concertación's inability to change the 1980 constitution and with the country's lackluster economic performance after 1997. In addition, the Concertación had, by 1999, been in power for almost a decade. There was some loss of enthusiasm for the coalition, as the initial goals of ensuring democracy and military subordination to civilian rule seemed mostly resolved.

36. DIRECON, *Chile Investment Review,* June 2004.

37. One member of this group is Patricio Arrau. See his website www.elkybalion.cl.

38. Patricio Arrau, a leading "neoliberal" Concertación economist wrote a proposal in 2002 entitled "Agenda Pro-Crecimiento, Propuestas de Reformas al Mercado de Capital," which provided a blueprint for how to reactivate Chile's economy. It was written with funding from SOFOFA, a major organization for industrial interests in Chile, and it distills the thinking of the "complacent" wing of the Concertación. The document can be found on Arrau's website: www.elkybalion.cl/pdf/SOFOFA-rmk2-final.pdf

39. A group of fifteen Concertación senators and deputies (the so-called Group of 15) in the "self-flagellating" camp signed on to a document that critiques the current economic model and recommends a more socially conscious strategy for both reactivating the economy and creating a more equitable society. The document, entitled La Concertación de Chile por un Desarrollo con Justicia," (Santiago de Chile: Terram Publicaciones, October 2002) ends, on page 46, by calling for Chile to "end its social and economic backwardness, to advance justice… and to create real, sustainable development." Richardo French-Davis, a leading CEPAL economist, also wrote a prescription for Chile's economic ills in late 2002; it was entitled "Un Shock Reactivador para Recuperar el Crecimiento con Equidad," and it circulated privately among influential intellectuals and Concertación party elites.

40. The 1 percent number was part of a complex econometric model of the economy that government officials used. The finance minister didn't want to overstimulate the economy by overspending beyond the parameters of the economic model.

41. See, for example, Manuel Riesco, "The Rise and Decline of Neoliberalism in Chile," June 2003, CENDA UCLA.

42. This group is composed of Iceland, Liechtenstein, Norway, and Switzerland.

43. Having said this, I should note that there were popular protests in South Korea while its legislature pondered ratification of the free trade agreement. Some analysts speculate that these protests were driven largely by internal political concerns; that is, domestic agricultural interests in South Korea were setting the groundwork in case their government began to negotiate other free trade agreements.

44. His predecessor, Frei, had implemented a sweeping educational reform in an attempt to improve education.

45. Javier Nuñez and Roberto Gutiérrez, "Classism, Meritocracy and Discrimination in the Labor Market: The Case of Chile," Working Documents Series No. 208, April 2004.

46. See, for example, Arturo León and Javier Martínez, *La estratificación social chilena*

hacia fines del siglo XX, Political Science Series No. 52. (Santiago: United Nations and CEPAL, 2001).

47. Chile had previously used a mechanism designed to put controls on the flow of volatile, short-term capital. This mechanism, called *encaje* in Spanish, required that short-term investors deposit one-third of the value of their investment in a Chilean bank. The *encaje* was designed to prevent the sudden outflow of short-term capital from Chile, resulting in an economic crisis, as had occurred in Mexico in the early 1990s. Because the United States was opposed to any regulation of capital flows, Chile agreed that it would not use an *encaje* unless a capital flight had already taken place. This compromise seemed to many to give away the store because the mechanism was designed to prevent a sudden flight of capital.

48. I want to thank Oscar Muñoz Goma, who brought up this point of view in conversations with me.

6

Peace at Home, Turbulence Abroad

The Foreign Policy of the Lagos Administration

JOAQUÍN FERMANDOIS

In this chapter I examine the foreign policy of the Concertación, focusing on the Lagos administration. I argue that the Concertación's foreign policy has been driven by economic considerations and that this focus, notwithstanding the criticism it has generated, is normal for governments during times of economic and political stability. For those in the anti-globalization camp, Chile's political diplomacy appears to have been replaced by "trade diplomacy" and the abandonment of a distinctly Latin American perspective. My analysis argues instead that this emphasis demonstrates the relative normality of Chile's foreign policy, which, under peaceful conditions, tends to dedicate more time and energy to economic matters and coexistence. President Lagos' good standing in the international arena reflects the current domestic economic and political peace, in contrast with the turbulence found in the international system. The challenge for the Concertación, and especially for Lagos' government, has been to balance its global openness with its need to maintain good relations within its region, notwithstanding the economic vicissitudes of some of its neighbors. This chapter will explore these challenges, as well as the principal foreign policy accomplishments of the Concertación.

The Lagos government's current international posture also highlights a central paradox for the government. Internationally, Lagos positioned himself as one of the leaders of the "Third Way," or *tercera via*; that is, as both a socialist and a democratic representative of the region, even while facing criticism at home, especially during the first few years of his administration. Lagos' socialism was limited to the important task of building up a leftist orientation inside the Chilean market model of development, with the goal of giving social content to the new Chilean road to development. Lagos has interpreted the message of the Third Way by explaining that "the fact that one employs a market mechanism does not necessarily mean that one would create a market society."[1] Domestically, the achievements of his administration have been mixed and subject to criticism from the right and left.[2] While critiques from the left point at the problems of the model as such, those from the right point to issues that are at the heart of the social and political debates of the current agenda: economic growth, security, unemployment, health reform, and the rights of unions versus "flexibility" of the labor market. Even though the economy stagnated from 1999 through 2002, a notable change in comparison to the economic growth of the 1990s, it is hard to deny that in light of the regional crisis, Chile's performance is certainly good. As a result, the Lagos administration has achieved some remarkable successes in foreign policy, most of them in the realm of international political economy. On the other hand, the repeated and greatly overstated assertion made during the 1990s that Chile would achieve full development by 2010—the year of the country's bicentennial—created frustration when the pace of growth slowed down.

In the next section I examine the Concertación's foreign policy goals, focusing on the Lagos period. After examining the management style of the Lagos government in terms of foreign affairs, I address the principal foreign policy focus of the Concertación: trade policy.

Concertación Foreign Policy Goals

Chile's foreign policy goals have changed substantially during the last decade and a half. After the isolation experienced during the military regime, the main goal in the early 1990s was to reinsert the country into the international arena. In the mid-1990s, Chile's efforts were geared toward achieving a greater degree of political integration and coordination with other Latin American countries; by 2000, the international setting had become more complex, in ways different from those imagined a decade earlier.[3]

The Lagos administration inherited a complex web of economic interrelations and a politically respected country. Since at least the mid-1990s, Chilean officials have been saying that the main goal of Chilean economic foreign policy (some critics would argue of foreign policy in itself) was "open regionalism."[4] This was an expression of Chile's general international political economy, which was driven by the notion that the political class of the 1990s had accepted the economic setting created by the military regime, including its policy of unilateral reductions of barriers and tariffs. It also meant that if the country adhered to a more protective set of tariff policies, like the one followed by MERCOSUR, it would have to pay a huge social and economic cost. Therefore, the Chilean government proposed that the foreign trade policies of the region should converge in a general and common policy of low tariffs.

Clearly the latter policy implied much more than economic considerations. Throughout the 1990s, the opposition had not made much noise about foreign policy, including trade policy, bilateral relations with neighboring countries, or inter-American relations. The only exception was a border issue with Argentina in 1993.[5] Thus, by the year 2000 Chile's performance in foreign policy was strong, despite the political uproar over the arrest of Pinochet.

In terms of its approach to trade, following a policy initiated by the military regime in the 1970s, the Concertación decided to widen and diversify its commercial ties. It extended its relationship with the Asian Pacific region while strengthening its ties within its own region, becoming a member of the Asian Pacific Economic Cooperation (APEC) in 1994 and an associate member of MERCOSUR in 1996. Chile also began negotiations with the United States on a free trade agreement, which turned out to be a very arduous and slow process. At the same time, Chilean spokespersons insisted on the importance of supporting the Free Trade Area of the Americas (FTAA, or ALCA in Spanish), a free trade agreement to include all the countries in the Americas. On the whole, the Chilean government's attitude could be described as one of being prepared, just in case the U.S. Congress approved a fast-track measure that would open the possibility of trade negotiations with Chile.[6]

During the same period, Chile was also in the process of negotiating a free trade agreement with the European Union (EU). This treaty negotiation has to be understood, like the others, as another step—albeit a big step—in its policy of negotiating trade agreements with a vast array of countries and trade blocs around the world.

From an ideological perspective, the Lagos project highlighted a mild contradiction between two camps within the Concertación, those with a more egalitarian view who proposed "growth with equality" (*crecer con igualdad*), in contrast with Chile's more modernizing sector, who were determined to achieve full development, inspired by the Third Way of British Prime Minister Tony Blair. The Lagos government not only used Blair's Labor government and the policies proposed by leaders of the aforementioned Third Way as a reference point; it saw ideological counterparts in Brazilian President Fernando Henrique Cardoso, Argentinean President Fernando de la Rúa, and to a lesser extent, Mexican President Vicente Fox. The references were to the policies of Cardoso in Brazil, who was a personal acquaintance of Lagos, and the new and presumably promising Argentine president-elect, Fernando de la Rúa. The latter, in a political decision that would have been unthinkable prior to the 1980s, had openly supported Lagos' candidacy before the 1999 election, and Chile in the 1990s enjoyed exceptionally good relations with de la Rúa's predecessor, Carlos Menem. The election of Vicente Fox as president of Mexico in 2000, which was a political turning point in that country, was seen by the Concertación as another electoral victory for progressive and reform-minded governments in Latin America.

Last of all, economic and political turbulence in the region created a more complex regional environment for the Lagos government. For example, Lagos' foreign policy decisions had to take into account the mounting Latin American economic crisis characterized by stagnant or recessive economies; the surge of populist movements and governments in several countries, especially that of Hugo Chávez in Venezuela; the devaluation of the real in Brazil; the collapse of state authority in extensive areas of Colombia; rampant narcotics trafficking in a number of countries; the crisis in Peru after 1999; and the Asian economic crisis, which was echoed by the currency devaluation in Brazil in January 1999. All of these threatened Chile's positions and goals.[7]

Lagos explained how his administration would reconcile the basic ideas of the Concertación with the Third Way approach in international affairs:

> We are the first government of the twenty-first century, a century which will be full of changes, of adjustment to the new reality of globalization, which touches the most diverse realms of human activity. A century in which the nations of the world will have to make an effort to find a new, more just, fairer, and more sustainable international order. A century where the classical idea of our sovereignties inside each of our countries will give way to a new, different attitude of implementing shared sovereignty over a wide array of global issues in a universal realm.[8]

This very important statement appears to indicate that the classical thesis of the left, that change in the international system is a premise for social change in individual countries, had been translated to fit the conditions of the post–Cold War system, that is, a liberal (economic) order with a human (social) face.

The Management of Foreign Policy

Lagos visibly enjoys conducting foreign policy. As is traditional in most Latin American countries, foreign policy is mainly presidential policy. Even though the Concertación mustered an impressive intelligentsia in foreign affairs, the president is still the central foreign policy maker in Chile at the beginning of the twenty-first century. Paraphrasing Manfred Wilhelmy, he is a promoter;[9] in other words, Lagos is the driving force behind his government's foreign policy approaches and decisions.

This power is clearly highlighted by the fact that Lagos appointed as his foreign minister Soledad Alvear, a well-known political figure without much experience in the field; as a result, Lagos has had significant and direct involvement in policy formulation. That is not the whole story, however. Alvear, a high-ranking official of the Christian Democratic Party (PDC) who is married to Gutenberg Martínez, also a high-profile Christian Democrat, had been an effective cabinet minister in both prior Concertación governments, including serving as minister of justice under Frei. Alvear was also pivotal in helping Lagos win the 2000 runoff election as his new chief of staff. As a result, Alvear was in a position to ask for a high-ranking post in the new government. She rejected the very important post of interior minister (*ministro del interior*) and, much to the surprise of the Concertación, demanded the post of foreign minister (or *canciller,* in Latin American jargon).

From the start Alvear was hard working. She learned quickly, and with her excellent bureaucratic skills she was able to organize effective task forces and build political support. She had shown these traits as justice minister under Frei, where she successfully promoted the single most important judicial reform in recent Chilean history. In contrast with the eroding position of the governmental coalition from 2000 to 2003, Alvear, together with President Lagos, has been one of the few center-left figures whose standing has grown in the past three years. Her popularity has increased due to the attention stirred up by the free trade negotiations with the United States, which concluded at the end of 2002. By 2003, Alvear had been singled out as the most likely PDC nominee for the presidential elections of 2005, along with Michelle Bachelet (of the PS), former minister of defense. Both women resigned in October of 2004 in order to devote themselves full-time to gaining the Concertación nomination. They are, by the way, the first women to be considered serious candidates by a major coalition for the highest office.

Alvear's appointment as *canciller* also had the effect of displacing Heraldo Muñoz, one of the most prominent internationalists in the Concertación coalition. Muñoz is a political scientist who has written extensively on Chilean foreign policy in the 1970s and 1980s, and he is one of Ricardo Lagos' most trusted aides. Prior to 2000, he had been ambassador to the Organization of American States and to Brazil, where he proved his value. Muñoz held the post of undersecretary of foreign affairs for two years before being replaced by a career official closer to the Concertación. In the aftermath of the Iraq war, Muñoz was sent to the United Nations (UN) as ambassador, probably in an attempt to mend relations with the United States.

Initially, Alvear had some difficulties on the job. She had no real prior experience in international affairs, nor did she have any special knowledge of international studies, and she distrusted not only the career diplomats, but also her fellow coalition undersecretary. When Alvear assumed power, she surrounded herself with her own politically oriented staff, signaling that she considered her position a political job (which, among other things, it is). Although her first declarations and public conferences were not very impressive, Alvear, a quick study, soon mastered the job by studying the issues relevant to the functions of the ministry. As a gifted politician, she has since been able to position herself as a leading public figure, aided by the high-profile nature of her position, especially through the conclusion of a free trade agreement with the EU in April 2002 and the much more celebrated and long-awaited agreement with the United States.

It is fair to say that under Alvear's leadership, the foreign ministry has successfully dealt with the changed reality of modern foreign policy and the ascendancy of the Foreign Ministry as a major actor in foreign policy matters, even though in 2004, disputes with Bolivia, Argentina, and Peru cast some doubt on Alvear's performance. This process of foreign policy adjustment had, in fact, begun under the military regime, which initiated Chile's greater insertion into the global economy. By the 1990s, however, the same open economy strategy led to the integration of Chile's economic and political institutions, most importantly the Finance Ministry and, to a lesser extent, the Central Bank. In this context the central task of the Foreign Ministry was not only to formulate foreign policy, but to coordinate the actions of the different foreign policy actors. This coordination has been challenging because the 1980 constitution established the autonomy of the Central Bank. The Central Bank plays an important role in controlling inflation, thereby contributing to the economic stability and international respectability of the Chilean economy.

The role of the Finance Ministry and its interactions with the Foreign Ministry have been even more important in terms of international economic policy than the role of the Central Bank. As a result, a new institution was born, the Dirección General de Relaciones Económicas Internacionales, or General Office for International Economic Relations (DIRECON). DIRECON was first established by the Foreign Ministry in the early 1990s, and it has since developed into a complex agency that links the Foreign Affairs and Finance Ministries in the process of international negotiations. Even if the costs of setting up this agency raised questions about overspending and unnecessary duplication of functions, the success of the whole process has muted its critics. The creation of DIRECON consolidated the trend of concentrating trade policies in the Foreign Ministry, with trade policies as the focal point of Chile's foreign policy.

Does this mean, then, that in Chile political diplomacy has been replaced by trade diplomacy? Although many people think that Concertación policy has meant an abandonment of a Latin American perspective, I prefer to stress that, under peaceful conditions, foreign policy is mostly dedicated to economic matters and coexistence.

Concertación Foreign Policy Focus: Trade and Treaties

During the 1990s, the Chilean government signed free trade agreements with many countries. These agreements reflect Chilean acceptance of the globalization process. In the programmatic language of the 1999 Lagos campaign, "It is no longer possible to enclose ourselves, nor to sustain autonomous policies." The election program also stressed "open regionalism" and the priority of the region in Chile´s international approach. Although there has been progress in relations with the Southern Cone countries, the main thrust of the economic foreign policy has been the global arena.

Free trade agreements are a code word for the political economy of the post–Cold War world. Under the old liberal (Manchesterian) assumption that trade brings peace and prosperity, the policies of the Washington Consensus were designed to take advantage of the process of economic reform in Latin America. In this context, the Initiative of the Americas of George Bush Sr., although it was not much of a success, helped the United States on a most vital front: reaching a free trade agreement with Mexico.

Since 1994, Chile has been one of the strongest supporters of that initiative. Overcoming the CEPAL (Comisión Económica para América Latina y el Caribe) legacy of Raúl Prebisch's structuralism, the elite Chilean economists inside the Concertación have taken advantage of the exceptional situation of the Chilean economy and called for a free trade agreement with the United States. For Washington, this policy has been a substitute for old-fashioned assistance policies, such as the Alliance for Progress in the Kennedy era.

The Process of Free Trade Treaty Negotiations

Chile's emphasis on free trade agreements with the EU and the United States can be considered a result of the recessive trends in the Chilean economy after 1998, which had created doubts about the future of the economy. As the stagnation continued for several years, free trade negotiations and treaties represented a political escape valve. The political and financial constraints imposed on policy makers by the existing economic system in Chile did not leave them with much space to maneuver in the area of fiscal policy and, as a result, success on the international front became increasingly important. Many hopes were placed on the signing of these agreements, and the agreements in turn have been considered major public relations accomplishments for the government. Given the sluggish performance of the economy at the beginning of Lagos' term, it became increasingly important for the government to show success in the international field, where Chile was still something of a star.

In the late 1990s and the early years of the new century, Chilean economic growth rates have been much better than those of many other Latin American countries, but dismally low if the country expects to reach real economic development. Between 1984 and 1997 the rate of economic growth was more than 7 percent, while from 1998 to 2003 it averaged a mere 2.4 percent.[10] More important, around half of the gross domestic product originates in the international sector of the economy. Chile did well in resisting the economic shock produced by the "tequila effect" (the Mexican crisis) in 1994. However, the country felt the tremors and waves of the "Asian flu" of 1997, which arrived on the southern shores in 1998 and, according to some, became more severe as a result of the delayed response of the Frei government.[11] The slower rates of growth were a huge barrier to development and to the task of overcoming poverty. Thus, the whole idea that the Chilean model was the right path to development came into question.

It is under these circumstances that the continuation of the free trade negotiations, an important achievement in itself, becomes critical, because they appear to counterbalance the lack of an outstanding leap on the economic front. With increasing unemployment and economic stagnation, the legitimacy of the model and of the strategy of the Concertación could be cast in doubt. The idea was that free trade agreements could help to promote a new economic takeoff and continued growth. They also had a soothing effect on the perception of economic insecurity and the glum prospects held by the general public and economic actors, which contrasted sharply with the over-optimism of the 1990s. And there is international recognition of Chile's relative success under the present conditions. Even pointing to the low technological development of the economy, Jeffrey Sachs affirms that "Chile is still a star."[12]

For a while, the negotiations with the United States appeared endless, especially given the reluctance of the U.S. Congress to approve fast-track legislation with Chile, which was a serious obstacle. The Clinton and the early Bush administrations were also reluctant to launch a more dynamic offensive on Capitol Hill. Finally, in December 2001, the U.S. Congress granted trade promotion authority, or TPA (the successor mechanism to "fast-track" authority) to the George W. Bush administration; this was the tool required to advance the agreement through Congress. If, in many aspects, the Latin American policy of the Bush administration looked to be in disarray or plagued by indifference, in this respect the administration showed resolution.

In the meantime, negotiations with the EU scored the first success. This could be seen as paradoxical, because at the beginning it looked very improbable that any agreement would be reached. In fact, the Chilean government's policy of prioritizing an agreement geared toward reaching full membership in MERCOSUR confused the Europeans and led them to believe that they were better off negotiating with the MERCOSUR bloc.[13] As with the negotiations with the United States, the Chilean government's soul was divided between the "Latin American priority" and the needs of the Chilean economy.

With regard to the free trade agreement with the United States, Chilean policy makers decided that their task was simply to be prepared by maintaining a financial and legal system that would be ready to go if the United States decided to proceed with the treaty—in effect, leaving the initiative in American hands.[14] On the U.S. side, in spite of the Bush administration's seeming indifference to the region, the White House continued the Clinton administration's policy of singling out Chile as a good partner and candidate for a free trade agreement. When Lagos visited the United States in mid-2001, Bush stressed the U.S. commitment to supporting his government.[15] Presumably, in the eyes of the administration, having a free trade policy with Chile and Mexico was tantamount to having a policy for Latin America.

It is important to note that the nature and extent of U.S. economic relations with Chile have changed dramatically in the last twenty years. Up to the 1970s, the United States was Chile's most important trading partner and the most critical point of reference in Chile's foreign economic relations. This remained true even after the U.S.-owned copper companies were nationalized in 1971. As the Chilean economy became more internationalized, the relative importance of trade with the United States decreased proportionally. Chilean foreign trade became more diversified, in terms of both products and trading partners. By the 1990s, Washington had lost the overwhelming economic influence it had held in the past because by then Chile's trade was divided evenly among each of the four regions: the United States, the EU, East Asia, Australia and New Zealand, and Latin America.[16] Furthermore, the feared "war of regional blocs" predicted at the end of the Cold War did not happen, at least not to the degree predicted.

With MERCOSUR negotiations blocked (at least from the Chilean point of view), Chilean policy makers argued that the only way to acquire international respect and solidify Chilean development was through an agreement with North America. The comprehensive agreement signed with Canada in 1997 was considered an important step in this direction. Although Canada was not an important trading partner (accounting for only 2 percent of Chile's trade), the Chilean government believed that this was a world-class agreement because it was made with an advanced economy. It was also considered likely to facilitate a treaty with the United States. On the other hand, Canada is an important source of foreign investment and, above all else, the agreement added prestige to Chile, given Canada's economic, technological, and political reputation. This latter factor was quite important, given the more complex nature of relations with the United States. Canada is perceived as a progressive country and her policies are attuned to the views of the new Chilean left. Thus, this agreement was another step in the policy of being prepared for a free trade agreement with the United States.

As I argued previously, signing the treaty with the United States had both international and domestic importance. Internationally, a free trade agreement with the biggest economy of the world would give Chile international prestige and would facilitate future trade negotiations with other countries. Domestically, during the years of economic stress, international negotiations were also an effective political maneuver that deflected attention away from domestic issues and emphasized the effectiveness of the government.

Negotiations with Europe

In May 2002 the Chilean government signed an agreement with the EU. In October 1994, Chile had formally asked the EU for a strategic association, perhaps signaling Chile's desire for greater convergence over the long term. In March 1995 President Frei traveled to several European countries to seek some form of association. The beginning of negotiations toward the agreement coincided with the inauguration of the Lagos government in 2000 and lasted until April 2002. Undoubtedly, the process was accelerated by the new administration and it was probably enhanced by the EU's desire to demonstrate its ability to open its economy to a developing country.

The treaty with the EU provoked varied reactions in Chile, as had the discussions around the limited treaty with MERCOSUR and the treaty with the United States. Although the majority supported the treaties out of either concurrence or indifference, the representatives of the traditional agricultural sector—including wheat, milk, and meat producers—and the anti-globalization actors such as the extra-congressional left, anti-capitalist groups, ecologists, and some groups within the indigenous Mapuche Indian community, opposed these agreements. Some of them argued, for example, that increased investment facilitated by the agreements would continue to erode the environment and result in the removal of indigenous peoples from their lands.[17] Although congressional opponents of the treaties were quite vocal, they did not build a real opposition bloc. In the case of the EU treaty, the real stumbling block was fishing rights, which many Chileans considered dangerously biased toward European interests. This criticism was made not only by ecological groups, but by others as well.[18]

In the final analysis, the treaty with the EU was widely supported, and it was a public relations success for the government. The agreement was the result of a close collaboration between the government and the industrial sector represented by the Sociedad de Fomento Fabril (SFF), along with the (reluctant) support of the workers' unions. As with many other facets of foreign policy in a democratic environment, the policy served other objectives as well.[19] The accord served to reinforce Chile's commitment to democracy and western concepts of human rights. This point was stressed by President Lagos, who affirmed that the "Treaty of Association with the EU reflects a shared will around common values and orientations." The president also identified this as the most important accord in Chilean history, because it enhanced Chilean markets and broadened cultural and scientific opportunities. According to President Lagos, "Chile is determined to promote an orderly and just globalization. Our friends from the EU have a long tradition of knowing how to link the relations between large and small countries; about how to debate a new political charter; about how to put in motion multinational parliaments; about how to develop a community led by responsible authorities in the most important public policy areas."[20]

It is interesting that Lagos' declaration mostly underlines the political dimensions of the treaty. It is also important to note that a treaty with the EU was not seen just as a step in negotiations with the United States; it was also a policy geared toward making the treaty with the United States more palatable, as well as a tool to combat criticism from the anti-neoliberal and anti-globalization groups. On the European side, Romano Prodi, the European Union Commission president, stated that the agreement was important because the Chilean state introduced reforms geared toward increasing the "transparency of public actions."[21] This issue has been a constant worry of Europeans with regard to Latin America.

If in its last years the Clinton administration did not show much energy in promoting a free trade agreement, things changed under the George W. Bush administration. What moved a somewhat isolationist administration in this direction? Seemingly, it was the same set of concerns that had dominated the Clinton White House and had pushed policy makers toward an agreement with Chile in the first place: The mounting crisis in the region, especially the Hugo Chávez regime in Venezuela, the crises of governance in the Andean countries, the clouds over Argentina, and the uncertainties over Luis Ignacio "Lula" da Silva's victory in Brazil accelerated the idea of using Chile as a "model."

From the standpoint of the U.S. State Department, in the absence of a crisis in the region, Latin America beyond Mexico is of secondary importance, since the "real" and "vital" interests of the United States in Latin America have been concentrated in Mexico. Although President Bush displayed much friendliness toward Mexican President Vicente Fox, his administration recognized the need to have a Latin American strategy. What better strategy could there be than to promote a treaty with what economists perceive as the best economy in the hemisphere, that of Chile?

It is interesting to note that in this case observers in the region tend to compare the current Mexican government with the Concertación, even though in political orientation the Fox administration has more affinity with the goals of the Chilean right. Nonetheless, both sides—Mexican as well as Chilean officials—promote this analogy because the parallels are real. Like the Partido Popular of Spain, the Chilean right has been disdained by presumed allies because of their "original sin," referring to the fact that Chile's capitalist transformation is associated with the Pinochet regime,[22] which has alienated many supporters of free trade and economic reform, or neoliberalism, in both Chile and Spain. To the extent that the United States had been supportive of these policies all along, the so-called sin served as a reinforcement for U.S. policy makers to formalize economic relations with Chile. Thus, supporting Chile was seen as tantamount to having a Latin American policy for an administration that otherwise had failed to find an anchor for its policies in the region.

Of course, this attitude played into the hands of the Chileans. The Chilean political soul since the late 1980s has been dominated by the concept of consensus, which includes, generally speaking, a positive view of American international political economy. This is a phenomenon common among all Chilean economists, both those within the Concertación and those in opposition think tanks. In this light, it is obvious that the American economy is the standard upon which economic success should be judged.[23] An agreement with the United States would leave the Chilean economy in good standing with the big economic powers; that is, with the United States, APEC (mainly East Asia) and the EU, and would be seen as proof of Chile's capabilities.

Even though the Bush administration engaged in the negotiations with new brio, the process moved fairly slowly until August 2002, when the administration won approval for the TPA. Approval of the TPA precipitated hectic negotiations that concluded with a free trade agreement in December 2002. The agreement was formally signed on June 6, 2003, in Miami, and was ratified on July 31, 2003, by a landslide vote in the U.S. Senate (66-31).[24]

The debates generated in the United States and in Chile were quite similar. On both sides representatives of the agricultural sector vocally opposed some provisions. In Chile, although traditional agriculture enjoys a form of protection that guarantees certain price ranges for agricultural products, known as *bandas de precio,* their representatives pointed to the generous agricultural subsidies that exist in both the United States and the EU. Ecological groups, on the other hand, were concerned about the potential for environmental damage resulting from the treaty; for example, that investment in the wood and energy areas might lead to the destruction of Chile's native forests. Another area of concern was U.S. anti-dumping measures, which Chile and other developing countries perceive as hidden protectionism. There were also musings that Chile was abandoning its regional interests and that it did not enjoy sufficient strength to negotiate alone with the United States (the latter an argument of former Foreign Minister Gabriel Valdés), as well as accusations of surrendering to neoliberalism, which came from the more orthodox left.[25] These critics point to the fact that after almost thirty years of economic reforms, Chile basically remains an underdeveloped country.

By and large, however, there was a consensus in Chile that the treaty was favorable for the country's interests. In the end, the United States made fewer trade concessions than expected. Nevertheless, the whole treaty was seen not only as favorable to Chile, but also as a gigantic step in Chile's economic international history. Chile achieved a position that it had not held since the United States became its main trading partner in the inter-war years. The consensus was that if Chile was going to be an export economy, a treaty like this was a must.

East Asia as a Market

It was the military regime that first played the "Asian card" by developing better economic relations with that region. This strategy served as a counterbalance to Chile's political isolation at the time, and it was feasible because Asian countries did not consider domestic affairs, such as human rights, an obstacle to economic relations.[26] This trend of opening links to Asia was enthusiastically and legitimately continued by the democratic Concertación governments. After removing some obstacles (including whether Chile was really a Pacific country), Chile was admitted to APEC in 1994 and has taken a prominent role in the organization ever since, especially considering the size of its economy.[27] East Asia evolved from being an adjacent market to becoming a main trading partner; however, the East Asian countries have not become major investors in Chile.

Within the Asian market, relationships have also evolved. For some years, Japan was Chile's main trading partner, displacing the United States. More recently, China has become Chile's main East Asian buyer. Even more important, Chile enjoys a large surplus in its trade balance with the region, especially with China. This surplus, in turn, allows Chile to finance its large trade imbalance with MERCOSUR, especially with Argentina, a deficit that totaled more than US$2 billion in 2002.[28]

A sign of Chile's importance is that it hosted the 2004 APEC Annual Conference of Heads of States. This was a real landmark for the country and, it was hoped, a step that would ignite the economy. A close relationship with APEC is evolving slowly over the long term. When he toured South America to demonstrate Beijing's new interest in the region, Jiang Zemin visited Chile in April

2001. It is important to note that in the case of China, the Chilean government has avoided any reference to the human rights issue in bilateral relations.

In conclusion, although economic relations with the East Asian countries are growing, Chile's main *political* relations are still focused on North and South America and the EU.

Ambivalence toward Latin America

As discussed previously, Chile´s policy toward Latin America suffers from an inner tension. The spirit of the Concertación, Lagos' ideas, and the traditional rhetoric of Chilean diplomacy all lead the Lagos government to stress the importance of Latin America. In reality, however, since the 1830s, European countries have come first, replaced in the 1920s by the United States, which has been at the center of Chilean international economics. The same pattern has held true for other nations in the Southern Cone.

Barring any new conflict or the formation of special organizations like the Rio Group, it is obvious that in peaceful times commerce will continue to be at the center of international economic relations and that, as in the past, the main partners of the Southern Cone countries will be Europe, the United States, and now, East Asia. On the other hand, Chile is part of South America, and regional trends influence the country. Historical ties to Bolivia and Peru have been delicate, and they will not easily be smoothed over

It was natural for the new democracy of the 1990s to build strong bridges to other Latin American countries. On the whole, they have been successful. In addition, one should take into account that after many years of discussing regional integration, what really brought the economies closer were the economic reforms implemented throughout the region. Trade links with neighboring countries increased, and by the mid-1990s, one-fifth of Chile's foreign trade was with Latin American countries, mainly Brazil and Argentina. At the same time, Chile inaugurated a new trend in its own economic life with direct investments by Chilean economic groups in neighboring Argentina, Peru, and Brazil. This was a completely new facet of economic life and regional relations. Contrary to many expectations, foreign investment in those countries by and large has not produced much conflict.

There have been some policy hurdles along the way. The most agonizing questions have resulted from the existence of MERCOSUR, the common market of Argentina, Brazil, Uruguay, and Paraguay. These countries formed a powerful economic association during the 1990s, and although they have not developed a common foreign policy, they nevertheless constitute an impressive political force. In 1996, Chile was invited to join and signed on as an associate member. Chile would be happy to be a full member of the group. The main problem is that the MERCOSUR countries' economic reforms have not been nearly as extensive as Chile's, and they have retained high protective tariffs. It is unimaginable, given the policies of the Concertación governments and their insistence on lowering tariffs, that Chile would be willing to raise tariffs in order to comply with MERCOSUR policies. Such a policy would unleash a major crisis, and it would endanger various free trade agreements.

President Lagos unequivocally explained the Chilean position: "We understand MERCOSUR with a clear political sense. . . . The crux of MERCOSUR, it seems to me, is how we make of this [association] a tool for advancement of our countries and our peoples."[29] Thus, Lagos stressed both the idea that Chile's alliance with MERCOSUR should be part of its foreign policy, in order to maintain a Latin American perspective, and at the same that keeping a responsible fiscal policy is important. In this vein, President Lagos has spoken a great deal about joining MERCOSUR, stressing its indubitable political significance, but he has also made it clear that Chile will not change its basic approach to international economic policy.

Regional leaders, on the other hand, have repeatedly invited Chile to join MERCOSUR, implying that Santiago will not be considered a real partner until it becomes a full member of the organization. Inside Chile, the economists and political leaders of the opposition decry any measure to close the gap with MERCOSUR (as, privately, do many people within the ranks of the Concertación). Those who oppose joining MERCOSUR have been reassured by the mounting crisis in the region, which makes any move toward full membership unlikely for Chile in the short term.

In fact, as a leading article in a major newspaper argues, "relations with MERCOSUR have been characterized more by political will than by concrete advances."[30] Privately, that is also the opinion of many government officials.[31] The impending crisis in the region, which has even threatened to involve Brazil, has led experts inside and outside of Chile to argue that the country should not abandon its prudent fiscal policy in order to avoid being an island in the region.[32] At the same time, Chilean officials struggle with concerns over being considered arrogant, which is the surest ticket to regional isolation.

Bilateral Policies in the Region

The political ambivalence toward MERCOSUR in general is a reflection of Chile's policy in the entire region. Argentina, Chile's most important and biggest neighbor, has been a historical paradox in terms of economic relations. The two countries have a long history of border disputes; twice, around 1900 and in 1978, both nations were close to war. Both times they were deterred by a combination of prudence, foreign arbitration or influence (from big powers), and fear of the consequences of a conflict. On the other hand, these two countries, which share one of the longest borders in the world, have never gone to war; they have much in common, and in general they have cooperated well with each other. Relations were perhaps better in the 1990s than in any other period since the 1902 arbitration.

As a result of these improved relations, Chile has been importing natural gas from Argentina, becoming energy dependent on its neighbor. Moreover, after a long domestic debate, in 1997 Chile and Argentina signed a mining treaty that regulates investment along the border. After heated discussion, the treaty was approved by Chile's Senate in August 2000. It is clear that this treaty would have been unthinkable in the past, and in fact opponents of the treaty did appeal unsuccessfully to the Constitutional Tribunal. The main objections on the Chilean side were strategic because the agreement allowed foreign investors from a neighboring country to acquire property along the border.[33]

Even though Argentine President Carlos Menem was widely held in Chile to be a promoter of good relations, there was much hope that the election of Fernando de la Rúa at the end of 1999 would make those relations even closer, since Lagos had many political affinities with the latter. De La Rúa fell from power in December 2001, however, due to the country's financial crisis. Chile also supported de la Rúa's successor, Eduardo Duhalde (2001–2003). After the first round in the presidential elections of May 2003, candidate Néstor Kirchner visited Brazil and Chile as a way of stressing the importance of bilateral links. Despite having a Chilean mother, Kirchner was presumed to have an anti-Chilean bias. Neither his populist rhetoric in international economics, clearly different from that of Lagos, nor Chile's trade deficit of nearly US$3 billion appeared to be real hurdles in bilateral relations. In the long run, what is important is the extent of Argentina's economic recuperation, since the size and depth of Argentina's crisis threatened the whole economic landscape of the region and made Chile's economic recovery more difficult.

The close links between former Brazilian President Fernando Henrique Cardoso and Chile are well known. Cardoso was one of the most distinguished intellectual exiles in Chile in the late 1960s, and it was in Chile where he became the father of the Marxist-rooted dependency theory. Later on, his own political evolution went hand in hand with that of his Chilean counterparts. From 1994 to 2002 his government strongly emphasized the importance of continuing the "economic reforms" already introduced by his predecessors. Lagos and Cardoso also stressed their affinities, and both of them took part in Third Way meetings. Thus, when other Brazilian officials criticized Chile for not joining

MERCOSUR as a full member, or for negotiating bilaterally with the United States and with the EU, President Cardoso always reaffirmed his understanding of the Chilean position.

Ironically, perhaps, the Lagos administration would have been pleased had José Serra been elected as Cardoso's successor, since the winner, Luis Ignacio "Lula" da Silva, was a reminder of the (so-called) old-fashioned left that in Chile strongly criticizes Lagos. But under the Lula administration, Chile and Brazil enjoyed the same good relations they had had in the past. Andrés Oppenheimer, a well-known Argentinean American columnist, said that Lula has the choice to align with Fox and Lagos or, catastrophically, to emulate Chávez. This statement, although exaggerated, describes what Lula's options are and in what measure Chile is seen as an "axis of hope."

We see a similar trend in relations with other neighboring countries. Chile enjoyed good relations with Fujimori's Peru, where in the 1990s Chilean businesses invested more than US$3 billion, an unheard-of sum compared with earlier investments. In 1999 Chile and Peru signed a final agreement in order to fulfill the 1929 treaty[34] ending the War of the Pacific. In spite of the onerous burden of the nineteenth-century conflicts, in 2000 and 2001, with the fall of Fujimori and the election of Alejandro Toledo, who was seen within the Chilean government as a sort of Cardoso, the future seemed bright for bilateral links. But troubles soon arose. First, President Toledo faced mounting internal difficulties. Then came a somewhat nationalistic backlash in Peru against one Chilean investor (Mr. Lucchetti, from the Luksic group), which has raised concerns about Chile's investments in that country.[35] There were also some minor border problems, which were resolved due to the calm responses of Presidents Lagos and Toledo. Although they avoided major incidents, much work remains to be done to solve these problems and to avoid isolation and a deterioration of relations.[36]

In the case of Bolivia, relations are very charged. Officially, the two countries have no diplomatic relations, but the reality is somewhat different. The general consuls in the two countries' capital cities are, for all practical purposes, ambassadors. Lagos sent former Defense Minister Edmundo Pérez, a businessman very close to Eduardo Frei, to La Paz as consul, and he has had made multiple gestures of sympathy to Bolivia, including attending the funeral of former president (and dictator) Hugo Bánzer Suárez. Consul Pérez and Minister Alvear saw an opportunity to improve relations by strengthening trade relations, specifically, allowing Bolivia to export natural gas to the United States and Mexico through a pipeline that runs to a Chilean harbor. This proposal produced a nationalistic backlash in Bolivia, however, as opponents of the deal claimed that a national resource was being sold to imperialist and Chilean interests.[37]

This claim was connected with a widespread protest against the government of President Sánchez de Losada, who supported the deal.

The protests revealed deep rifts in Bolivian society and Sánchez de Losada fell from power in mid-October 2003, mainly due to this issue. His successor, Carlos Mesa, linked the gas issue to Bolivia's demand for an outlet to the ocean (*salida al mar*) and transformed it into a continental issue. In January 2004, at the Guadalajara Presidential Summit (Cumbre de las Américas), Mesa raised the issue. He obtained support from Hugo Chávez of Venezuela and garnered some mild declarations from other leaders.

The Bolivian situation has been compounded by the tensions in Chilean-Argentinean relations resulting from Argentina's decision to reduce its supply of natural gas to Chile, beginning in March 2004, in order to avoid gas rationing in Argentina. This action of Argentinean President Kirchner has been widely seen in Chile as unilateral and in violation of previous accords. In Chile, the administration was embarrassed on this issue, even though President Lagos has shown strong leadership in the face of these external difficulties. The opposition attempted to use these problems to weaken the position of then Foreign Minister Soledad Alvear, and a sense of isolation, perhaps exaggerated, still permeates the country's mood. President Kirchner criticized the appointment of Ignacio Walker as Alvear's successor because some months earlier Walker had written in an op-ed piece that Peronism had fascist traits. Although calling Chile "isolated" might exaggerate the situation, within the region Chile has been criticized both by the opponents of neoliberalism who see in Chile a "false model" and by those who have old, historical grievances dating from the nineteenth century. All this has soured somewhat what was otherwise an optimistic regional environment.

Keeping its promise not to have a high profile, Chilean regional diplomacy has been low key, with two arguable exceptions: Chile's response to the failed coup in Venezuela and a problem involving Cuba. In the Venezuelan case, Chile did not condemn the revolt quickly enough. In fact, the Chilean ambassador, who ostensibly showed some "understanding" for the coup, was later sacrificed by the administration.[38] The whole affair highlighted the mixed feelings of the Chilean left inside the Concertación, which does not trust Chávez but cannot support a coup, even if supported by many Venezuelans.

The rift with Cuba took place in February and March 2002, a result of suspected Cuban support of terrorism in Chile, which the Cuban government strongly denies. Castro's treatment of two Chilean envoys, one of them none other than former Foreign Minister Gabriel Valdés, was heavy-handed. At the same time, he ostentatiously received the leader of the Chilean right, Joaquín Lavín, and wrote an insolent letter to President Lagos.[39] Cuba also strongly rejected Chilean protests over its execution of three would-be hijackers and the imprisonment of dozens of dissidents in April 2003.[40] Inside Chile there are mixed feelings about Cuba, just as there are about Venezuela. In the 1960s, the current leadership of the left wing of the Concertación had been admirers of Castro, but in the 1980s almost all distanced themselves from the Cuban government, and the Chilean transition was perceived as a defeat for Castro's policy of confrontation with Pinochet. On the other hand, almost all Chilean political leaders have rejected the U.S. policy of isolating Cuba, and Castro still enjoys a certain measure of support among some minor but vocal groups in Chile. Anti-Americanism, never fully dead in Chile, demands a certain degree of sympathy for Cuba.

New Themes and Challenges and Old Realities

Human rights, gender, and environmental issues, as well as the problems of minorities, are themes that have appeared in the international studies agenda with the end of the Cold War. All of these issues have had some relevance in the Lagos administration. The growth of the so-called Mapuche problem, referring to the demands of the main indigenous group in Chile, and the support they have garnered from nongovernmental organizations around the globe, while not a grave problem in Chile, could threaten the legitimacy of the nation-state over the long term. Public opinion in the United States and western Europe tends to sympathize automatically with Chile's ethnic minority.

Regarding human rights, the Lagos administration has accepted initiatives geared toward "internationalizing" human rights laws, and this policy has influenced the commandant of the army to distance himself remarkably from the Pinochet regime. Concerning gender, on the other hand, the administration has not had to confront any major issues, as the Concertación governments in the mid-1990s did with the Cairo and Beijing women's conferences.

Environmental issues, like minority rights, have a huge international component. For example, the debates over the creation of Parque Pumalín, which is almost 300,000 hectares in size and is located in the far south, link internal and international factors.[41] These are real *intermestic issues*, to use a term from international studies.

The old power realities of international politics die hard, as was demonstrated when the Iraq conflict knocked on Chile's doors. As had happened in both world wars, Chile was confronted with an impossible problem that stretched its capabilities. In the 1990s, relations with the United States were probably the best they had been since the mid-1960s. When Lagos visited Washington in April 2001, he was warmly welcomed by George W. Bush, and Chile was singled out by the Bush administration as an example of economic success. The September

11 attack in the United States initially had the effect of bringing Chilean and U.S. policies even closer, as Chile supported the war against terrorism and the UN-backed intervention in Afghanistan. In the second half of 2002, however Chile became a two-year member of the UN Security Council. It is probable that Washington, already planning the war, thought that Chile, as a would-be favored trade partner of the United States, would support U.S. policy. Washington put pressure on Chile, first gently, then not so gently. In Chile, polls indicated that 98 percent of the population was against the war. Only some groups on the right favored supporting the United States, perhaps in part simply to annoy the government, forgetting their own stance against "American interventionism" during the Pinochet regime. In turn, a few people in the Concertación condemned the Saddam Hussein regime for its human rights abuses.[42] The vast majority sided with the government's decision not to support the United States, at least not without UN backing.

What emerged was a built-in tension between having close relations with the United States on the one hand and sustaining a position of sovereignty that reflected the national and regional mood on the other. In the UN Chile and Mexico took a similar stance, and there was much consultation between the two nations. Chile's strong-minded ambassador to the UN, Juan Gabriel Valdés, took perhaps an overly visible and opinionated position, a bit harsher than the administration wanted. The White House responded by sending Undersecretary for Latin American Affairs Otto Reich to Santiago to try to change the Lagos administration's position, but to no avail.[43] Chile refused to support the war despite the possibility that the United States would retaliate by rejecting the free trade agreement. Stressing its independence, Chile went so far as to propose the postponement of the war for three weeks, only to be rebuffed disdainfully by Washington. This failure of Ambassador Valdés led to his replacement by former Minister Heraldo Muñoz, and Valdés was sent to Buenos Aires. For a while, the White House showed some muscle and threatened a reprisal through the free trade agreement, but U.S. Secretary of State Colin Powell later signaled that Chile had been pardoned, and arrangements were made to forget the incident. Still, Washington signaled its displeasure with Chile by signing the agreement in Miami rather than in Washington, and it was signed by the U.S. trade representative Robert Zoellick rather than Secretary of State Colin Powell. In the final analysis, the treaty looked good, and Chile stood its ground on Iraq. As a small country Chile could not accept a unilateral action by the United States. Besides, "preventive war" as a general doctrine is not a concept that pleases the small players of this world.

Another emerging challenge for Chile is the presence of the Chilean armed forces in Haiti. This could initiate a new stage for Chilean foreign policy and one that might be very difficult. Prior to participating in this police action, Chile had only sent observers to UN missions. The volatile situation in Haiti may transform the "peacekeeping" mission into a "peace-enforcing" one, which is a very different task.

Conclusion

The principal goals of Chilean foreign policy—the insertion of Chile into the global economy, the diversification of trade, and cooperation with the largest powers—have largely been completed, and they constitute some of the principal achievements of the Concertación. However, relations in the region have been complicated by historical conflicts that, along with the current Latin American crisis, have accentuated the differences between the political economy of many of the region's countries and Chile's general strategy for development.

Whereas in the early 1990s, Chile focused on the consolidation of democracy, the last ten years have seen an emphasis on international trade-related issues. Perhaps the stability of the Chilean political situation enabled a focus on an international economic strategy.

Of particular note, in 2002–2003, Chile signed two key free trade agreements, with the United States and with the EU. Although these agreements may not lead to much economic change—despite the claims to the contrary from the Lagos administration—they do constitute a recognition of Chile's international role. It is important to note that the Bush administration signed the agreement despite some disillusionment with Chile's lack of support for U.S. policies toward Iraq in the UN Security Council.

By 2003 and 2004 the domestic political and economic situation began to improve. Politically, there has been a strengthening of Lagos' image and the outlook for the future of the government coalition. Economically, there is renewed optimism as a result of signs of economic reactivation.

Chile's foreign policy, however, has to be placed in the context of the Latin American crisis of the late 1990s. While internally Chile's economy seemed stalled as a result of the Asian crisis and the lack of a strategic push from the administration at a regional level and even beyond, what began to be called the Chilean model gave Chile and the Concertación added international stature. Such stature had seemed unattainable in the early 1990s.

Overall, at the international level there are several clouds on the horizon, notwithstanding the success of the Chilean economic model. The main challenges for Chile's foreign policy arise from within the region. While the strategy for Chile's global economic insertion is progressing well, there are unpredictable factors within its own region that could emerge as problems. Potential sources of unrest are the instability in Argentina, the continuing demands from Bolivia for an outlet to the sea, or even the smaller but persistent troubles with Peru. At a larger level, the political and economic crisis in South America creates an uncertain context for Chilean foreign policy in the region.

Notes

1. "La tercera vía y sus tareas en el mundo global. Cumbre de Líderes Progresistas," London, July 12, 2003, http://www.presidencia.cl.

2. For a critique from an anti-globalization view, see Nira Reyes Morales, "Mito y realidades del modelo chileno," *Le Monde Diplomatique,* November 2002 (Spanish-language edition).

3. For dilemmas of Chilean foreign policy at the beginning of the democratic regime in the 1990s, see Alberto van Klaveren, "Continuidad y cambio en la política exterior chilena," in *Argentina y Chile: ¿Desarrollos paralelos?* ed. Torcuato Di Tella (Buenos Aires: Grupo Editor Latinoamericano, 1997); for a general overview of Chilean foreign policy in the 1990s, see Joaquín Fermandois, "Una década de transformaciones: relaciones exteriores de Chile, 1988–1998," in Eve Rimoldi de Ladmann, ed., *Política exterior y tratados. Argentina, Chile y MERCOSUR* (Buenos Aires: Ciudad Argentina, 1999).

4. One internationalist and officials of successive Concertación governments have used this terminology. Alberto van Klaveren, "América Latina: hacia un regionalismo abierto," in *América Latina en el mundo,* ed. Alberto van Klaveren (Santiago: Los Andes, Prospel, 1997).

5. In this case, a Latin American tribunal had awarded land to Argentina in Laguna del Desierto, in the far south. Although the tribunal conceded all the disputed territory to Argentina, the whole problem was a moot issue by 2000. Early that year, Chile and Peru agreed to resolve certain aspects of the 1929 Peace Treaty (of the 1879–1883 War of the Pacific). Again, there was not much uproar in the Chilean press or the Congress about the agreement.

6. For a new assessment of the interplay between internal and external factors in Chilean foreign policy at the end of the twentieth century, see José A. Morandé, "Chile: The Invisible Hand and Contemporary Foreign Policy," in *Latin American and Caribbean Foreign Policy,* ed. Frank O. Mora and Jeanne A. K. Hay (Lanham, Md.: Rowman & Littlefield, 2003).

7. For an analysis of the early foreign policy of the Lagos administration, see David R. Mares and Francisco Rojas A., *The United States and Chile: Coming in from the Cold* (New York: Routledge, 2001), 111–21.

8. Presidencia de la República de Chile, "Palabras del presidente de la república en reunión con el cuerpo diplomático," March 29, 2000, http://www.presidencia.cl.

9. Manfred Wilhelmy, "Analyzing Chilean Foreign Relations," *Latin American Research Review* 17, no. 1 (1982): 244–54.

10. Banco Central de Chile, *Síntesis estadística de Chile, 1997–2001* (Santiago: Banco Central de Chile, 2002). This summary has been my main statistical source. For a study of recent trends, see Rodrigo Vergara, "Reformas, crecimiento y desaceleración: lecciones del caso chileno," *Estudios Públicos* 91 (Winter 2003): 127–52.

11. For a vivid counterpoint between Minister of Economy Alvaro García and an economist close to a liberal think tank, Juan Andrés Fontaine, see *El Mercurio*, July 5, 1998.

12. *El Mercurio*, February 9, 2003.

13. *El Mercurio,* September 18, 2000.

14. See *El Mercurio,* January 26, 2002, on an inconclusive meeting between the Chilean and American delegations.

15. Mares and Rojas, *United States and Chile,* 118.

16. Dominique Hachette, "La reforma comercial," in Larraín and Vergara, op. cit., 295–340.

17. Jorge Calbucura, "El precio del modelo: la enajenación del territorio mapuche," *Rocinante* March (2004): 14–15.

18. "La pesca y el acuerdo con la UE," *El Mercurio,* April 30, 2002.

19. For a general report on the negotiation process, see *El Mercurio*, May 5, 2002.

20. Cited in *Diplomacia* 92, July–September 2002.

21. Romano Prodi, "Un paso fundamental para la consolidación de las relaciones entre Chile y la Unión Europea," *Diplomacia* 92 (July–September 2002): 357–99.

22. Arturo Fontaine, "Sobre el pecado original de la transformación capitalista chilena," in *El desafío neoliberal: el fin del tercermundismo en América Latina,* ed. Barry B. Levine (Bogotá: Editorial Norma, 1992).

23. For an early assessment, see Felipe Larraín and Juan E. Coeymans, "Efectos de un acuerdo del libre comercio entre Chile y Estados Unidos," *Cuadernos de Economía* 94 (December 1994).

24. Joseph Ramos and Alfie Ulloa Urrutia, "El tratado de libre comercio entre Chile y Estados Unidos," *Estudios Internacionales* 36, no. 141 (April–June 2003): 45–68; *El Mercurio*, August 1, 2003.

25. *El Mercurio*, November 30, 2002. For an anti-globalization point of view, see Marcel Claude and Rodrigo Pizarro, "TLC Chile–Estados Unidos o los adoradores del significado," *Le Monde Diplomatique,* January–February 2003.

26. Manfred Wilhelmy and Rosa María Lazo, "La política multilateral de Chile en Asia-Pacífico," *Estudios Internacionales* 30, no. 117 (January–March 1997).

27. Pilar Armanet, Pilar Alamos, and Luz O'Shea, *Las relaciones de Chile con los organismos multilaterales de la Cuenca del Pacífico* (Santiago: Instituto de Estudios Internacionales, 1996).

28. *El Mercurio*, May 26, 2003.

29. Presidencia de la República de Chile, "Cumbre de MERCOSUR, Asunción, June 18, 2003," http://www.presidencia.cl.

30. *El Mercurio*, July 21, 2003.

31. See critical comments by an observer close to the Concertación in Eugenio Tironi, "Condiciones de ingreso al MERCOSUR," *El Mercurio*, October 1, 2000.

32. Felipe Larraín, "¿Latinoamericanismo fiscal?" *El Mercurio*, October 8, 2002; *Financial Times*, reproduced in *El Diario*, October 6, 2002.

33. *El Mercurio,* September 3, 2000. María Teresa Infante, "Tratado minero en-

tre Chile y Argentina. Una visión global," *Estudios Internacionales* 34, no. 135 (July–September 2001): 22–42.

34. This treaty was the final peace treaty of the Pacific War (1879–1883), which Chile had fought against Peru and Bolivia. The treaty gave back to Peru the Tacna province but not the province of Arica, which Chile retained. It further stated that Chile was required to ask for Peru's permission before giving away to a third party (that is, Bolivia) any territory that had formerly belonged to Peru.

35. Sometimes they provoke nationalistic responses in Chile too. See Sergio Villalobos, "Visita del presidente del Perú," *El Mercurio,* August 1, 2002.

36. Editorial, *El Mercurio*, May 19, 2002. Peru's official view appears in an interview Peru's foreign minister gave to the Chilean press, *El Mercurio*, February 16, 2003.

37. See the interview with Consul Pérez in *El Mercurio*, August 11, 2002. For a Bolivian view, see Ramiro Orías Arredondo, "La diplomacia del gas boliviano: integración energética y geopolítica en la región," *Estudios Internacionales* 135 (July–September 2001).

38. *El Mercurio*, April 21, 2002.

39. *El Mercurio*, March 11, 2002.

40. *El Mercurio*, April 11, 2003.

41. The park, which is privately owned, is an attempt by a foreign capitalist to prevent the economic exploitation of a vast area and to protect its fragile ecology. Critics of this effort claim that it undermines the security of Chile.

42. Joaquín Fermandois, "¿Morir por Irak?," *El Mercurio*, October 16, 2002.

43. *El Mercurio*, March 10, 2003.

7

Cooperation or Confrontation between the State and the Market?

Social Security and Health Policies

SILVIA BORZUTZKY

In this chapter I present an overview of both the Chilean pension and health-care systems, emphasizing the changes that have taken place during the Frei and Lagos administrations. To begin, I summarize the major reforms enacted by the Pinochet regime in social security and health care; I also trace the evolution of social security and health care since 1990 and examine the Lagos administration's performance in both sectors. Ultimately, the goal is to identify whether the reforms enacted by the Concertación governments are expanding and strengthening the market; I also discuss the role of the state in these areas. Finally, I explore the extent to which social security and health policies have dealt with the great inequalities that have always plagued Chilean society and that were made much worse by the Pinochet regime, which strengthened the application of the market economic model.

Both the social security and the health-care systems were substantially modified by the Pinochet regime. Whereas pensions were fully privatized under a defined-contribution, fully funded system, the health-care system experienced partial privatization and a substantial transformation in terms of both its institutional structure and financing. Most important, these policies were central to the economic model developed by the Pinochet regime, which strengthened the role of the market and the private sector and reduced the socioeconomic functions of the state.

Both the 1980 constitution and the neoliberal economic model embedded in the constitution were the result of the will of General Pinochet and his advisors. Given the nature of the transition and the support for free market economic policies among the new governing elite, the economic structure established during the Pinochet regime has not been substantially modified by any of the

Concertación governments. In fact, the Concertación has avoided changing basic economic and social policies.

During the Lagos administration, the pension system has experienced marginal changes. In contrast, health care has been very much at the forefront of the political discussion due to persistent problems in both the private and the public components of the system. A major bone of contention has been the proposed Plan AUGE (Plan de Acceso Universal con Garantías Explícitas, or Guaranteed Universal Health Access Plan). This originally entailed a new form of financing health care for a number of preestablished diseases, as well as a guarantee that those suffering from one of these diseases would receive full and prompt medical attention.

As I argue in the conclusion, it is clear that in the social security area the market has been strengthened and that the changes implemented in the last ten years are geared to benefit the middle- and upper-income groups while reinforcing existing socioeconomic inequalities. In terms of health care, the picture is more complex, since the Concertación governments found a sector that was starving for resources and for a serious and coherent reform. Here, the success of the Lagos administration hinges on the funding for their newly created Plan AUGE. Although the plan was designed to eliminate old inequities, AUGE is creating new ones. In the new two-tiered system, the critical distinction is whether the disease is or is not covered by AUGE. The future of the health-care system also hinges on the willingness of the public sector to increase its financial commitment to health care. But in health care, as elsewhere, the administration seems to be driven more often than not by a market logic that emphasizes efficiency, autonomy, and competitiveness rather than the overall improvement of the health-care system.

Social Security Policies

Since its inception in 1924, the social security system, structured around a common fund system, expanded in a very amorphous and unique form. By 1973 it covered about 75 percent of the population through more than six hundred different funds and massive legislation full of privileges and special benefits to those interest groups that could exercise political or economic power.

In the case of Chile, the "massification" of social security benefits[1] was followed by a massification of privileges and exemptions that totally distorted the basic notions of equality and universality that should be at the core of a social security system. As a result, the system was very expensive for the state, the insured, and the employers. Moreover, the majority of the population received insufficient pensions. Attempts to reform the system during the Alessandri and

Frei administrations (1958–1964 and 1964–1970) were frustrated by the power of the interest groups that received sizeable pensions and other benefits.[2]

The 1980 Reform

As is true of Chilean health-care policies, the framework and characteristics of current social security policies were established by the Pinochet regime. The 1980 reform privatized social security and established a fully funded, defined-contribution system. While it is clear that the social security system needed a major reform and that the reform should include the elimination of the privileged pensions, such as pensions based on years of service and the *perseguidoras*, it is not so clear that the system needed the kind of reform implemented by the Pinochet regime. (*Perseguidoras* was a special privileged pension received by high level civil servants. The amount of the pension was equal to the salary received by the person performing the job.) As I have argued elsewhere, the social security reform was a byproduct of the power and ideology sustained by the economic advisors of General Pinochet known as the "Chicago Boys." Their ideology, as developed by Minister José Piñera, the author of the reform, argued that the old system had failed to achieve its goals and that instead of creating a more egalitarian society it had created a system full of privileges and inequalities. The minister proposed and created a system based on the private administration of individual accounts and the elimination of the employer's portion of the social security tax.[3]

The transference of account administration to the private sector involved the creation of a new type of enterprise: the Administradoras de Fondos de Pensiones (Pension Fund Managing Corporations, or AFPs). The AFP is a for-profit entity that charges a commission for the administration of individual accounts. The accounts contain funds from a 10 percent tax paid only by the worker. Pensions, in turn, are provided either directly by the AFP, indirectly through an annuity bought from an insurance company with the funds accumulated in the account, or through a combination of the two. In the case of disability and survivors pensions, the benefit is paid directly by the AFP. As of December 1999, 52.06 percent of retirees had chosen to obtain pensions directly from the AFP, while 39.8 percent had opted for an annuity. Only 1.66 percent had chosen the combined system. In the first case, the pension is determined annually by the AFP, based on the life expectancy of the affiliate and the rate of return of the capital. In the annuity case, the funds are permanently transferred to an insurance company, which determines the amount of the pension, as well as funeral and survivors benefits, if this is what the retiree wants.[4] Thirteen AFPs are operating in the market today.

The new system was compulsory for all the workers who joined the workforce after December 1981, while those already employed could choose between the old and the new systems. It is quite ironic that the military and the police retained their state-financed systems. Clearly, this is an indication that they found the market to be good enough for the rest of the society but not for them.

From an administrative standpoint, the system entailed the disappearance of the old funds and the creation of a unified administrative system under the Instituto de Normalización Previsional. The instituto administers the *bono de reconocimiento,* or recognition bond, which represents the number of years that the insured contributed to the old system. These monies are transferred to the AFP at the time of retirement.

Impact of the Reform: Winners and Losers

The reform has affected the entire society, as well as the state, but not all Chileans have been affected in the same manner. The reform entailed changes in coverage, and there has been a great deal of argument about the extent of the coverage provided by the fully funded, defined-contribution system. In 2001, the Superintendencia de AFPs reported that 59.5 percent of the workforce was currently contributing to the system, while 69.7 percent had made a contribution during the preceding year.[5] Data for February 2003 show a marked decline in coverage since 2001, as the AFP system now covers only 52.5 percent of the economically active population and 2.72 percent is still enrolled in the common fund system. Thus, a total of 55.23 percent of the population is covered by a pension plan, the lowest percentage since 1989 and much lower than the coverage provided by the old system, which covered more than 70 percent of the population.[6] The self-employed who did not have coverage in the past remain outside the system.

Contrary to the expectations created by the framers of the program, the value of the pensions offered by the fully funded, defined-contribution system has not changed dramatically either. The value of an average pension in the fully funded system is 12 percent higher than the value of a pension provided by the common fund system, but in the case of disability pensions, the pension provided by the common fund system is 23 percent higher than the pension provided by the fully funded system.[7] The replacement ratio is 80 percent in the case of old-age pensions and 67.9 percent for those who opt for early retirement.[8]

The fully funded, defined-contribution system has reinforced the gender inequalities that exist in the workplace and in society. To the extent that the value of the pension depends on an employee's wages, years of contributions, and life expectancy after retirement, the pension received by women is markedly lower than the pension received by males. Women spend fewer years in the workforce, receive about 30 percent less than men for comparable jobs, and live longer than men. Two issues are very critical here: (1) the fact that women's pensions are estimated to be between 52 and 76 percent of men's pensions, which condemns many women to poverty;[9] and (2) the fact that many women do not even qualify for a private pension and have to opt for a state-paid minimum pension, which is not only insufficient but also represents an added burden for the state.[10]

The law allows the AFP to charge two different commissions for the administration of the fund. All the AFPs except one charge a fixed commission, which is a percentage of the deposit or of the taxable wages. The commission charged as a percentage of the taxable wages is called the additional commission, and a fraction of this charge is used to pay the premium to the life insurance company to cover the disability and survivor's pensions. Furthermore, if the insured changes from one AFP to another more than twice in the same year, he or she must pay an "exit charge." Most of the AFPs also charge a commission, known as *retiro programado,* for the administration of the pension fund after retirement. Finally, a commission is charged for the administration of the voluntary savings accounts, which are discussed later.[11] The commissions and other charges are high as well as regressive. As a percentage of the average salary, the value of the commissions has decreased from 3.57 percent in 1982 to 2.43 percent in 2003;[12] however, the charges are still quite regressive. For instance, for an insured person with an income of about US$1,609 the administrative cost fluctuates between 25.6 percent and 37.9 percent of the deposit, while the cost for an insured person with an income of US$1,300 fluctuates between 24.1 percent and 30.2 percent of the deposit.[13] The fully funded system has also had a very powerful effect on the owners of AFPs due to the massive transfer of funds from the public to the private sector of the economy. By March 2003, the combined amount of capital accumulated in the hands of the AFPs amounted to 55.77 percent of the gross domestic product (GDP).[14]

The performance of the individual accounts administered by the AFPs has ranged from 29.7 percent in 1991 to –1.1 percent in 1998.[15] Since the inception of the system, the average rate of return has been 10.3 percent.[16]

Regarding the impact on the state, the establishment of the fully funded, defined-contribution system has not reduced the role of the state but has simply changed it. The state continues to have a large involvement since it is responsible for paying the pensions of those who stay in the common fund system; for paying the recognition bond at the time of retirement for those who began in the common fund system and then transferred to the fully funded system; and for paying the minimum pensions, as well as the welfare pensions. The two most expensive items are the recognition bonds, which should diminish over the years, and the minimum pensions, which are expected to increase over the years. The system has produced and will continue to produce a budget deficit of about 4–5 percent of GDP per year.[17]

Major Reforms Undertaken between 1998 and 2003

The Concertación governments, which have ruled Chile since 1990, have been committed to maintaining the system designed by the Pinochet regime. A number of reforms have in many ways strengthened the system while a few new modalities, such as unemployment insurance, multifunds, and voluntary contributions, have been introduced during the Frei and Lagos administrations. The new modalities are based on individual savings and private administration of the funds.

Unemployment Insurance

One of the most interesting modifications recently introduced has been a new form of unemployment insurance. The insurance is based on a system of tripartite contributions that combine individual accounts designed specifically for this purpose with a national solidarity fund. The system covers all workers except domestic workers (who account for 27.9 percent of the economically active female population[18]) and minors. The system provides automatic coverage for all workers who join the labor force after the enactment of the law; it is optional for those who are already employed. The fund is formed with a 0.6 percent tax paid by the worker, a 2.4 percent tax paid by the employer, and a state contribution of about US$9 million per year. The funds go to two different accounts: The worker's entire contribution plus 1.6 percent paid by the employer forms the worker's individual account. The remaining 0.8 percent paid by the employer plus an annual state contribution of US$9.4 million forms the national solidarity fund.

The law distinguishes between two types of benefits: The individual account is used to pay benefits in case of unemployment, regardless of the reason. The benefit paid depends on the amount accumulated in the individual account. The law requires a minimum of a year of contributions, and the benefits are divided into a maximum of five payments of up to 100 percent of earned wages after eleven years of contributions. For those with fewer years of contributions, the benefit amounts to as little as 27 percent of the wages. In the case of temporary workers, the requirement is six months of contributions, and in this case the contributions are paid by the employer only.

The national solidarity fund, on the other hand, is used in cases in which unemployment results from an employer's decision, and it complements the subsidies provided through the individual accounts. The solidarity fund can be used only twice in five years, and the amounts received by the worker are equivalent to up to 50 percent of the wages the first month, decreasing to 30 percent by the fifth month.[19]

The unemployment insurance program is administered by a private, for-profit corporation dedicated only to this task, and the administrator is entitled to charge a commission for the management of the funds. Before adjudicating the administration, the government asked for bids from both national and foreign companies. Ultimately, a conglomerate of AFPs won the bid and will administer the system for ten years. The same institution, known as the Unemployment Insurance Administrator Corporation (Sociedad Administradora del Seguro de Cesantía), has the obligation of paying the benefits. Since the funds belong to the insured, unused funds at the time of the insured's death are part of his or her estate. The system began operation in October 2002. The government and the AFPs expect that within the next ten years the unemployment insurance coverage will be about the same as the coverage provided by the AFPs, and that the fund will amount to about US$3 billion dollars.[20]

Voluntary Contributions

In order to increase national savings, the social security system has included since its inception a system of voluntary contributions. However, the system has been rather restricted and has had a limited impact. Law 19,768 of 2001, which went into effect in March 2002, expanded drastically the extent of the law and the type of financial institutions where these voluntary retirement accounts could be held. Thus, according to the 2001 legislation, workers in both private and public pension systems are allowed to set up voluntary retirement savings accounts. Their goal is to stimulate private savings and to augment the value and replacement rate of pensions. The law also is aimed at reducing government involvement in the system via minimum pensions in hopes of injecting a new dynamism in the capital markets. The contributions are nontaxable (taxes are paid at the time of retirement) and the funds can be deposited either in an AFP, a bank, or a mutual fund; a life insurance company; or an investment fund. As of April 2002, the preferred option has been mutual funds.[21] The new legislation also allows workers to withdraw the funds before retirement. According to Alvaro Clarke, the plan has not actually generated much new savings, but mostly serves as a substitute to other forms of savings. Clarke also argues that given the nature of the tax structure, this new modality benefits mostly high-income groups.

The latest proposal in this area includes the idea of establishing a form of 401K plan. Given the rapid growth of 401K plans in the United States and the assumption that they have served to generate new savings, the Lagos administration has made a serious effort to develop them. The proposed 401K plans will again entail a tripartite effort among workers, employers, and the state. According to its proponents, this modality could be expanded to other areas such as health, and it is expected to benefit lower-income groups.[22] As in the United States, the incentive for employers will be tax benefits, as well as increases in productivity. According to the plan, the workers will be allowed to withdraw a limited amount of money for specific purposes before retirement and to borrow from the account without paying taxes. In order to avoid the kind of problems generated by the Enron scandal, companies will not be allowed to invest in their own shares.[23] All the voluntary contributions and accounts can be combined with the mandatory individual account at the time of retirement.

Multifunds

Until July 2002, the AFP administered two types of funds: Type 1 was open to all the affiliates in the AFP while type 2 was reserved for those contributors within ten years of retirement. New legislation enacted in June 2002 allowed the AFPs to establish at least five different funds. The critical difference between each of these funds is the proportion of the deposit invested in instruments of "variable income" (*instrumentos de renta variable*), which are riskier but have the potential to generate a larger return. The goal of the reform was to create a variety of options for the contributors so they could adjust the investment to their preferences.

As a result, the reform is expected to generate a higher degree of contributor participation in pension decisions. The reform is also expected to generate better service and more transparency on the part of the AFP. Those who are more than fifty-five years old, however, must stay with the traditional plan in order to secure their investments. Each fund is regulated in terms of the proportion of investments going into high-risk instruments. Moreover, each type of fund must pay at least a minimum interest based on the historical performance of the fund.[24] Finally, new legislation has permitted the investment of funds abroad and established new regulations in this area. Administrative fees are quite high, averaging 13 percent of the worker's contributions. Affiliates may change from one fund to another, but the AFP may charge a fee if the person changes more than twice in the same year.[25]

Health Policies

This section outlines the legacy of the Pinochet regime and discusses the current problems and policies affecting the health-care system. Special emphasis is placed on the Plan AUGE, as well as on some of the other reforms proposed by the Lagos administration.

The Legacy of the Pinochet Regime

Although concerns for public health in Chile can be traced back to the origins of the country, it was in the mid-twentieth century that the state began to play a very active role in the provision of health. In 1952, the National Health Service (SNS—Servicio Nacional de Salud) was created. Its functions were to provide medical attention to blue-collar workers and indigents, to supervise the general health conditions of the country, and to be responsible for general preventive medical functions. White-collar workers and civil servants received limited medical services through SERMENA (Employees Medical Services), created in 1960. The entire system was based on the separation between blue- and white-collar workers already existing in the social security system.[26] By 1973, the SNS employed about 120,000 people and provided coverage to about 70 percent of the population.

The Pinochet regime introduced substantial modifications to the Chilean health delivery system. As with social security, the policies were framed by the idea of the subsidiary state, which aimed at withdrawing the state from the provision of social services and regulatory activities and transferring those responsibilities to the individual and to private health-care providers. The policies evolved from the drastic reduction of funds in the early years to a major transformation of the system in 1979.

From an institutional perspective, the most important reform took place in 1979, when the government ordered the replacement of the National Health Service and SERMENA with the National System of Health Services (Sistema Nacional de Servicios de Salud), which provides services in a given geographical area and does not distinguish between blue- and white-collar workers. The system provides benefits on the basis of twenty-seven Autonomous Regional Health Services (Servicios de Salud Autónomos). However, primary-care facilities were transferred to the municipalities, creating a new source of inequality in the nature and extent of the care, given the huge income disparities among the different localities.

The creation in 1981 of ISAPRES (Instituciones de Salud Previsional) signaled the introduction of a new market-oriented approach to health. ISAPRES, modeled after U.S. health maintenance organizations, are "private entities that offer a series of medical insurance and workman's compensation packages in return for a basic 7 percent payroll contribution plus an additional premium of 2–3 percent depending on the size of the package."[27] Until 1998, the government offered a 2 percent subsidy to low-income citizens joining an ISAPRE. The subsidy was later eliminated due to its negative effects on both the public health system and the health of the low-income groups, who often were attracted to the ISAPRES by their propaganda not by the quality or quantity of their services. In fact, for many, the services provided by the ISAPRES were worse than those offered by the public system, and came at a much higher cost.

Thus, since 1981 the Chilean health system has been formed by two main branches: the public and the private system. Employees or workers have the option of depositing the 7 percent mandatory health tax into either the public or the private system. The public system is administered by FONASA (Fondo Nacional de Salud, or National Health Fund), which in turn provides the insured the option of receiving attention, either through one of the public hospitals or through a system of vouchers financed partly by FONASA and partly by the insured. The vouchers allow the insured to get attention from participating physicians and hospitals.

If the insured chooses the private system, the 7 percent goes to the selected ISAPRE, which in turn offers a variety of plans. Depending on the plan chosen by the insured, his or her contribution has to be augmented by at least another 4–7 percent of wages. Given the cost of the system, only 26 percent of the insured receive attention through the private sector; 62 percent through FONASA, and 3 percent through the armed forces and police medical services. The public system is also responsible for the provision of preventive medical services, such as vaccination programs, prevention of contagious diseases, and maintenance of water and sewage services for the entire population.

Concertación Policies: Increasing Health-Care Spending and Regulating the ISAPRES

The Concertación faced a number of critical problems in the health area, including lack of resources, the unregulated and discriminatory actions of the ISAPRES, and the redefinition of the relations between the private and the public health-care sectors. This section examines the actions of the Concertación governments in these three areas.

The Pinochet regime's market legacy was not limited to the administrative reorganization of the health system and the creation of the ISAPRES. The market policies also affected the health sector through a constant reduction of funds. The legacy here was one of insufficient resources, resulting in a poor and decaying infrastructure, poor salaries, lack of equipment, and long wait periods. In view of these problems, a central goal of the Concertación governments has been to increase health-care spending.

In 1990 public health-care spending amounted to $157,616 million while the total spending amounted to $464,136 million. By 2002 public spending had increased to $596,673 and total spending to $1,326,894.[28] Thus, in seven years public spending on health increased by 279 percent, while the total increased by

186 percent.[29] Health spending amounts to 2.9 percent of GDP and 12 percent of total public spending.[30] Of the public health budget, 48 percent is financed through a fiscal subsidy, 33 percent comes from taxes paid by the insured, and 17 percent comes from other sources.[31] Official statistics for 2001 (the most recent year for which there are available data), indicate that per-capita health spending is US$303 per person. Public health spending amounts to 44 percent of total health spending and 12.7 percent of public expenditures, and the cost per person is estimated at US$133. Private health-care spending amounts to 54 percent of total health spending, which is very expensive given the small percentage of people covered by the system. Within the private health sector, private insurance pays for 40.3 percent of the cost and 59.6 is directly paid by the users.[32]

The rapid increase in investments has not translated into a sizeable improvement in services. The public health-care sector continues to be plagued by enormous problems, including poor medical care, long waiting lists, limited services in rural areas, and lack of equipment and medicines. Part of the problem still lies in insufficient resources, as President Lagos has recognized in several speeches,[33] but a major reason for the problems is the inefficiency of the system. For instance, although funds have increased, the number of surgeries performed in the public system fell by 7.1 percent.[34]

Prior to 1990, the ISAPRES were fairly unregulated, and the affiliated workers had to confront a number of problems, such as persistent discrimination against the elderly and women. As a result, only 2.5 percent of the affiliates are sixty-nine years or older and only 31.8 percent of them are women.[35] In other words, the ISAPRES have consistently refused to insure those who for reasons of either gender or age are likely to incur high medical costs. Concertación policies have been implemented to regulate the ISAPRES through the creation of the Superintendencia de ISAPRES. This regulatory organism, established in 1990, has reduced most of the abuses and discriminatory practices of the ISAPRES. Despite the efforts of the government, public perception of the ISAPRES has deteriorated rapidly due to accusations of fraud and discrimination against the elderly and the sick. The worst year for the ISAPRES was 1999, when they lost about 12.2 percent of their affiliates and the industry also registered heavy losses.[36]

Another major bone of contention has been the financial relationships between the ISAPRES and the public system represented by FONASA. In practice, the public system acts as a catchall system, since those affiliated to the ISAPRES can at any time transfer to the public system. However, returning to an ISAPRE is much more difficult. Moreover, it has become common practice for individuals who are subscribing to one of the ISAPRES to seek medical attention in the public sector, either because the ISAPRE does not cover a particular ailment or because of the poor distribution of services provided by the ISAPRES throughout the country.[37] Thus, by the winter of 1998 about 20 percent of those served by the public system were in fact enrolled in and paying fees to an ISAPRE.[38]

Challenges under the Lagos Administration

In spite of the efforts of the Aylwin and Frei administrations, the Lagos presidency has had to confront major challenges in the health area. Some of these challenges are new, such as the need to provide coverage for catastrophic illnesses; and some are longstanding, such as the problem of insufficient funding for the health sector, the redefinition of the relationships between the public and the private sectors, the need to improve the performance of the sector, and the need to reorganize and increase the efficiency of the public health system. The Lagos administration has dealt with all these problems through five different bills. The following sections discuss the creation of a system of protection against catastrophic illnesses, the budget increases, and the Plan AUGE, which in the view of the administration will provide a comprehensive solution to many of the problems afflicting the sector.

Catastrophic Illness

Chileans are living longer. Life expectancy has increased from 54 years in 1952 to 76.7 years in 2002;[39] consequently, the chances of suffering a catastrophic illness have also increased.[40] Until 1999, a major point of criticism of the ISAPRES was the lack of coverage in the case of catastrophic diseases. Since 2000, the ISAPRES have agreed to include a clause in all their contracts providing basic protection in the case of a catastrophic illness.[41] In order to be eligible for this benefit, the insured has to pay an additional fee. The major advantage of the new arrangement is that the benefit does not depend on a specific list of diseases but defines a catastrophic illness in terms of the cost and includes all diseases costing more than the deductible.

Insufficient Funding

Despite the rapid increase in spending, the most critical problem in the health-care system is still insufficient funding. Here the record of the Lagos administration has been one of recognizing the depth of the problem and trying to confront it through renewed funding and organizational changes.

The 7 percent wage tax is insufficient and does not cover the basic needs of either the public or the private system. In the case of the public system, the wage tax covers only about 50 percent of the budget, and the other 50 percent is financed through fiscal subsidies. As I argued previously, the increases in budget allocations for health have turned out to be insufficient. The end result is a system still plagued with problems, including long waiting lists for basic medical attention; lack of basic resources, such as medicines and equipment; and poorly paid personnel.

On the other hand, the private system is expensive and geared to serve only the high-income groups. Thus, in practice, the state system has been left with the task of caring for the poor, the elderly, and the very sick. These groups have high health expenditures and generate small contributions. In order to solve these problems, the Lagos administration has pursued a multidimensional approach that includes budget increases and a comprehensive reform of the system.

Regarding budget increases, President Lagos promised to increase health-care spending focused on the most critical services. Between 2001 and 2003 the health budget increased by about 15 percent. While the budgets for hospitals increased 4 percent, the budget for ambulatory care increased by 14 percent.[42] Between 1999 and 2004 the budget for primary care was doubled.

Plan AUGE

In April 2002, the Ministry of Health announced that it would send to Congress a new plan designed to provide coverage for fifty-six basic diseases, encompassing about 1,600 different diagnoses. The controversial program is called Plan AUGE. It is important to note that *auge* in Spanish means power, dignity, or glory, giving the acronym particular significance. Since the original plan was substantially transformed by Congress, what follows is a discussion of both the Ministry of Health's original plan and what the Chilean Congress finally approved.

The Original Plan

The goal of the plan was to create an integrated health system with a public and a private component. The key to understanding the plan is the notion that the state will ultimately guarantee the comprehensive and speedy treatment of fifty-six different pathologies by both public and private health-care providers. Among the main benefits that the plan was expected to provide were integral maternity care, including a pre- and postnatal subsidy; and care for patients with diabetes, hypertension, epilepsy, HIV/AIDS, cancer, and neurological diseases, among other conditions. Together, these diseases account for about 80 percent of the health-care spending and also about 80 percent of deaths.[43]

I should emphasize that the plan did not involve the provision of new benefits. On the contrary, it involved a new means of financing benefits that both the public and private sectors were already committed to providing but that in practice the public sector could not afford and the private sector often refused to pay for. In fact, what the plan really entails is a set of four guarantees: (1) guaranty of access, which forces both public and private health-care providers to make available the required medical attention for those suffering from one of the preestablished illnesses; (2) guaranty of opportunity, which ensures prompt attention; (3) guaranty of quality, which ensures access to medical attention in the form and conditions established by the law; and (4) financial guaranty that the money is there to pay for the required services and that the insured will never pay more than 20 percent of the expenses.[44] The plan was going to be financed by increasing the value added tax by 0.5 percent and by increasing taxes on alcohol, tobacco, and gasoline.[45]

One of the most controversial features of the plan involved the idea of forming a solidarity fund (*fondo de compensación*) by taking 0.6 percent of the 7 percent health tax paid to the ISAPRES. The monies would be used to finance a maternity fund to cover the pre- and postnatal subsidy paid by the government to women enrolled in both the private and the public system. Thus, the government saw this fund as a mechanism to obtain reimbursement for the maternal subsidy paid to women enrolled in ISAPRES, which accounts for 80 percent of the money spent in the maternal subsidy. The solidarity fund was also expected to provide $15,000 million to $18,000 million (Chilean pesos) to defray part of the cost of AUGE and part of the health-care costs incurred by the older and sicker members of the public sector. The administration argued that the fund would bring about a degree of solidarity and equity in the provision of health care by transferring resources from the upper to the lower income groups, from men to women, and from the healthier to the sicker.

The administration sees AUGE as a critical step in the improvement of public health in Chile. In the words of former Minister of Health Osvaldo Artaza, the plan "entails a commitment to make available to the beneficiaries the infrastructure, the technology, and the personnel needed to satisfy their primary health care needs."[46] The plan, according to its proponents, is a mechanism geared to create a truly universal and integrated health-care system that does not discriminate between low- and high-income patients, since the health-care providers in both the private and public sector must comply with the same regulations and should provide the same type of services.

Opposition to Plan AUGE

Opposition to the program came from many different quarters, including the ISAPRES, the Colegio Médico de Chile, the right-wing political parties, and even members of the government coalition. One of the most vocal opponents of Plan AUGE has been the Colegio Médico de Chile, the Chilean equivalent of the American Medical Association. According to the Colegio Médico, the plan is destined to fail because it is built on the basis of an already bankrupt system. Moreover, they oppose the plan because they perceive it as a way of reducing the government's commitment to the provision of health care and because it entails the establishment of bureaucratic controls on medical decisions and practices in order to contain costs. In fact, the plan assigns protocols to each disease covered, including the types and number of exams that can be ordered and the medicines that can be prescribed.

Physicians have also questioned the logic used in the selection of pathologies included in the plan. For instance, the Chilean Society of Pediatrics and Infant and Adolescent Neurology points out that while the plan covers rare diseases, such as cystic fibrosis (there are only ten to fifteen cases per year), it does not provide any coverage for attention deficit disorder or depression, which together affect about 15 percent of Chilean children and have serious consequences for the educational system and society as a whole. Dr. Tomás Mesa, the association's president, states, "We do not know what criteria were used to select the diseases. We believe that there was a criterion based on cost and incidence, but the scientific societies should have been consulted."[47] The administration's criteria are certainly difficult to understand. For instance, the plan covers depression in women between the ages of twenty and forty-four but not in women more than forty-four years old, who are much more likely to suffer from depression; it covers drug and alcohol dependency only for those between fifteen and twenty-four years of age and psychosis only for those between the ages of fifteen and twenty-nine.[48]

Others see the plan as nothing but a step toward the privatization of the system, since it will force hospitals to compete in the provision of benefits and services and to make the most efficient use of their resources in order to be compensated by the state. Some projections of health-care spending appear to indicate that AUGE will allow the government to reduce health-care spending in the future.[49]

The ISAPRES, for their part, opposed the establishment of the solidarity fund, arguing that it involved an illegal form of taxation. They argued that the administration was establishing a new tax on the middle class and was attempting to destabilize the ISAPRES. They also threatened to take the case to the Constitutional Tribunal if the fund was approved by congress.

The Final Bill

In July 2004, after months of negotiations, the Health Committee of the Chilean Senate approved a compromise bill. In order to obtain the support of the right-wing Alianza por Chile coalition, the administration had to withdraw from the plan the creation of the solidarity fund.[50] According to Minister of Health Pedro

García, the government decided to compromise in order to get support for a bill that otherwise would have died in Congress. García has promised that the government will include the idea of the solidarity fund in the bill that modifies the legal structure of the ISAPRES.[51] The compromise bill also forces the Ministry of Finance to supply the funds needed to implement the program, which the government expected to get from the solidarity fund, as well as the funds that were expected to come from new taxes, since the discussion of this issue was also postponed. The compromise bill calls for guaranteed care for twenty-five diseases in 2005, forty in 2006, and fifty-six in 2007. The bill establishes a 20 percent maximum copayment if the actual cost of the treatment is higher than the estimated government cost. Anything over that 20 percent will be paid either by FONASA or the ISAPRE.[52] The bill also creates a system of pre-judicial mediation in the event of malpractice suits, in order to contain growing concerns over the high cost of damages for medical negligence and also to satisfy at least one of the many demands made by the physicians.[53]

Withdrawing the solidarity fund from the project was a major blow to the government plan. The solidarity fund was not only a key element in the financial strategy of the government, but also a critical component of the plan from the standpoint of equity. Recall that the fund was designed to take monies from the upper-income groups affiliated with ISAPRES and to redistribute those monies among persons considered more vulnerable and in greater need of health-care services: women of child-bearing age, adults over sixty-five years old, and children under two years of age. By approving the plan without the fund, Congress not only protected the interests of the ISAPRES and their subscribers, but also deprived the plan from its redistributive purpose.

The physicians continued opposing the plan but were not nearly as successful as the ISAPRES in their attempts to influence the legislative process.[54] There were two central concerns on their minds: The physicians argued that (1) the plan limits their independence, since the number and type of exams they can order are limited by the diagnosis; and (2) AUGE brings even more inequities to the health-care system because it entails preferential financing for certain types of illnesses while others will remain without adequate financial support. From their standpoint, the elimination of the solidarity fund and the limited number of illnesses covered by the project compromise basic notions of equity and justice.[55]

The physicians opposed without much success the implementation of a pilot plan that began in 2002 and provides guaranteed attention for three ailments: cancer in children; chronic renal failure, and congenital cardiopathies. Once again, they argue that the entire approach forces them to discriminate among their patients, which they consider unethical.[56] It is important to note here that the Colegio Médico has always had a voice in health policies and that they have always favored a large role for the state in the system, while allowing physicians to retain a degree of autonomy and independence.

Another major area of controversy is the financial basis of the reform. Even members of the administration recognized that there was no political support within the government coalition for an increase in the value added tax and that new sources of revenue needed to be identified. In fact, decisions regarding the financial structure of AUGE were also postponed. In the meantime the plan will be financed with general revenues. The approval of the plan without adequate financing creates a major dilemma for the government, which needs to cover not only the cost of the plan, expected to be about US$150 million, but also a US$435 million deficit produced by the recently signed free trade agreements with the United States, the EU, and South Korea,[57] as well as the cost of the program Chile Solidario (another government social program), which will cost about US$150 million.[58] New financial arrangements were also added to the ISAPRE bill still under discussion in the Chilean Congress. The discussion of the ISAPRE bill was slow and controversial, since the government included the solidarity fund and financial provisions for the Plan AUGE in it. The bill was approved by the Congress, after discussion in the Senate, in January 2005. Ultimately the success of the plan will depend on the resources devoted to its implementation, and the action of Congress in creating a plan without the resources required to implement it do not bode well for the future.

Other Health Policies: ISAPRES, the Administrative Reorganization, and the Attempt to Privatize New Hospitals

The government is also pushing for new legislation to deal with the question of the solvency of the ISAPRES and the need to protect the affiliates in cases of bankruptcy. Although this is not a new concern, the need to deal with it has become urgent given the bankruptcy and financial scandals that affected the ISAPRE Vida Plena, which left about 15,000 people without coverage.[59] The new law was approved in April 2005.

Another controversial dimension of the government policy was the decision to privatize new hospitals. The idea of privatizing new hospitals emerged from the lack of government funds to cover the estimated US$600 million per year needed to improve the infrastructure and equipment of hospitals,[60] and the belief that the private sector could administer them more efficiently.[61] The plan developed by the Ministry of Public Works, which had scant credibility given a series of financial scandals in 2003, aspired to build five new hospitals over the next twenty years. The ministry intended to use the same model that has been applied in Chile to the construction of new roads and prisons, under which the private enterprise that undertakes the construction of the project is also in charge of its administration. As with Chilean highways, the building company would charge a "toll" for the use of the hospital facilities. In the words of a ministry spokesperson, "The profits for the company responsible for the construction and administration of the facility will result from the 'toll' charged to patients for the use of the facilities and clinical services. To the extent that these are profitable projects, based on users' fees, the government can rely on private funds for the construction of new facilities."[62]

Opposition to the privatization of new hospitals was immediate and massive. The Colegio Médico reacted by arguing that the big losers in this scheme were all the taxpaying Chileans who would be forced not only to make their required contributions to the health system, but also to pay a tariff for the use of the facilities. The policy was expected to have a particularly negative impact on those affiliated with the public health sector, who would be forced to pay for the use of the public hospitals.[63] Most important, the plan was immediately rejected by members of the government coalition. Socialist and Christian Democratic members of the health committees of the Chamber of Deputies and the Senate expressed anger and disdain, arguing that the government had produced the project "behind their backs." In fact, after less than two weeks of heated discussion, President Lagos ordered his ministers to lower the project's profile and to present the idea only as a preliminary study, although the president had publicly announced the model just a few weeks earlier. As one would expect, the right-wing coalition supported the idea in Congress.[64]

While the idea of charging a fee for the use of hospitals might have been abandoned, the idea of introducing more autonomy and competition among hospitals has not. Policy makers in the Ministry of Finance, for instance, have argued that the process of granting autonomy to the hospitals should continue in order to lower costs and enable better and more efficient use of resources.

Finally, the Lagos administration has embarked on a massive administrative reorganization of the health-care system, which would include the establishment of a new supervisory bureaucracy charged with controlling both the private and the public components. The administration is also drawing up proposals to better integrate public and private health-care facilities by establishing an integrated network that will cover the entire country.

Conclusions

The situation in the pension system is quite clear. The Pinochet regime transformed Chile's social security program into a compulsory, private pension system with a subsidiary role for the state. The state exercises this role through the provision of minimum and welfare pensions, as well as the provision of pensions for the military, the police, and those who opted to stay in the common fund system. The minimum and welfare pensions are there to maintain at least a veneer of social/state commitment to the social security system.

Policies enacted since the mid-1990s have certainly strengthened the role of the market through the introduction of new savings mechanisms administered by the private sector and controlled by the state. These reforms are geared toward increasing savings among the middle- and upper-income groups, while introducing more accountability and transparency into the system.

To the extent that the Lagos administration, like all the other Concertación governments, is determined to maintain the fully funded, defined-contribution pension system, we are going to see a continuation of some of the problems that I have highlighted elsewhere, including lower pensions for women than for men; a very high and regressive system of commissions; and the accumulation of a large amount of capital in the hands of the AFPs. By and large these policies have been designed to serve the interests of the upper and upper middle classes, but they have not increased the capacity of the lower income groups to save for the future.

The Concertación governments in general, and the Lagos administration in particular, are determined to maintain the market model while reducing poverty. In the area of social security, the main problem that this administration and others in the future will face is the dramatic reduction of coverage that has resulted from the implementation of the fully funded, defined-contribution system. The challenge here is for the policy makers to find ways of expanding coverage to its pre-1980 levels in order to guarantee a minimum pension for at least 70 to 75 percent of the population.

Health policies and the provision of health benefits are at the core of the social functions of the state. Any assessment of Concertación policies has to take into account the magnitude of the problems experienced by the system in 1990. General Pinochet's policies created an unregulated, discriminatory system of private health insurers and reduced the quality of the services provided by the public sector through dramatic budget reductions. Budget increases in the last ten years have not produced the desired results, and the Lagos administration has been faced with problems that require not only more resources, but also conceptual changes. These changes are seen in the Plan AUGE.

What is important to note here is that the goal of Plan AUGE was not to create a "kinder" or "gentler" health-care system, but to create a new financial structure and to guarantee that all patients affected by one of the illnesses included under the plan receive the same standard of care. Thus, benefits will depend on the nature of the disease, not on the patient's affiliation with a private or a public insurer. In its original form the plan had the potential of achieving a degree of integration and equity through the solidarity fund, but the amendments introduced in Congress deprived the plan of its compensatory mechanism. Moreover, Congress did not create new sources of funding, which entirely undermined the plan's financial objectives.

In addition, the entire plan is built upon a discriminatory element, since access to and quality of care depend on the type of illness experienced by the insured. In an environment of already very scarce resources and without new funds to satisfy the requirements of the plan, the results of this approach are easily predictable: Those who are experiencing other types of diseases will not only be deprived of the quality care guaranteed by AUGE, but will actually receive worse care than they would have received in the past. A study done during the pilot phase of AUGE confirms that patients experiencing non-chronic renal failure, not covered by the plan, had much longer waiting periods than patients with chronic renal failure, which is covered by AUGE. The reason is simple: While the number of physicians serving the selected patients did not increase, the demands on them increased, given the nature of the protocols required for an AUGE patient. In other words, the AUGE patients are using more resources while the overall resources have not increased.[65] One can expect this to happen throughout the system. This paradox will result not only in longer wait periods, but also in a scarcity of other resources, such as access to radiological exams, laboratory tests, and other services.

Was AUGE inspired by a need to ration resources? Was the purpose to control and change the way in which medicine is practiced in Chile? Does AUGE limit the freedom of physicians to choose appropriate treatment once a diagnosis is made? The answer to all these questions is yes. Will it bring about better health care for all? No, not unless the public sector is willing to increase health spending. Thus, the arguments presented by the Colegio Médico are well founded. AUGE will force physicians to discriminate between AUGE and non-AUGE patients because, when treating AUGE patients, they have to adhere to strictly regulated, preestablished protocols that demand comprehensive and speedy care. This type of regulation certainly has the potential to save money, but it also has the potential to create a two-tiered, bureaucratized style of medicine. If fully implemented, AUGE will change the way in which medicine is practiced, as well as the role of physicians in the process.

There is no doubt either that the reform aims at creating autonomous and competitive hospitals. While the administration had to give up its plan to privatize the management of new hospitals and to charge users' fees in the new facilities, it has not given up its plan to give more autonomy to existing hospitals and to force them to compete with each other. The government's proposed changes in health-care administration will give hospitals the power to administer their own resources and to compete, thus reducing their dependency on the fiscal budget. AUGE creates incentives for the hospitals to compete by selling AUGE services to insurance companies and ISAPRES.[66] Hospitals will also compete for AUGE patients, who offer a guaranteed payment, and will have no incentive to care for non-AUGE patients.

The most critical issue here is funding. AUGE is creating a two-tiered health-care system, and so far the notion that AUGE should entail a new form of financing health has not come to pass. If projections about future health spending with AUGE in place are true, the plan will reduce fiscal involvement in the health area.

Here again we see a socialist government pursuing policies that are guided by notions of efficiency not equity. But because this is a socialist government, policy makers appear to be trying to walk a fine line between two opposite goals and values: the neoliberal logic and the need to improve health care. The neoliberal logic calls for efficiency, competitiveness, and privatization, which are at the core of the new policies. On the other hand, there is a well-recognized need to improve basic health services for the majority of the people, to solve the financial and administrative problems that plague the public hospitals in Chile, and to better coordinate the private and public sectors.

In the final analysis, an examination of the health policies produces the picture of an administration that would like to improve health-care delivery without spending the required resources. The weakness of this commitment was seen clearly in the administration's willingness to compromise on the most critical aspects of AUGE during the congressional debates. To the extent that Concertación governments are determined to continue market-oriented policies and that the right-wing alliance has a veto power in Congress, the market will prevail, despite the needs of Chilean citizens. Moreover, projected reductions in health spending resulting from the implementation of AUGE only confirm that the government's aim is to continue the process of disengagement, and that costs for the insured will increase while benefits will decrease. In brief, although these policies have been presented as aiming toward the provision of comprehensive health coverage, they are ultimately geared to reducing the functions of the state in the area and creating a two-tiered health system.

It is also clear that the Concertación policies have not been geared to ameliorate the very large income gap that exists in Chile and that, in fact, many of the policies have reinforced the inequalities that exist in Chilean society. It should come as no surprise that, although poverty has been dramatically reduced by the Concertación governments, income distribution appears to be slightly worse than it was during the Pinochet years. For instance, data comparing income distribution between 1987 and 1998 show "that inequality has increased slightly since 1994; the Gini coefficient decreased between 1987 and 1994, but increased again, returning to its 1987 level in 1998 (O.5465 in 1998)."[67] According to this same study, the income of the top 1 percent of the population increased from 12.02 in 1987 to 13.22 percent of gross national product (GNP) in 1998.[68]

Social policies are undoubtedly one of the factors that influence income inequality. As I have shown, social security policies have reinforced the inequities produced by the market. In health policy, the sizeable increases in health spending are probably the most important government contribution to reducing health inequities. Thus, AUGE seems to be eliminating some forms of inequities while creating new ones.

In conclusion, while in the social security area the state continues to reinforce the market even twenty-four years after the reform was implemented, in the health area there is a clear preference for market-oriented solutions to the numerous problems affecting the sector. As Karl Polanyi argued, "The road to the free market was opened and kept open by an enormous increase in continuous centrally organized and controlled interventionism."[69] In the name of the market, the Chilean state continues to intervene in the provision of both health care and pensions.

Notes

1. This term was coined by Carmelo Mesa-Lago in his pathbreaking book, *Social Security in Latin America: Pressure Groups, Stratification, and Inequality* (Pittsburgh: University of Pittsburgh Press, 1978).

2. For a detailed discussion of the problems see Silvia Borzutzky, *Vital Connections: Politics, Social Security, and Inequality in Chile* (Notre Dame: Notre Dame University Press, 2002), chaps. 2–5.

3. Ibid., chaps. 6 and 7.

4. Asociación de Administradoras de Fondos de Pensiones (AAFP), *Serie de Estudios,* No. 8 (June 2000), 1–2.

5. Superintendencia de Administradoras de Fondos de Pensiones (SAFP), *El sistema chileno de pensiones*, 5th ed. (Santiago: SAFP, 2002), 121.

6. Ibid., 122. Data for 2003 obtained from SAFP, "Estadísticas principales," 2003, 1.

7. SAFP, "Boletín estadístico mensual," 2001, 199.

8. AAFP, "Calidad de las pensiones que entregan las AFP muestra eficiencia del sistema," *Serie de Estudios* 17 (Sept 2001): 1–3.

9. Alberto Arenas de Mesa and Verónica Montecinos, "The Privatization of Social Security and Women's Welfare: Gender Effects of the Chilean Reform," *Latin American Research Review* 34, no. 3:7–38.

10. Fabio Bertranou and Alberto Arenas de Mesa, eds., *Protección Social pensiones y género en Argentina, Brasil y Chile* (Santiago: Oficina Internacional del Trabajo, 2003).

11. SAFP, *Sistema chileno de pensiones,* 92–93.

12. SAFP, "Estadísticas principales," 2003, 9.

13. SAFP, "Boletín estadístico mensual," no. 148, December 1998, 3, 28.

14. SAFP, "Estadísticas principales," 2003, 5.

15. This is an average for all the AFPs.

16. SAFP, "Estadísticas principales," 2003, 7.

17. Borzutzky, *Vital Connections,* chap. 7.

18. Canadian International Development Agency, "INC Gender Profile: Chile." February 2002, www.acdi-cida.gc.ca/cida_ind.nsf/0/8fc0e492cd4f032385256bf20067d924?OpenD.

19. SAFP, "Seguro de Cesantía," www.safp.cl/seguro.

20. AAFP, "Serie de Estudios," no. 22, March 2002, 1.

21. Alvaro Clarke, "Desafíos para estimular el ahorro voluntario en Chile," unpublished manuscript, May 2002.

22. Ibid.

23. *Estrategia Worldwide,* June 17, 2002, www.estrategia.cl/histo/200206/17/valores/cuatroci.htm.

24. SAFP, *Sistema chileno de pensiones,* 173–78.

25. Barbara Kritzer, "Recent Changes to the Chilean System of Individual Accounts," prepared for the Division of Program Studies, Office of Research, Evaluation, and Statistics, Office of Policy, Social Security Administration, available from www.ssa.gov/policy/docs/ssb/v64n4/v64n4p66.html.

26. René Merino, "Desarrollo histórico y visión futura de la salud in Chile," in *Síntomas del sistema de salud chileno, su diagnóstico y tratamiento,* ed. Rafael Caviedes et al. (Santiago: Ciedess, 2002), 17–32.

27. Brian Cartin, "The Effectiveness of the Reform," in *Do Options Exist? The Reform of Pensions and Health Care Systems in Latin America,* ed. María Amparo Cruz-Saco and Carmelo Mesa-Lago (Pittsburgh: University of Pittsburgh Press, 1999), 210.

28. All amounts in Chilean pesos. One U.S. dollar equals about six hundred pesos.

29. "Reforma a la salud: ¿dónde están los usuarios?" *Libertad y Desarrollo*, Temas Públicos, No. 578, May 17, 2002, p. 5, www.lyd.com.

30. "Gasto fiscal en salud: más recursos y menos resultados," *Diario Estrategia,* 26 Junio 2003: 1–2.

31. Pan American Health Organization, "Sistema Regional de Datos Básicos de Salud—Peril de Salud de PAFS 2001—Chile," pp. 11–12, www.paho.org/spanish/sha/prflchi.htm.

32. Organización Mundial de la Salud, "Core Health Statistics," www3.who.int/whosis/country/indicators.cfm?country=CHL&language=spanish.

33. See for instance, Ricardo Lagos, State of the Nation speeches for 2001, 2002, and 2003. All speeches are given on May 21 of the relevant year.

34. "Gasto fiscal en salud," *Diario Estrategia.*

35. It is important to note that 10.2 percent of the Chilean population is more than sixty years old.

36. *El Mercurio* online edition, May 29, 2000, www.elmercurio.cl; Superintendencia de Institutos de Salud Previsional, "Annual Statistics," www.sisp.cl/estd/e-sintes.

37. Borzutzky, *Vital Connections,* 237.

38. *La Tercera* online edition, September 1, 1998, www.latercera.cl.

39. Organización Mundial de la Salud,"Core Health Statistics."

40. María Eugenia Salazar, "Las enfermedades catastróficas y su cobertura," in Caviedes et al., *Síntomas del sistema de salud chileno*, 119–30, see esp. 109.

41. Ibid.; Superintendencia de ISAPRES circular 59.

42. *El Mercurio* online edition, February 10, 2003, Diario. "Salud se impone duras metas para 2003." elmercurio.com/resp.asp?id=298773&rep=298.

43. Ministerio de Salud, "Plan Auge," www.minsal.cl/ici/info.asp?cbc=102&rela175-169.

44. See Law 19966, Article 4.

45. The tax on hard liquor was going to increase from 27 to 28 percent, while the tax on wine and beer was expected to increase from 15 to 18 percent. Taxes on cigarettes and cigars were also going to increase to 61 percent, while a new tax on diesel was going to be levied. Ministerio de Salud, "Financiamiento del Sistema AUGE," www.minsal.cl/ici/info.asp?cbc=102&rela=175-166.

46. Osvaldo Artaza Barrios, "Mensaje del Ministro de Salud a los médicos de Chile," *EMol, El Mercurio Online,* January 2003, www.emol.com/noticias/documentos/artaza.asp.

47. Victor Hugo Durán, "Médicos critican baja cobertura mental del Auge," *El Mercurio,* February 4, 2003, www.emol.com/noticias/deportes/detalle/detalle_diario.asp?.idnoticia+010402200300.

48. Victor Hugo Durán "Nuevo boicot médico contra el plan AUGE," *El Mercurio,* February 1, 2003, www.emol.com/noticias/deportes/detalle/detalle/_diario,asp?idnoticia+010102200300.

49. "Estado posee recursos necesarios para financiar el Plan AUGE," *Diario Estrategia,* August 5, 2002, www.sii.cl/SIIPRENSA/2002/0805/11.htm.

50. Consejo Regional Santiago del Colegio Médico de Chile, "Las Isapres eliminaron 'su piedra en el zapato,'" www.medicosdesantiago.cl/noticia.php?num=374.

51. *El Mostrador* online edition, "AUGE, Minsal justifica exclusión de fondo de compensación, May 12, 2004, www.elmostrador.cl/modulos/noticias/constructor/detalle_noticia.asp?id_noticia=13.

52. *El Mostrador* online edition, "Senado aprobó en general el plan AUGE" and "Alianza retira disputada indicación del plan AUGE," May 19, 2004, and July 12, 2004, www.elmostrador.cl/modulos/noticias/constructor/detalles_noticias.asp??id_noticia=13.

53. *El Mercurio* online edition, "Comisión de Salud despacha el AUGE," July 16, 2004, http://diario.elmercurio.com/2004/07/16/nacional/portada/noticias/E1B)1DB8-0F22-4CA.

54. Consejo Regional Santiago, "Las Isapres eliminaron su 'piedra en el zapato.'"

55. *El Mostrador* online edition, "Senado aprobó en general el plan AUGE."

56. Carlos Villaroel, president of the Colegio Médico, argued, "Nobody can force us to discriminate among our patients. We are not going to accept it. If the plan becomes law it will be 'dead letter' because we are not going to obey it. If this means sanctions we are going to confront them and we are going to lead a movement of civil disobedience against unjust laws." Durán, "Nuevo boicot médico contra el plan AUGE."

57. The deficit is the result of the reduction in tariffs entailed in the agreements.

58. Nelly Yanez, "Lagos arremete contra quienes dudaron del TLC," *El Mercurio* online edition, May 29, 2003, http://diario.elmercurio.com/rep.asp?id=335540&rep=298.

59. Mauricio Campusano, "Lagos insta al congreso a acelerar la reforma de la salud, *El Mercurio* online edition, April 9, 2003, www.emol.com/noticias/todas/detalle/detalle_noticia.asp?idnoticia=109408.

60. The deficit in this area is estimated to be about US$450 million. See "Concesión de hospitales: el costo de la ideología," *Libertad y desarrollo*, Temas Públicos, no. 635, July 18, 2003, www.lyd.com.

61. Others estimate that the cost could amount to US$120 million per year.

62. Victor Hugo Durán, "Las razones del MOP para entregar administración hospitalaria a privados," *El Mercurio* online edition, July 6, 2003, http://diario.elmercurio.com/rep.asp?id=348214&rep=298.

63. Ibid.

64. Victor Hugo Durán, Polémica desata ingreso privado en la administración de hospitales," *El Mercurio* online edition, July 7, 2003, http://diario.elmercurio.com/repasp?id=348569&rep=298; Durán, "Cómo se cayó la concesión hospitalaria," *El Mercurio* online edition, July 8, 2003, http://diario.elmercurio.com.rep.asp?id=348951&rep=298.

65. Fernando González F., "Implementación del Plan AUGE en pacientes con IRC," *Revista del Colegio Médico de Chile* 131 (2003): 545–51. It is also interesting that the plan covers only patients with chronic renal failure, while excluding those who need acute care.

66. Interview by the author with Jaime Crispi, Santiago, June 2003.

67. Alberto Valdés and Norman Hicks, "Pobreza y distribución del ingreso en una economía de alto crecimiento" in Rosita Camhi, ed., *Chile sin pobreza: un sueño posible* (Santiago, Fundación Miguel Kast, Fundación Libertad y Desarrollo, 2003), 110.

68. Ibid.

69. Karl Polanyi, *The Great Transformation: The Political and Economic Origin of Our Times* (Boston: Beacon Press, 1944), 140.

Conclusion

Coping with the General's Long Shadow on Chilean Democracy

ALDO C. VACS

As President Ricardo Lagos prepared for his July 2004 formal visit to the United States, he expected that the meeting with President George W. Bush would give him the opportunity to display his administration's accomplishments before Chilean and international audiences. The encounter at the White House was seen as an occasion to celebrate the bilateral free trade agreement signed six months earlier and to highlight the significant role played by a politically stable and economically sound Chile as a Latin American partner of the United States. To Lagos' chagrin, however, a few days before his departure for Washington, D.C., revelations about a financial scandal featuring General Augusto Pinochet overshadowed the anticipated festivity. A U.S. Senate report accused the Riggs Bank (a U.S. bank) of violating anti–money laundering regulations by helping General Pinochet to hide millions of dollars in deposits. The report forced President Lagos and other members of his administration to address a new set of charges against the former dictator and contributed to an intensification of an already uncomfortable domestic political situation created by a Chilean court ruling declaring Pinochet competent to stand trial for human rights abuses.[1] Inevitably, the focus of attention shifted away from what Lagos and his Concertación partners expected would be an upbeat political event, concentrating instead on the new accusations of misdeeds involving Pinochet. Once again, the ghost of the authoritarian past returned to haunt a Chilean democratic administration and served as an untimely reminder that the legacy of Chile's authoritarian regime has not yet been fully confronted nor effectively dealt with.

Twenty-five years after Pinochet's electoral defeat, Chile's political system and civil society are still coping with the general's long shadow and attempting to overcome some key negative sequels of his dictatorship. This book represents a significant attempt to analyze Chile's recent political, social, and economic evolution and to assess to what extent the post-authoritarian administrations, especially the Lagos presidency—the first one led by a socialist since the end of the dictatorship in 1989—have dealt with this troubling legacy while trying to promote the consolidation of an authentic democracy. The authors offer a critical and balanced evaluation of the progress made in this direction by successive civilian Concertación administrations, while carefully examining their shortcomings in different ambits. In order to carry out this undertaking, they examine the impact of the stances and policies espoused by the Concertación administrations on the restructuring of Chile's political and party systems, the evolution of civilian-military relations, the treatment of the human rights question, the transformation of church-state relations, the formulation and implementation of a new foreign strategy, the handling of the market economy, and the management of the inherited social security and health programs.

Patricio Navia's chapter analyzing the evolution of Chile's current two-party system and the chances of reemergence of a three-way split does not arrive at a definitive conclusion about the future of Chile's political landscape. However, it does highlight the tensions affecting the current system, and it helps us understand the relative rise of political apathy among Chilean citizens, the concomitant decline in political participation, and the softening impact on political competition of the broad consensus on the preservation of the free market economic model.

Gregory Weeks' study of the course of civilian-military relations since 1990, with its particular emphasis on the Lagos years, suggests that although progress has been made in redirecting these relations in a more democratic direction by trimming military autonomy, there still are important legal and political constraints on the capacity and willingness of elected officials to assert civilian supremacy over the armed forces.

Elizabeth Lira's examination of the treatment of the human rights question since the return to democracy highlights the progress made by Concertación administrations in uncovering the truth about the dictatorship's violations and abuses, in seeking to protect civil rights, and in offering reparation to the victims and their relatives. She also indicates, however, that domestic political divisions and confrontations over the nature of the dictatorship have led to a vacillating approach that has prevented the resolution of the human rights issue in a way that would allow final closure or satisfy either side of the political spectrum.

The analysis of church-state relations in William Lies' chapter sheds an interesting light on the recent evolution of this relationship. It focuses on the transformation of the church's role from that of a key adversary of the authoritarian regime to a strong opponent of several legal, educational, and health initiatives of the democratic administrations that the church sees as contradicting Catholic doctrine.

In his chapter, Joaquín Fermandois argues that since 1990 the foreign policy approach followed by the three successive Concertación administrations has shown a remarkable continuity. He ascribes this continuity to the enduring consensus among politicians on the preservation of the free market and trade liberalization economic model. Other factors are a nationalistic emphasis on Chile's sovereignty and independence and the favorable international perception of the economic policies and political orientation followed by the post-Pinochet democratic leaders, particularly among the developed countries.

In examining the economic policies adopted by the Concertación, Lois Hecht Oppenheim notes that trade policy has become a cornerstone of Concertación economic policy and that the coalition's policy of negotiating trade agreements at all levels differs from the unilateral approach to trade during the Pinochet era. Despite this innovation, she concludes that although changes have been introduced in the economic model implemented under Pinochet, these alterations are not significant enough to represent a transformation of the general free market export-led strategy and that nothing indicates that there will be significant shifts in this regard in the future.

Finally, Silvia Borzutzky compares the social security and health policies pursued by the Pinochet regime and by the Lagos administration. She contends that the emphasis on free market solutions and privatization approaches continues to predominate not only in the case of widely supported programs such as the privatized retirement system, but even in cases such as the provision of health services where the market-oriented approach generates opposition among substantial segments of the population.

As a whole, these studies offer a comprehensive analysis of Chile's recent evolution and the fundamental political, economic, and social aspects of its current situation. They also represent a critical assessment of the impact of Lagos administration policies on the quality of Chile's democracy and its prospects for consolidation and deepening in the coming years. Their collective work indicates that, in fifteen years of power, the Concertación administrations' cautious, incremental approach to post-authoritarian reform has attained significant gains in consolidating the liberal democratic regime, developing a suitable party system, improving civilian-military relations, addressing some important human rights issues, introducing several elements of a secular agenda, improving the country's international position and prestige, furthering economic growth and stability, and attempting to lessen the negative consequences of free market imperfections on social security and health conditions. In the institutional sphere, the 2004 agreement between the government and opposition parties to reform the 1980 constitution so as to eliminate some of its blatantly nondemocratic clauses, including the elimination of non-elected senators and the restoration of presidential authority to remove the commanders of the branches of the armed forces, represents an important step in the direction of deepening and consolidating the political regime's democratic features.

Other recent developments reveal a growing determination to expand political participation and to enforce the principles of legal equality and judicial independence. The first was the decision by the two principal Concertación parties to support women for the presidency. Michelle Bachelet, former minister of defense under Lagos, who is supported by the Socialist Party and the Party for Democracy, and Soledad Alvear, former minister of foreign affairs, nominated by the Christian Democratic Party, to be these parties' presidential nominees. When Alvear withdrew, Bachelet was declared the Concertación candidate. The second development was the Supreme Court ruling in late 2004 to uphold a lower court's decision that Pinochet is competent to stand trial on murder and kidnapping charges. Yet another positive sign is that, in comparison with other Latin American countries, Chile has exhibited a remarkable record of economic growth, social peace, and political stability since the return to democracy. The economic crises, explosions of popular discontent, attempted coups, violent political confrontations, and forced presidential resignations that have occurred in the last few years in countries such as Argentina, Bolivia, Brazil, Ecuador, Peru, and Venezuela have not affected Chile, or if they have had some kind of repercussion, as in the cases of the civilian-military confrontations and financial crises, their impact has been much less intense than in the rest of the region.

It is important to remember, however, that these positive developments have been accompanied by or associated with the persistence of a number of negative circumstances that affect the democratic quality and socioeconomic welfare of significant portions of the population. From this perspective, some of the main challenges that Chile's civilian governments still face result from the continued presence of political, economic, and social conditions inherited from the military authoritarian regime, which prevent the completion of the democratization process. These challenges include the establishment and consolidation of a regime characterized by undisputed respect for popular sovereignty, the promotion of broader political participation, the comprehensive application of the rule of law and the principle of legal equality, full enforcement of human rights provisions, and the appropriate promotion of social justice. Having listed these shortcomings, I should mention that until 2004 the post-Pinochet administrations were unable to eliminate important constraints on democracy imposed by the constitutional framework inherited from the authoritarian regime and faced a lingering incapacity to assert unequivocal civilian supremacy over the military, hesitant efforts to solve the human rights issue, the partial failure to establish more cooperative relations with other countries in the region, a limited ability to promote progressive secular policies, and a relative incapacity to address the negative outcomes of the application of an unrestricted free market model, particularly in terms of income distribution.

Although some very important constitutional reforms were implemented in late 2004, several institutional and legal features that restrict popular sovereignty and hinder the manifestation of majority rule remain in place, including the maintenance of the binomial electoral system and the conservative bias in the configuration of electoral districts. The presence of the binomial system in turn favors bipartisanship and coalition building while making it difficult for minority parties and groups to attain political representation. In the area of civilian-military relations, the reassertion of civilian authority over the armed forces and the lessening of military intervention in political, national security, and judicial affairs have not completely eliminated the participation of military authorities in some of these decisions nor the budgetary autonomy and privileged position of the armed forces in terms of expenditures for equipment and personnel. In the human rights area, although important progress has been accomplished regarding their enforcement and the provision of information to and reparations for victims and their families, effective prosecution and punishment of those responsible for the most egregious human rights violations have been up to now very difficult to carry out, as the long and convoluted legal saga of General Pinochet demonstrates.

In the arena of foreign relations, Chile's gains in global esteem and independence have not been accompanied by a comparable increase in its influence and leadership in the region or by a decrease in tensions with some neighboring countries. Although some secular-oriented legislation and policies have been enacted despite opposition from Catholic Church leaders, the political influence of the Catholic hierarchy remains substantial, particularly in areas such as sexual education and reproductive rights. Finally, the most significant area in which it is possible to detect shortcomings affecting Chilean democracy is in the exclusion from political debate of the fundamental components of the free market economic model and the refusal to consider that Chile's income distribution and social welfare problems might be the result not of market "imperfections" or policy timing, but rather of the existence of a free market system. However, the importance of the market model is such that it generated a dual process: On the one hand there is consensus on the need to preserve the general model, while on the other there is consensus on the need to ameliorate its consequences. This, in turn, led to the formulation of anti-poverty and employment programs and the implementation of social policies that have only partially reduced poverty and marginally improved access to health, old-age, and educational services for the less affluent sectors of the population.

As the Lagos administration comes to an end, it is clear that some of these challenges remain unresolved. It is appropriate to ask if these problematic issues emanating from the dictatorial past are likely to be successfully confronted by the coming administrations. This is by no means a question that can be answered easily or with unqualified assurance. Sooner or later General Pinochet will no longer be a relevant actor in Chile's political arena, and his exit will eliminate or lessen some of the problems and constraints faced by the civilian governments as they try to modify his legacy. It is also clear, however, that his eventual disappearance will not wipe out the structural changes his regime imposed, nor will it extinguish the social, economic, and political actors and conditions that underpinned these transformations. Pinochet's authoritarian regime has cast a long shadow on Chile that the Chilean people have recently begun to confront. Chilean political actors have recently begun to face the predicament of either maintaining some important authoritarian and inegalitarian components of the current political, social, and economic arrangements or of trying to modify them in a more democratic and equitable direction. In the former case, political and socioeconomic stability and tranquility could be expected to prevail but at the cost of preserving some of the existing undemocratic and inequitable situations affecting the country's political system and society. There may be an inherent risk that an economic crisis could lead to widespread conflict and instability. In other words, the expected benefit of promoting more politically democratic and socioeconomically equitable conditions should be weighed against the risk that measures taken to attain these goals might generate growing economic difficulties, social tensions, and ultimately, political instability.

It is evident that a cautious approach has prevailed since 1990. The Concertación administrations of Presidents Aylwin, Frei, and Lagos have chosen to deal gradually and very carefully with the manifestations of the authoritarian heritage and have tried to alter the status quo in incremental and nonconfrontational ways. This approach has led to positive results in fields such as human rights, civilian-military relations, and political participation but has fallen short of modifying some crucial undemocratic and inequitable components of the inherited political, social, and economic models. As I mentioned, this is especially noticeable in areas such as the electoral system, autonomy of the armed forces, enforcement of human rights legislation, improvement of income distribution, eradication of poverty, access to education, and social security and health coverage. However grave these problems are, nothing seems to portend that in the coming years there will be substantial ideological and policy shifts in the way they are treated. The January 2006 victory of the Concertación candidate Michelle Bachelet augers for a greater degree of social and political change than we have seen to date by the Concertación. On the one hand, the Bachelet administration will most likely represent a government of continuity in terms of the general economic free-market, open economy approach. However, in the area of social policy there will be important changes, with a greater emphasis on pension, health, and educational reform. President Bachelet, the first woman elected president in Chile, also made the issue of political style a priority during her campaign. With an atypical personal biography for a politician, she has promised a government that is more participatory and grass-roots. Likewise, she has committed her government to gender equity and demonstrated her commitment to this principal by having gender parity in both her cabinet and subcabinet level appointments.

Bachelet's election, which means a fourth consecutive Concertación government for Chile, raises serious issues for the right-wing parties. It is clear that to keep their influence and increase their changes of political success the right-wing coalition needs to reconsider its approach to the nature of the political system and to social policies.

With the victory of the Concertación and Michelle Bachelet, Chile's democracy will no longer be threatened by military intervention or populist revolts, and there is the hope that Bachelet will be able to deepen political participation and promote democratic decision making, along with ameliorating some of the negative social consequences of the economic model.

Notes

1. Terence O'Hara and Kathleen Day, "Riggs Bank Hid Assets of Pinochet, Report Says," *Washington Post*, July 15, 2004, A01; Larry Rother, "Pinochet Continues to Haunt Chile's Civilian Government," *New York Times*, July 18, 2004.

Contributors

Silvia Borzutzky is an associate teaching professor and director of the Political Science Program at Carnegie Mellon University. She is the author of *Vital Connections: Politics, Social Security and Inequality in Chile* (Notre Dame University Press, 2002) and numerous articles dealing with Chilean politics, social security policies, globalization, and international relations. Borzutzky is a member of the editorial board of several journals, including *Revista Bicentenario* and the *Journal of Societal and Social Policy.*

Joaquín Fermandois has been a professor of contemporary history at the Catholic University in Santiago since 1984. He received a Guggenheim Scholarship in 1989. Fermandois is the author of several books, including *Chile y el mundo, 1970–1973, La política exterior del gobierno de la Unidad Popular y el sistema internacional,* and *Abismo y crecimiento: Gustavo Ross y las relaciones entre Chile y Estados Unidos, 1932–1938.*

William M. Lies, C.S.C., is the executive director of the Center for Social Concerns at the University of Notre Dame and holds a concurrent appointment in the Department of Political Science. His research focus is on Latin American politics, religion and politics, and public policy. As head of the Center for Social Concerns, Fr. Lies gives his time to community-based learning and research throughout the university.

Elizabeth Lira is a Chilean psychologist, researcher, and professor at the Jesuit University Alberto Hurtado. She has worked on human rights issues and political violence from a clinical and psychosocial perspective. Lira has received numerous awards, including the 1983 National Prize from the Chilean Association of Psychologists, the Nevitt Sanford Award from the International Society of Political Psychology in 1998, and the 2002 Humanitarian International Award from the American Psychological Association. She is the author of more than thirty papers and numerous books. Lira has recently coauthored several books on political reconciliation and reparations in Chile during the twentieth century.

Patricio Navia is an assistant professor at the Center for Latin American and Caribbean Studies at New York University and professor of political science at Universidad Diego Portales in Santiago, Chile. He has published articles in the *Journal of Democracy, Social Science Quarterly, Comparative Political Studies,* and *Democratization* and also writes political analysis for several Chilean newspapers. His book *Las Grandes alamedas: el Chile post-Pinochet* was published in Chile in 2004.

Lois Hecht Oppenheim is professor of political science and former vice-president for academic affairs at the University of Judaism, Los Angeles. Her book, *Politics in Chile: Authoritarianism, Development, and the Search for Democracy* (Westview Press, 1993, 1999) is in its third edition (forthcoming). Oppenheim is the author of numerous articles about Chilean politics. She is the recipient of a Fulbright Senior Lectureship to Chile and has been a visiting professor of sociology at the University of Chile, a visiting researcher at Comisión Económica para América Latina y el Caribe (CEPAL), and a visiting researcher at Programa de Economía y Trabajo (PET), all in Santiago.

Aldo C. Vacs is a professor of government and director of the Center for Latin American Studies at Skidmore College. He holds degrees in political science, sociology, economic policies, and planning from institutions in Argentina, Brazil, Chile, and the United States. Vacs is a contributing editor to the *Handbook of Latin American Studies* published by the Library of Congress and an associate editor of *Latin American Politics and Society.* He has published extensively on Latin American politics, international relations, democratization, and international economic issues.

Gregory Weeks is assistant professor of political science at the University of North Carolina at Charlotte. He is the author of *The Military and Politics in Postauthoritarian Chile* (University of Alabama Press, 2003) and *U.S.–Latin American Relations* (Longman, forthcoming), as well as numerous articles on Chilean politics, civil-military relations, and U.S.–Latin American relations.

Index